THE BLUE MOUNTAINS SING

of rivers, old men, trails and trout

RON H. RADER

ISBN: 978-0-9890280-0-4

The information in this book is accurate and complete to the best of my knowledge. It is offered without guarantee on the part of the author. The author and Windswept Publishing disclaim all liability in connection with the use of this book.

I have tried to recreate events, locales, and conversations from my memories of them. In order to maintain their anonymity in some instances , I have changed the names of individuals and places. I may have changed some identifying characteristics and details such as physical properties, locations, and story details. Some names and identifying details have been changed to protect the privacy of some individuals.

Book design: Aaron Barnhart

Front Cover art: "Ancient Hills" and Back cover art :"Remembrance" by Robert A. Tino
Robert is an east Tennessee native who has spent his artistic career painting the beauty of the Great Smoky mountain region.
www.robertatinogallery.com

Contact the author at: ronrader@live.com

Written for and dedicated to:

Jane, my loving wife, for her patience and support that made this a reality, my Rader family who love and entertain me, my grandchildren who give us hope, the locals yearning for more reminders of their mountain days past, the teachers, both current and past, who asked me to write it, the children of today and tomorrow, the mountain's fisherfolk, campers, hikers, and all outdoor lovers, the visitors and newcomers who hunger to learn more of our past, those who graciously coached me, edited my manuscript, and befriended me, and all who remain deeply in love with our Great Smoky Mountains.

"A man might own a whole country and be a stranger in it. If I belonged in this place it was because I belonged to it. And I began to understand that so long as I did not know the place fully, or even adequately, I belonged to it only partially. That summer I began to see, however dimly, that one of my ambitions, perhaps my governing ambition, was to belong fully to this place, to belong as the thrushes and the herons and the muskrats belonged, to be altogether at home here . . .

But now I have come to see that [belonging] proposes an enormous labor. It is a spiritual ambition, like goodness. The wild creatures belong to the place by nature, but as a man I can belong to it only by understanding . . ."

—Wendell Berry, *The Long Legged House,* 1965

CONTENTS

Once there was a place where simple was revered. The pace was slower and life balanced. Everything mattered. People mattered. Nature mattered.

Once there was a place where people relied on others and others relied on them.

Once there was a place where man and nature were in balance. This place had more trees than people.

Once there was a place where words meant everything. It was a place where words had one true meaning and word was kept.

Once there was a place where honesty abounded. A place where life rode the two-way bond of respect.

Once there was a place where greenness was revered, and both life and success came from the earth.

Once there was a place where man and the outdoor life around him rode as equals on nature's carousel.

Once there was a place where man and animals lived in harmony and interdependence, as did neighbor and neighbor.

Once there was a place where people lived as if "under God," their country and prayer meant everything, and in this place, hope grew in capital letters.

Once there was a place where you could fish, swim, and drink the same clear water.

Once there was a place where civility reigned. Kindness, courtesy, respect, and self-sacrifice were the threads that joined its people, one to another.

Once there was a place where its people and its visitors began to ignore its earlier revered way of life. The people grew too busy to nurture it and overlooked its value. They took its living gift for granted. Its once treasured life went unnoticed. Forgotten, its value lost, this life gradually faded and then disappeared.

This once near heavenly place is just another place now, and it bears the sameness of so many others, except now, this one is veiled with sadness.

Prologue

For years, this book simmered and rolled around in that spot where many books are born. It began and grew as I recalled my boyhood experiences in Sevier County. It evolved into a written chronicle for my sons and grandchildren. I figured someday they might pause and wonder what life was like in Sevier County pre- and post-World War II. In fact, each of my three sons had already asked about those differences between the *Then* and the *Now*.

"How does our life really differ from your 'born and raised' times in the 1940s and 1950s? Have the three cities—Gatlinburg, Pigeon Forge, and Sevierville—really changed a lot?" As they grew older, they asked more often because they were now adults and lived here. Their deductions that followed were identical: "I wish I had lived back when you grew up here. Everything seemed simpler, safer, friendlier, less crowded, and more pastoral." I guess it was.

I am a part of the mountains. I always have been. I believe they are a part of me. The mountains and their people shaped who I have become. With this book, I honor those mountains and the people who were a part of them.

These chronicles are sketches of my childhood and young manhood. My book depicts how I experienced life around me. It is filled with my own perceptions, views, biases and is heavily colored by my own interests. Each of my classmates, friends, and acquaintances has their own colorful accounts of our life in these mountains and foothills. I'm sure they place a high value on their memories; I just happened to write mine down. Each of our stories may differ, but each story is also colored and interwoven with sameness. In that era, our rural life was a tapestry sewn with threads routinely common to most of us who lived the mountain life, and many paths of similarity linked us all. Gradually, those threads grew into bonds. They became treasured links that bound us tightly to one another, for we were the kids of the 1940s and 1950s.

I have seen it grow in recent years, this need to understand and revisit the past. Newcomers to our area seem to have an almost insatiable hunger to know more of who we once were. I suppose because they think those earlier times were so richly unique. Well, they're right; they were one-time-only memories of our past. Our heritage, history, and culture of Pigeon Forge, Gatlinburg, Sevierville, and the Great Smoky Mountains with the national park are unmatched anywhere in the world. What these newcomers seek is exactly what I try to recapture—the views of a native son, a boy's firsthand account of life lived in those days. It's been my experience that our newcomers seem a whole lot more interested in our heritage than we locals are.

Born in 1938, I recount those years from my earliest memories through the years of 1955, my Sevier County High School graduation year. Those were the "golly gee" years where every minute was eventful and exciting. Whether my life was speeding up or down, its adventures unfolded faster than Saturday's cliff-hanging, Jungle Jim serial episodes at Sevierville's Pines Theater.

If my boyhood were a pie, its slices were made from a recipe's meld of many Sevier County locales. I was constantly in and out of fun places with fun people. My journey zigzagged into the Great Smoky Mountains National Park (the Park) and its woods, rivers, and trails.

I was in the constant company of Park employees who befriended me like Dutch uncles and aunts , as did many folks , young and old, in the three towns. They know who they are. Not to be overlooked are the many folks who lived in neither town but lived on those farms and the many settlements, the "in-betweens," scattered throughout the mountains and foothills. They, too, know who they are, and I'll never forget any of them.

All were special in my growing-up years. Left out, but not forgotten, are the scores of others who deserve a place in the book. Sadly, they are bumped only due to the lack of space and maybe my dimming recall. Yet, they move in the endless parade of thoughts, memories, and hometown images that still drift in the creeks of my mind.

Unlike many folks, my family never moved. I spent my entire childhood and teen years in Pigeon Forge, son of local grocery store owner parents, and a parallel side of my life as a Great Smoky Mountains National Park brat.

As young boys, we swam and fished the Little Pigeon River in summer, and in the winter, we trapped mink and muskrats and at season's end sold their pelts to earn Christmas money. In between, we'd dig ginseng and hunt arrowheads. I grew well into my teen years surrounded by the mountain settler mores and customs. These sound, basic virtues were espoused by most others in the community even though we were just about to enter a whirlwind of change. Getting ready to go into the wilderness might be the way some folks these days recall it. Tourism, visitors, motels, retail, construction, and subdivision growth were about to explode around us. It would bring change that even Nostradamus could not have predicted. If he did, he never told us.

As kids of that era, we were very fortunate. Pigeon Forge probably had seventy-five to one hundred families, and Gatlinburg had far fewer. Most folks knew everybody else, and socially, Gatlinburg was an equal extension of Pigeon Forge and vice versa. The whole area was very Mayberry-esque. Life was good. WWII came and went. Prosperity followed. Most folks farmed or worked with Tennessee Valley Authority, The Great Smoky Mountain National Park, or another government agency. It was the Roosevelt era. Other folks owned retail stores or motels. Some were beginning to court the growing tourism trade. Most of my classmates and friends enjoyed the same life quality, and most of us fell into that broad, middle-class range.

What a privilege it was to grow up here and enjoy hometown folks. They surrounded me with their friendship, concern, and mentoring. I especially appreciated their laughter and our shared fun. They remain young and very much alive and well in my memory. I was truly blessed to have lived during such a magnificent era and in a wilderness that only God could make.

That Pigeon Forge, my Pigeon Forge, was my boyhood home and my hometown. There was nothing to do indoors, except maybe to be sick or read. We all wanted to be outside where all the action was. You either found it or created your own excitement and entertainment. We entertained ourselves and nature played a big part in it. It had to be outside, for there was nothing else. Our outdoors were unique, and they made the perfect playground. So we immersed ourselves in all things outdoors—the woods, waters, and farm life. These places will always earn a special niche in my soul.

One thing is certain, I am a product of these foothills of the Great Smoky Mountains. The oft- heard local exclamation, " I was born and raised here," is not born of haughty pride or a better-than-thou aloofness; instead, it is an expression of humble gratitude. Translated it means: "I was so blessed to have been a part of those earlier times; I hope one day you can somehow experience the same joy I experienced growing up here. I truly bonded with the people and the land."

As one old timer put it, "In our own family we git to talk about, fuss, argue, and fight with each other. If you ain't in our family, we don't put up with nobody else talkin' about or botherin' family. You had better know it right up front. Here where we live, families stick together. We help each other through thick or thin no matter what. We stick together 'cause, well, 'cause family is all we got. Yessir, family is all any of us has got. It's the one place we all call home, and in the end, our mountains and our past is all we got."

My hometown, its people, its colorful characters, and my friends shaped me and became as much a part of my character and personality as anyone.

Along with my parents, they helped raise me, and few even realized it. So I apologize to any and all of you for any of my errant ways, character defects, or any of my obvious oversights, slights, and personal eccentricities that may have disappointed you. However, since most of you had a hand in raising me, you must now share a bit of the blame for any of my shortcomings, missteps, or double dribbles. The good news is you get some of the credit for any of my few redeeming virtues.

These perspectives and experiences are solely my own. I write these chronicles because I have a deep love for the area, and because I have to. I write to recapture that era the way I experienced it—as a childhood memory. My string of life sketches speak of southern boyhood, of coming of age in a small East Tennessee town deep in the foothills of the Great Smoky Mountains. I chose episodes that were important to me.

Most of my characters are real; sometimes their names are not their real ones. A few characters are composites. Composing random slices and episodes of my early life into compressed stories, I wrapped them around fictional settings or characters to depict the reality of that era. Several eclectic adventures have been rolled together and ascribed to one character for brevity. I have made every attempt to be accurate and factual in regard to dates, statistics, and other specifics. I worked diligently to be accurate with titles, citations, incidents, and other items. My recall at seventy-four may be a bit hazy, so I ask for your patience. However, my goal is to write anecdotes and stories that reflect the times. If I erred in any of these areas, I apologize in advance. I invite you to pencil in your own corrections that you believe to be more factual in your book's margin and read on. I intend for you to find your reading pleasure in the color and adventure of my word journey, not in the accuracy of the book's scholarly, statistical, historical milestones. My intent is to depict the area's ambience of the 1940s and the 1950s.

All facts and statistics herein were researched and drawn from The Great Smoky Mountain National Park Service documents, its library, their online websites, and other related government documents. Any fact or statistic that relates to the mountains, the flora, fauna, locations, culture, environment, and history of the area is attributed to those Park documents that are intended to provide the public with a deeper knowledge of our mountains. I could not have written this book without the assistance from their vast knowledge base and their online websites.

In addition, I've drawn on seventy-four years of my own personal experiences as a native son. The years of outdoor jaunts and activities with park staff made great contributions to my content. I drew on my close friendship with Art Stupka and John Morrell—my treasured mentors—and from our many conversations for much of my factual content. In addition, our discourse enabled me to create meaningful anecdotes. I attribute most of the older factual information to them. Finally, all current facts were gleaned from the latest information provided by the Great Smoky Mountain National Park. Much of their environmental, weather, flora and fauna, wildlife, cultural, and historical timeline information was woven into conversations between my characters.

I took the high road on this word journey. There is more than enough tragedy, negativity, and, yes, evil in this world. I did not plan to add to it at the expense of any individual because of his or her choices, actions, or behavior. I seek to write of the best in people, and most deserve it. I consider any obstacle, challenge, downturn, bad choice, or prior mistake anyone may have suffered in his or her own life as simply a pothole in his or her road—a temporary inconvenience. I hope each person has moved on because I intend to treat him or her as if that were the case. I plan to do the same in my life.

If I, herein, have offended any person or reader for that matter, or erred in any way, I apologize in advance, for that is certainly not my intent. I quote a phrase from the "Physicians Hippocratic Oath" to underscore my intent. Let it serve as my writing pledge and commitment *"to do no harm"* within my word journey that follows. I hope you'll read my story with the same intent.

Enjoy.

CHAPTER ONE

My Great Smoky Mountain Boyhood

My Pigeon Forge of the 1940s and 1950s

A trailing dust storm was building in my rearview. I didn't care. I was fourteen. It was an Uncle Remus day. Nothing could spoil it. Drunk on my freedom from our grocery store, the wind in my face, and the exhilaration of a midday in June, I felt like a bluebird really could be on my shoulder—except for the force of the wind. I pushed my foot deeper on the accelerator. At thirty-five mph, the dust cloud took on a high, arching fishtail that only speedboats could make, ones I'd only seen on Movietone News at the Park Theater. An elderly lady was in dire need of her groceries. Her need was growing. Her starvation could be real, unless I acted quickly and bravely. I pressed on.

I began to sing, then shout, the words to "Oklahoma." With the windshield down at forty-five mph, the wind pressed my skin; my cheeks reverberated. Suddenly, I stopped singing and shouting my song. The wind's force and my fears of a June bug splatting down my throat made it seem like a good idea. Besides, as the jeep's speed increased, my entire face fluttered like a spaniel's lips with its head poked out your mother's side of the family car.

By now, the dust wall rolling up close to my bumper was tall and wide. In fact, it obscured my view of everything above and to either side. I knew it. This was a hurricane. Maybe it was as big as the one that chased Humphrey Bogart in Key Largo. Dust now spewed through the rusting, saucer-shaped hole in the passenger side floor. Now I was really in danger; my hurricane was loaded with dust—a howling dust storm. I must escape. Pigeon Forge was in danger. The Smoky Mountains were in danger. The people must be warned.

I didn't know if a 1946 Willy's jeep had a top speed limit or even if it could go past fifty-five mph, but I knew I had to try. I was in great danger.

THE BLUE MOUNTAINS SING
of rivers, old men, trails and trout

An old lady and a cow were probably starving. This very, very old lady was depending on me to get through. Her groceries were in danger, and she really needed food , and her cow really needed bran. I only hoped I could get there before they both starved. I had no choice. I must go faster. At fifty-three mph, dust literally boiled from the force of the wind and the jeep's speed, and dust was now circling up and around the floor, sides, and even rolling back over the hood, encircling me in loops and rolls.

Suddenly, I knew the truth. I was in the North African desert, fleeing a sandstorm; General Rommel and his tanks were in desert pursuit. Talcum clay dust accumulated on my hair, clothes, and the groceries. I couldn't read any labels on the groceries or the gauges on the dashboard. The floor disappeared under a growing clay carpet. My black tennis shoes were terracotta, and only the tops of my socks were visible. My only thought was, I must go faster. This storm has created a dilemma of life or death for everyone.

"I am in a violent and extremely dangerous sandstorm," I screamed to the wind. "Few people have ever survived your fury, but by the grace of God, I will, I can. I am strong. I am an American." Frantically, my mind searched for the escape answer to my survival. Then it came to me. What would Tarzan do?

Just then my turn off to Mill Creek sped by. Dadgummit, I cursed to myself—if I'd had goggles like Rommel's, I'd never have missed my turnoff, I thought. Slowing down to twenty-five, I made a U-turn in what was soon to be a grassy median. Slower, I headed up Mill Creek Road. Passing my Uncle Harry's farm on the right, I reached the big, white, two-story house with nine cats lying on and around the porch. Chickens eagerly moved around and through the yard feeding on something too small for me to see. Standing near a carpet of zinnias that sported nearly every color in the rainbow, Miss Emma unlatched the gate from the same post that held her mailbox.

"Land sakes, you got here quick, Ronny. Seems like I just got off the phone with Louise at the store. Lord, lord, honey that road bunch still not through on that road and still not got that dust settled down. Honey, it looks like you brought most of it with you. I'm sorry you had to go through all that mess. Lord child it's all over you—in your hair, in your eyes, and there's sweat streaks running rivers of mud down your neck. Bless your heart. "

I stepped out, dramatically beating dust from my clothes, and assumed my most pitiful look, mentally replaying the many trip dangers that I'd heroically overcome. I swaggered toward Miss Emma, hoping she noticed my best hero gait, and handed her the first bag of groceries.

My Great Smoky Mountain Boyhood

She stepped to the well pump mounted over the cistern that caught rainwater from the roof.

She pumped. Icy water soaked the dishtowel she had just whisked from her apron, and she said, "Let me get this stuff off your face and out of your eyes. Bless your heart child." I flexed my shoulders and unloaded all grocery bags, lifting the fifty-pound bag of cow bran as if it weighed mere ounces. "I hope your mother appreciates how hard that unpaved dirt road makes it on good workers like you. I'll tell her next time I see her. I'm making a cake for their bridge club on Thursday—I'll tell her then. You be good and don't work too hard in this heat and dreadful dust and this sun. Don't you over-do it, honey."

I grinned and said, " I won't, Miss Emma. You be sure and tell Mom that other part, too, you know about me needin' some off time, and don't forget the part about not having to work too hard at the store."

Three weeks later, my speedy deliveries got me in trouble. I didn't realize that weather could create high tail winds on my speeding jeep. It could easily multiply the force and spread of my trailing dust storm by ten. My mother was on the receiving end of the calls. Angry, agitated, irate women called with long renditions. Their key words were "dust, destruction, interruption, cleaning, customer, never again," and higher pitched ruinous phrases that described "ruined lunches, hairdos, bridal shower outdoors, and two teas."

At the end, my name was always attached as the cause. The first to call was Edna from Edna's Beauty Shop, followed by Irene's Diner, and next came the Tuesday bridge club. My interruption of the monthly meeting of the Daughters of the American Revolution brought on fiery conviction. According to the caller, they were mad enough to take up arms and show me that same pioneer spirit their forefathers used to win the revolution. All guests at the backyard bridal tea called, individually.

Mrs. Cincpac, the matronly Norwegian owner of twelve tourist cottages, called to say that she had just finished hanging the fifty-ninth sheet of her sixty freshly washed, still dripping bed sheets, outside, as was her weekly ritual. And that's when I blazed by her place in some kind of Nazi jeep, speeding like a bullet being chased by a mile-high dust storm—one for which I was solely responsible. She invited my mother to come see what seventy-five mile an hour of unpaved highway dust does to sixty wet bed sheets.

Well, I don't know how, but I survived my punishment and continued to drive. After that, I checked wind speed, calculated my course, and learned when to drive fifty-five plus.

Many of my earliest boyhood memories are vivid. Some seem like they only happened last summer. I grew up in a middle class family in Pigeon Forge, a small 1940s village in the foothills of the Smoky Mountains. My dad was employed as General Supply Clerk for The Great Smoky Mountains National Park (GSMNP – hereafter referred to as the Park) where he retired in 1955 after thirty-six years, the same year I graduated from high school. My parents owned a traditional small town grocery store. Actually, it was an old time general store trying to become modern, judging by its growing product lines. My mom, Louise Ogle Rader, owned and managed the Pigeon Forge Shopping Center located at the corner of River Road and Main Street in the center of Pigeon Forge. My brother Rick was five years younger than I, and we were best friends.

Mom found a partner in her friend Veryl Smith. Moving from Elkmont around 1950, where they had operated the general store concession inside the Park and lived in Park Service housing at Elkmont, Veryl and Homer Smith were family friends and became business partners in our grocery store. Homer served as Park dispatcher at Park Headquarters, maintained the power plant at Elkmont's lake, and was Park overseer and Park liaison to the Appalachian Club and the several homes there. The Smiths and children, Sonny and Mary Lou, lived at the ridge top across from The Wonderland Hotel, just above the lake and overlooking the private boys' camp—Camp Club LeConte for Boys. Veryl had grocery business experience from the Elkmont concession, and my mother owned the vacant store building and land, so the business partnership with my folks was a good one.

The Pigeon Forge Shopping Center store evolved into a one stop for all your needs. The store offered groceries, dry goods, clothing, shoes, boots, fresh produce, fresh meats, and cheeses along with animal feed, cattle bran, kerosene, seed, and products to meet other farm needs. A small, disorganized, honor-system library was on the second floor. The rear wall of our store housed a small bedroom-sized, square room, Pigeon Forge's local post office. Its front wall was completely filled with small, letter-size lock boxes. At its center, framed by tiny mailboxes, was a small service window. Made of slender brass bars, the service window swung open for service and was locked closed at day's end. It framed our petite, gentle postmistress, Miss Mildred. She, like my mother at the store's front counter, was congenial, always smiling, called everyone by name, and was the epitome of customer service and graciousness. She was someone who would always go the third mile to meet any need. She, my mother, and Mom's business partner, Veryl, served as the town's information center. Their work made them central to the town activity, information, and gossip. Like it or not, they listened to births, deaths, hysterectomies, affairs, surgeries, divorces, wrecks, fires, homicides, robberies, marriages, possible upcoming marriages, have-to marriages, scorned women, "dear john" men, preachers leaving, moving, and having to move, latest ailments, itemized lists of pills required daily, smooth salesmen with outside- the-county news, and finally, the weather. Only the town barber, Tebo Watson, our neighboring grocer across the street, Shirley Butler, or Doc Williams, the nearest pharmacist in Sevierville, were as informed on local news.

Our store nestled directly across the street from Butler's Grocery Store at the bridge's southeast end and at riverside across from the Old Mill. Its covered concrete porch and landing bordered the only road to Gatlinburg and the river.

At noon, a daily ritual took place. Farmers, carpenters, concrete finishers, masons, and a gathering of other Mayberry-esque characters gathered at our "Pigeon Forge Shopping Center."

First they'd buy their "every-day-for-lunch makings" inside our store and then sprawl, sit, or stand on the shaded porch. The level of the concrete porch floor was unusually high. It made both a perfect seat as well as curb for the two-lane highway to Gatlinburg. Even during dog days of summer, the concrete was always cold, so it made a refreshing spot for the lunch-goer or the bored passenger awaiting the next Trailways bus to Sevierville and beyond.

The dinner crowd relaxed on the storefront's porch and sat on its four wooden benches. Each bench was supported by thick concrete ends with wooden bench seats and backs. The wood was inscribed with scrolled RC and Pepsi advertisement logos, and here and there carved initials and hearts revealed loneliness and boredom from years past. It was here that they would catch up on local news, gossip, and tell a few good lies. Their midday dinner was often one loaf of Merita bread, one-half pound of baloney, two slices of that *rat cheese* (cheese sliced from a huge round hoop of Wisconsin sharp cheese), an RC "dope," and a Moon Pie. Partnering up, they usually split the cost and shared. Most of them got B.C. Headache Powder and poured it into the soft drink. Headaches were common, especially in hot summertime.

Overhead, tacked above the large, glass storefront picture windows, were rows of metal advertisement signs. In the first, The Lone Ranger astride Silver was obviously on a serious mission. He sternly shouted reassurance with his hardy cry of "Hi-Ho Silver." This was a cry that only Tonto could really understand. Tonto, his loyal, dedicated sidekick always knew where the bad guys were and always made Kemo-Sabe look good. The horse-riding duo's theme song made the William Tell Overture into an iconic tune. This was a front yard battle cry that every youngster knew by heart and could only be sung if the singing rider slapped thighs and urged an imaginary horse across the front yard. The famous masked man from the Merita Bread metal sign gazed down at the dinner bunch. So did the bellhop, Johnny, from Phillip Morris cigarettes, except he called from a different metal sign. Johnny shouted anxiously to anyone who might listen, "Call for Philip Morris."

None of the adult porch crowd ever seemed to grasp the seriousness of this drama hanging just over their heads. Yet, no youngsters failed to marvel at this "Best of the West" action hero aloft near the ceiling. In fact, they dreamed of their next store visit, when they could gaze longingly at the colorful sign to once again return to those days of yesteryear and be a part of their favorite masked rider's next adventure.

The porch's noonday talk rose and fell, its topics unconnected, random, and rarely with closure. The conversations of men at rest slid quickly from one topic to another, driven by the epiphany of the moment. Their murmuring chatter would rise and fall in volume, its level driven by emotion. One hot April day it drifted from the porch through our open doors into the store. Upcoming county elections and the candidates were the topic of the day.

The gravelly voice of Basil Regan could be heard clearly: "I don't care if he wuz in the war or even if he lived through the Battle of the Bulge. He cain't beat Tate. Tate's popular. He's kin, probably kin to about everbody settin' here today. He's been sheriff two terms and still finds time to cut the best flat top haircut of any barber in three counties much less airin'. Now, I know you can say you never know when he's goin' to show up at the shop and barber. And I know you can name fifty people who went, waited for two hours while the other two barbers cut heads of other folks not needin' flattops. And you can tell me you got mad and left, sayin' your time was wasted awaitin'. I still say he can sheriff better'n anybody we ever had."

Claymore Vaughn, mechanic at Floyd's, growing uncomfortable with the heated exchange, redirected with, "I hear tell they are tryin' to give those two boys the chair. You know, them two that killed Charlie Perry and Josie. Said they wuz tryin' to find Charlie's big hoard of cash. Everbody always said he must have a big wad stashed summers since he wouldn't take anythin' but cash."

The oldest of the lunch bunch, a finish carpenter, said, "My daughter that lives in Atlanta said some magazine, I believe she said *True Detective*, was tellin' the whole story, and it's supposed to be out next month."

The McBride brothers, master stonemasons, spoke up almost at the same time. "Anybody know if the crappie air still bitin'? I'm bout ready to switch to trout in the mountains. I know the redbud blooms are plumb gone and granny's yaller jonquils bloomed plum out three weeks ago. I thank it's time to head to Deep Creek or Walnut Bottoms."

The youngest of three roofers, all brothers, said, "If we can finish shinglin' the roof on that new motel today, or tomorrow, we're goin' to dig ramps."

"Where you going to dig 'em?" the house painter in the bunch asked. The oldest of the three quickly retorted, "Oh, I don't know maybe Cosby, maybe Del Rio, maybe Newport."

The miller brushed more flour dust and chaff from his hair and clothes and smacked his bib overalls several more times, saying, "Ramps nothin', you boys air on a whiskey trip. Now you may get some ramps along the way acomin' or agoin', but I'd bet my bottom dollar you boys got your mouth set on a fresh run moonshine in a six-case of them gallon jars. Everybody knows it ain't all gonna be trout, so fess up boys. In Newport, Del Rio, and Cosby, it's moonshine first and trout third."

Lynn puzzled, the youngest of three generations of wood carvers and broom makers, asked, "What's the second?"

"I ain't a sayin'." The miller was quick and defensive. "But if you ever go up there, you'll figger it out real quick—specially if you stop in any of them beer joints along the way." Several in the group snickered.

"Hello, Jase." They almost spoke as one. A man, looking to be in his mid-forties, sauntered up shyly. His demeanor was tentative, as if he was unsure if the group would let him join in. "What you been up to, Jase?"

"Oh, nuthin," he said as he put his left foot on the concrete edge and rested his weight on his right foot, still on the pavement. His always good-natured smile spread even wider. Tanned, muscular, thick through the chest and shoulders, his widow's peak of brown hair framed an unlined face that belied his age. He always wore a spotless white T shirt under clean, worn bib overalls. Jase, now reassured that he was included, pulled out a screen-door spring. The slender, rope-like wire coil was about two feet long. Most of Jase's conversation was a string of responses of "uhhuh, yeah, huh uh, no" to questions from the lounging dinner crowd. Jase never smoked, chewed, or whittled like the others. Instead, he gripped a screen-door spring by its ends, one in each hand, jump rope style. Holding it extended out from his chest, he began to twirl it as if someone was jumping inside its one-foot arc. He watched its spin as intently as a youngster fixates on a yo-yo. It was as if he might be watching unseen, tiny figures jump the spring.

The contractor jumped to his feet. " Hit's time for me to git atter it boys. I've got concrete to pour, and it's gonna really be hot." The rest straggled to their feet and proclaimed in tired, dreading sighs what their own rest of the day looked like.

Sitting on the concrete porch with your feet touching the soil, the fine

THE BLUE MOUNTAINS SING
of rivers, old men, trails and trout

gravel and pavement of U.S. 441 was both comfortable and an adventure. This river road carried not only all locals south but also every visitor to Gatlinburg and the Smokies. Each car passed within ten feet of the concrete porch's edge. And it was separated from the pavement edge by a neutral, narrow band of loose gravel. Anyone sitting relaxed with legs outstretched was tickling disaster. Although I never saw anyone actually suffer a crushed limb, the passing traffic often came close enough to spray gravel and dust onto the store porch.

A dirty store porch was my immediate responsibility, and according to my part-time job description (that I never ever saw and that was ever-changing), it included sweeping, cleaning, hosing, mopping all floors, and the front porch. In theory, a clean front porch would welcome the prospective customer and indirectly promise fine customer service inside. A clean store porch meant a continuing absence of tobacco juice stains, cigarette butts, empty RC, Coca Cola, Nehi, Orange, Dr. Pepper, 7Up, and other empty anythings.

The leftovers from the after-midnight porch loungers was an interesting mix. The into the early morning beer drinking crowd was different from the dinner bunch at midday. Their after-dark lounging on our store benches left nothing that ever made my job easier. Most enjoyed cigarettes and a beer as they converted a discarded automobile tire into a blazing bonfire at roadside at the end of the bridge. Mostly they talked through their boredom into the early morning hours.

Most locals were oblivious to this spectacular mountain range view that our porch offered. They were so accustomed to the mountain grandeur that commonly loomed around them, their interest always seemed focused on the news of the day.

At the front door of our store, the bridge lay at the juncture of River Road and Main Street and led over to the Old Mill. It ran nearly easterly and westerly and parallel to the highest peaks of the Smokies some twenty miles to the south.

The scene remains constant and picturesque even today. In the 1940s, the bridge, the dam, the constant motion of the mill wheel, the river current rush in the raceway, the cascading waterfall from the top rim of the dam, the millpond pool, its surface undisturbed, stretched south nearly as far as the eye could see, until finally the Smokies rose skyward at pool's end. The smooth surface of the water made the mountains appear as if they had a slick, perfectly level driveway leading toward their base and touching their foothills.

My Great Smoky Mountain Boyhood

Our Smoky Mountain range viewed from Pigeon Forge's north end near the Wears Valley road intersection with US Highway 441. A 1954 view of Mt. Leconte.
(Tennessee State Library and Archives)

From the dam to the rapids south beyond the Methodist church, thick weeping willows bordered the pool. The banks that held them were blanketed in honeysuckle tangles and occasional kudzu. Pale green foliage framed both banks of the Little Pigeon as far as you could see. Here and there, the mottled grey, white, and beige of the sycamore trees dappled the green. On nights of full moon, the silvery white bark literally glistened and glowed eerily. Of the sycamores that hung out over the water, nearly every one offered at least two or three good limbs for a rope swing. It was a nature setting that even a movie producer couldn't improve on.

The homes above the dam faced the millpond and had small front yards. Their waist-high, concrete retainer walls held yard soil back and, curb like, defined the shoulder of Hwy 441, the only road to Gatlinburg and the Smokies . This one-mile stretch of homes for fifteen plus families was called Stringtown. It began at the Old Mill Bridge and the Pigeon Forge Shopping Center, stretched south past the Pigeon Forge Methodist Church, and ended somewhere further south near Broady's Dairy Farm and Joe Carr's motel. It probably ended at the Judge Ben Robertson home with his adjoining tourist cottages.

Mostly white, mostly two story, mostly wood clapboard, most with front porches, the Stringtown homes were fairly upscale and well kept, with some owned by the same family for two generations or more. The property behind

THE BLUE MOUNTAINS SING
of rivers, old men, trails and trout

View of Stringtown's riverfront homes from Methodist Cemetery Hill. Circa 1919
(Pigeon Forge Library & Jim Whaley)

each home was undeveloped pastureland, farmland soon to become a four-lane highway. Its borders would be split into commercial lots and later, retail stores, restaurants, and motels. But in the late forties and very early fifties, it still remained as pastoral, beautiful open countryside.

Each pasture parcel was rectangular and stretched back southwest towards the Methodist Cemetery hill. Acreage may have varied a little, but several homes had six to ten acres, narrow cookie cutter strips laid side by side evenly like dominoes. Many families had a cow, chickens, a garden, and the occasional horse or pony. Several families sold fresh milk and eggs from their back yards to locals.

If you left the bridge and walked south upriver, the first building on your right was our general store, next door to Arlie Robert's filling station and garage. A broad gravel parking lot formed a roadway that separated his two buildings from our property. The residential area began there.

Mr. John and Emma Emory's house was the first house on your right, white clapboard and one story. The George Fains and children, Jack and Helen Ruth, lived in the second house, a white clapboard two-story home. The next-door neighbors to the Fains were Mr. Joe and Ellen Davis in their rather large, two-story, white frame home with a screened-in front porch overlooking the river. Helen Davis was the "Helen" in the county's weekly Sevier Country News Record column, "Ruth's Letter to Helen." The Davis house would later be rumored as haunted by a ghostly female figure always seen late at night dressed in ballroom gown finery from the Civil War period.

Ruth, in fact, was Adra Ruth, the wife of Judge Ben Robertson. She was the choir director at Pigeon Forge's First Methodist Church for many years. Her weekly column kept folks informed of the latest local news and happenings in and around the greater Pigeon Forge area. Several small communities made up the greater area: Williamsburg, Banner, Gnatty Branch, Gumstand, McCookeville, Boogertown, Possum Hollow or Ridge Road, Pine Mountain, Wears Valley, Waldens Creek, and Pine Grove, along with a number of colorful and aptly named "hollers" and evolving residential housing additions.

In Ruth Robertson's case, she kept the town informed—a sort of local Paul Harvey of written words. Folks could hardly wait to get the weekly paper to see what latest happenings had bubbled up. I remember quite distinctly as a young boy in each Sunday's Methodist service, Mrs. Robertson would select one special hymn of the morning. She'd precede our singing of the hymn with its story. Usually the author or composer was divinely inspired by some tragedy, life downturn, or human trial, and out of frustration, hurt, and pain created the verses we were about to sing. I'd have to give her a high mark for creativity. Every child in the congregation waited until after Miss Ruth's story before they lost focus, began to fidget, and aggravated others.

The fourth house south belonged to the Householders, Myrtle, Stan and their children, Pauline and Marjorie. Myrtle was my second-grade teacher and helped perpetuate that belief held by all youth that everything will remain just as it is—constant, unchanging, solid, dependable, and reliable. The Deloziers, Ruth and Asa ("Ace") and sons James and Bill, lived in the fifth house. This was the same one-story, white clapboard house with riverfront screened-in porch that was the first home of my grandparents, Dr. John W. and Blanche Wayland Ogle. It was the site where he first began his medical practice in 1921. The small outbuilding next door served as his medical office. My grandmother would return here to her first home from Five Oaks Farm sometime in the 1950s and remain there until her death at 103—the cycle complete.

Next door lived Bill and Alda Householder. Their house, the sixth, was quite different from the rest. It was made partially of sandstone and was quite beautiful. The two story home had a screened back porch and open front porch with a marble floor. Alda had four beautiful daughters, Billy, Helen, Sue, and Juanita. Juanita, a gorgeous blonde with blue eyes, would later have a daughter, a beautiful clone of herself, that she named Sandy. Sandy would later marry her high school sweetheart, Gary Wade, an attorney and Sevierville's youngest mayor, who later became a Tennessee Supreme Court Justice. In 2012, he was named Chief Justice of the Supreme Court.

Alda's home was special for several reasons. Not only were her daughters my babysitters on occasion, but her home had a southerly adjoining vacant lot that was nearly an acre, covered in lush Bermuda grass, and, thanks to Alda's graciousness, served as the neighborhood football field for all of us. It cornered the intersection of US 441 and Ogle Lane. Ogle Lane was the gravel road that led to my ridge-top home, "Windswept," the Methodist cemetery, and the homes of many of my classmates and friends. Continuing past our home our neighboring families and children were: Bill and Mamie Duggan and son Jack, Ed and Thelma Ogle and daughters Janice and Patsy, the Sherman Colliers, the Junior Weares and son Jerry Lynn, Uncle Dave and Mollie Ogle, Cleo and Beulah Travena and daughters Charlotte Ruth and Wanda, and several other families that lived further past Mill Creek.

The riverfront's seventh home belonged to Bill and Ruth Quarrels, Clara and Bobby. Their large, two-story, white clapboard home had a second floor screened porch overlooking the river. To the south, the next several homes seemed to match from all outside appearances. Next door, upriver, was the Oliver and Mary Trotter home, followed by the Fillmore and Berthinie McMahan home, Ernest and Flo Conner, children and my sitters Ruth, Jean, and Jack, and the Pigeon Forge Methodist parsonage, which later housed the Bill Steele family.

The twelfth home was the Vic and Ruby Allen and son Billy residence. It was two-storied, white clapboard and had a large, wrap-around front porch decorated with ornate wood trim. The Allen family had several tourist cabins that formed a U-shaped tourist court at the rear of their home. The thirteenth home belonged to Mel and Ethel Lawson and children, Earl and Mary Jean, and they, too, had several tourist cabins at the rear. The Lawsons would later move from the river to a large white, two-story home that stood at the foot of our hill on Ogle Lane. The home next door to the church was the fourteenth and belonged to Vic and Dis Marshall. It was set back farther from the river and included a tourist court.

Beyond the church, the Sam and Lena Roberson home looked out on the river. Sam owned the Exxon gas station that would later be Ward-Beal Exxon. Jim Myers lived in the sixteenth home, upriver. A pasture separated the Myers home and the Bob Robertson home. This seventeenth Stringtown home was family, and a close neighbor of the Judge Ben and Ada Ruth Robertson home. The Judge's home was quite stately and large, surrounded by a grove of several huge oak trees. Their tourist court of several cabins at the side and rear always looked shady and inviting. The Robertson home, the eighteenth, probably marked Springtown's end. They represented "Stringtown "at its best.

School in a small town like ours was definitely an adventure. Pigeon

My Great Smoky Mountain Boyhood

Forge Elementary—there was only one local elementary school—was about a mile and a quarter north of our hilltop home that looked down on River Road and the Stringtown homes. School-bus service had not yet arrived. You either rode your bike or walked to school, complete with a lunch box or bag. From our home's front porch on Windswept, our ridge top overlooked all of Pigeon Forge; you simply loped down a shortcut that traced the front slope of our hillside pasture where it intersected the downhill main gravel road. The walk was three hundred yards out the flat gravel lane. It led to our mailbox, Highway 441, and the banks of the Little Pigeon river. At the intersection of the two was the Householder home to my left and on my right the Quarrels home.

The walk was easier on the asphalt ribbon of our two lane US 441. It linked us to Gatlinburg, five miles away, and then to Newfound Gap in the Park. Five miles further northwest lay Sevierville, the county seat. I turned left, northwest, and downstream, for a three hundred yard walk past a string of very nice riverside homes past my grandmother's home to the Old Mill corner, where the roar of the dam and our grocery store would greet me.

Crossing the Old Mill Bridge, I passed the Old Mill to my right and the red barn housing the Pigeon Forge Pottery on my left. And just past the mill to my right, local blacksmith Arlie Roberts would look up from his metalwork, nod, and continue pumping the charcoal firepot bellows.

Jogging the last one-quarter mile to the Pigeon Forge Elementary School ball diamond, I'd climb through the fence, run up the hill to the gymnasium front, and begin my climb up the wide wrap of sixteen concrete steps. Their oversized, sprawling, quarter-moon shape always seemed better suited for the Lincoln Memorial, especially after a jog up the hill.

The school was heated with large, canister-shaped, coal-heated stoves, their potbellies hidden by metal, cylindrical-shaped covers that served as protection and to radiate heat. They looked like giant vegetable cans, dull aluminum grey and without labels. Each room had a stove at its center. We drank outside from a pump-handled well that squirted individual water streams along a sixteen-foot, galvanized pipe. Punctured with equally spaced spout holes and mounted on a horizontal concrete bench, it worked well as a multi-person fountain as long as someone pumped. The biggest aggravation was the pumper. Once the spouts of water rose high enough for drinkers to drink, pumpers thought it was a great prank to stop and run.

The school's hallway walls were covered in wooden, square, individual cubicles that allowed just enough room for a lunchbox or bag. Our bathrooms were outside. They were wooden privies with four wooden seats and a

THE BLUE MOUNTAINS SING
of rivers, old men, trails and trout

sloping wooden urinal trough for boys. Icy winter days made this activity very special, as did a hot day with flies and humidity. Our playground was a walk down the hill at recess for a quick baseball or marble game. It was part of Sam Robertson's river bottom that was bounded by the river and probably contained twenty acres. The school property, our ball field, and playground lay at the foot of the hill in a fenced-off, six-acre tract of the large, river-bottom pasture. It was flat, low-lying, flooded often, and seemed to hold water. Its outfield was often wet from heavy rain, and the river backup and poor drainage added more baseball misery to the low, spongy, marsh-like terrain. This area is now adjacent to Patriot Park. Our baseball field was huge, flat, and, most of the time, the outfield was full of bulrush clumps—wetlands. This memory is distinct because I was small for my age and maybe quick, so they always sent me to centerfield. Any baseball hit beyond second base was destined for four to six inches of water—the "Frog Pond." I don't remember ever having dry tennis shoes or socks after the morning recess. A gas station and small retail outlet now occupy that area adjacent to Patriot Park.

Basketball was the only winter game in town. There was no little league or any organized athletics outside school athletics in the Pigeon Forge area. I lived and breathed basketball during the winter. Somehow I had mastered first-grade requirements quickly; I was moved to the second grade the same year, and throughout my school years was one year younger and one grade above my age level. Short for my age and one or more years younger than my classmates, I was determined to excel at basketball or any sport for that matter.

During basketball season, I got up at four thirty a.m. and walked about a mile and a half to the elementary school so I could practice basketball shots until school started. The "unlock the doors and start the fires janitor" for a few winters was Clifford Rauhuff, a classmate and the tallest player on our team. Clifford started the fires in each stove at five a.m., so I made sure I got there when he opened the first door. I helped him turn all lights on and quickly have the entire gymnasium to myself. I shot fouls and layups until the school bell rang. I later got a bike and was able to get there quicker, especially when a four fifty a.m. January wind chill urged me on.

Even though I was probably the smallest and shortest player on the Pigeon Forge Tiger Basketball team, my early morning practice earned me some playing time. We were proudly clad in orange-and- black uniforms. Our principal, math teacher, and coach, Frank Marshall, was jubilant when, in our eighth grade and last elementary year, we won the 1951 Sevier County Boys Basketball Championship, complete with trophy. Mr.

My Great Smoky Mountain Boyhood

Marshall hauled our teams, both boys and girls, to and from games in the back of a pickup truck with a camper bed. He had wooden benches made especially for the team. At every away game, we could be seen pouring out of the back of his truck, not unlike an unending parade of circus clowns exiting a small vehicle.

Mr. Marshall was a disciplined teacher. I had him as a math teacher from fifth grade on. I'll be forever grateful for his politically incorrect teaching style and his determination that we master all multiplication tables, addition, and subtraction. He used flashcards and rote learning unmercifully. Each individual was expected to come to the front of the room, face a blackboard of problems, and mentally calculate the answers. Sometimes the problems were inscribed on the window shades, which he'd pull down to display the challenge of the day. The goal was to quickly recite your mistake-free answers aloud and to beat Mr. Marshall's stopwatch. Students who were either uncaring, did not run through the drills quickly enough or completed their drills with mistakes, were in trouble.

He invited all less-than-excellent performers of the day out in the hall where we were asked to bend over long tables. Requesting that every head be bowed and every eye closed, he would pace up and down behind us. The every head bowed and every eye closed part was strange and unnerving to most of us. The only other place we ever heard it was at the Baptist church revivals where ministers waited down front. It was an oft repeated phrase as the minister led us through our thirty-third refrain of the hymn, "Just as I am."

Mr. Marshall admonished the group about the perils that poor math skills would create in our future. Once he had created enough anxious tension, he would deliver a light smack,at random, to backsides with the big wooden paddle he always carried. His fear factor on us was infinitely more terrifying than any pain his stroke ever delivered. Secretly, he considered all of us to be his promising young math scholars. To this day, due to his dogged determination, I can still instantly add, subtract, multiply, and divide most numbers mentally. When I see someone counting on fingers or using any method other than mental calculations, I smile. His flash cards leap to memory, and I recall Mr. Marshall's persistence. He wanted to ensure that we would never go out into the world unprepared. His efforts and influence created some of the finest and most meaningful gifts I ever received from a teacher.

I spent my entire seven years at Pigeon Forge Elementary school. Our black and white class photo stirs bittersweet emotions. Life dealt with

THE BLUE MOUNTAINS SING
of rivers, old men, trails and trout

Pigeon Forge Elementary School – Circa 1944

Pigeon Forge Elementary - Front row: Edna Chance, Joan Ogle, Sue Ella Marshall, John Thompson, Homer Henry, Charlotte Ruth Travena, Donnie McNew, Marion Temple Householder. Back row: Dorothy Rolen, Nelle Huskey, OraLee Woodruff, Freddie Kasermann, Harold McCoy, Pat Whaley, and Ronny Rader
(Ron Rader family collection-)

each of us differently. Some came, went, and transferred, but all were my classmates at one time or another.

The early 1940s brought cataclysmic change to our tiny foothills village. Construction on the new highway began. According to Veta King's book, *Pigeon Forge*, it all sprang from an original Indian path. She described a Cherokee footpath known as the Indian Gap Trail that crossed the Great Smokies from North Carolina and passed through the Pigeon Forge Valley en route to its junction with the Great Indian Warpath. US 441 still passes through nearby Sevierville, and closely parallels this ancient trail. However, it crests the mountains at Newfound Gap rather than Indian Gap. From Sevierville, the Warpath headed west toward the Overhill Cherokee towns along the Little Tennessee River.

By late 1940s, the construction of our new four-lane highway sliced through most everybody's back yard that lived along the river. The town's center was in rapid change, and our pre-teen years, revolved around that change.

The beginning construction involved heavy equipment, huge scraping giants, bulldozers, and huge dump trucks. It began in early spring. The earth was moved, scraped, trucked, and treaded into fine dust by every tread imaginable, metal or rubber. It was driven over continually by construction. As a result, the activity converted the once

30

rich, river-bottom soil into a fine, reddish-tan dust, shoe-top deep and the texture of talcum powder.

Dust quickly became everyone's enemy. First, the merchants downtown complained, then the homeowners complained, then folks with dust-covered gardens, flowers, and crops complained, and then everyone complained. The Tennessee Highway Department tried to help. First, they sprinkled the entire two or three mile length with water trucks, but it quickly evaporated in the hot summer sun. Next they sprayed used motor oil on the clay roadway. The oil helped, but the continuous scraping quickly neutralized it, and it disappeared as new dust appeared.

A few weeks of that and the whole town was edgy and disgruntled. Winds added insult to injury. In fact, on some spring days when high winds swept through the unobstructed road plain, a reddish-tan dust reminiscent of the Southwest's Dust Bowl days seemed reborn here. This talcum dust lifted high on the westerly prevailing winds and mixed with the mountain's smoky blue haze. The puzzling blend created a new mountain look that only artists, photographers, and weather forecasters could have found interesting. Business owners and vacationers were furious.

An unfinished roadbed generated another civic nightmare. How could law enforcement folks enforce the non-established driving regulations and non-existent laws? Pigeon Forge law enforcement officers were more than frustrated. The dust along with the unpaved roadway had affected the enforcement of already murky driving laws. The new, temporary, unwritten "Let's get through this and everybody work together" directions were mainly rumor. Deputies and Tennessee Highway Patrol officers knew anyone living to the southeast of the road had to drive on and through the raw road base to get to and from their homes. The formal road signs read: *Construction equipment only—No traffic allowed*. The local word of mouth was: "It's OK to drive on the new, unfinished roadbed; just don't get caught." The local law enforcement looked the other way.

The newly scraped four lanes stretched from The Sandpike (Wears Valley Road) intersection to the Park boundary at the upper end of Pigeon Forge. If the center of Pigeon Forge was the hub of a wagon wheel lying on its side, and you stood on the hub and faced the Smokies, every road on your right was a side road. Each road led to a community that formed the greater area of the Forge. The new road sliced a perpendicular line through every ingress and egress road, directly or indirectly, on its way to Pine Grove. The communities most affected were Wears Valley, Walden's Creek, Pine

THE BLUE MOUNTAINS SING
of rivers, old men, trails and trout

Unpaved highway borders downtown Pigeon Forge. Circa 1950
(Pigeon Forge Library)

Mountain, Flannigan Addition, Ogle Road, Mill Creek, Conner Heights, and even Caney, Banner, McCooksville, Gumstand, and Boogertown.

To reach any one of these outlying areas, a driver travelled on one or more of the unpaved four lanes. The two lanes nearest the river were paved first and completed in 1949.However, due to lack of funds, the right side, the two lanes furthest from the river, were left unpaved until around 1952 or 1953. So from 1949 until 1953, the unpaved road portion was a sea of dust or mud and heavily used by locals. Some of my best adventures began on these unfinished portions of the new road bed.

The road and our need for grocery store deliveries set the stage for problems. As grocery store owners, Mom and Veryl wanted to be service oriented and neighborly. So they chose to deliver groceries. It was especially helpful for those store customers who didn't own a car, for those folks who lived so far back in the mountains that poor roads made it difficult to get to the store , or other folks handicapped by illness, a downturn in life, or other tribulations. Most of them really needed the help of grocery delivery. If there was a road, a logging road, or even a wide trail that was not overly steep, we tried to deliver. I delivered groceries by Jeep at age fourteen.

I viewed my summer part time work as boring. As a preteen boy who enjoyed the outdoors , it was a penance I had to pay. My folks explained it logically. Your help in the family business, for which you are fairly paid, teaches you many virtues along with discipline and work ethic. You don't have to be a grocer all your life, but everything you learn as a retail grocer converts to a skill that will help you somewhere else in life. Experience here will be invaluable in learning to deal with customers, especially the difficult ones.

Try as I might, I laid awake at night trying to come up with a counter argument that would rebut their stance, but I never did win this argument.

My Great Smoky Mountain Boyhood

Center of Pigeon Forge – Circa 1954

Our two story, brick grocery store is in upper right. Dairy Queen directly behind to left of Arlie Robert's garage. Note the paved four lanes
(Pigeon Forge Library)

It held water, and I could never punch a hole in their position. I tell you right now that any argument or position that you run into that is truthful, logical, rational, or reasonable, brother, you're gonna have your work cut out for you trying to disprove it. If I hadn't been a young boy imprisoned in the family grocery store I mighta made a good lawyer. Oh political correctness, where were you when I needed you.

You may not be aware of the demands of a grocer's life. We opened at seven a.m. , closed at seven p.m., and a few nights we stayed open to nine p.m. My part time work, chores after school, and summer job days were quite varied. Since my mother and her good friend and partner, Veryl, operated the store while their husbands worked at the Park, I was a part time employee and a partial one at that as was Veryl' s son Sonny.

When either of us was there, the lucky part-timer stacked and stocked all shelves after the merchandise was delivered from the distributor. We collected and separated all soft drink return glass bottles in their respective bottle wooden cases. All fresh produce had to be unloaded, stripped, freshened, and arranged. This included stripping brown leaves from lettuce and cabbage, trimming green onion tops, removing overripe tomatoes, potatoes, melons, and other vegetables. We also took customer orders at the meat counter, sliced, weighed, and wrapped the cheeses and meats. We often greeted and waited on customers, ran the cash register, bagged groceries, and carried groceries to car on request. The heavy lifting happened at the rear of the store where we restacked all twenty-five and fifty pound bags of flour, meal, horse and cow bran, refilled customer's five gallon kerosene cans. The kerosene was pumped from our five hundred gallon storage tank, and—we responded to the "come help with this, we need you."

My Dad, ever the World War II veteran from the European theater, never lost his fondness for the army surplus Willy's Jeep with four wheel drive. In 1948, he bought a used one , and we used it around home as a second vehicle and as a delivery vehicle at the store. I learned to drive on its gear shift despite its stubbornness. I was twelve, nearly thirteen, and couldn't wait for my permit, a release way too far in the future.

Now the new road had created somewhat of a dilemma. The town was small, a lot like Mayberry without the sheriff. Everybody knew everybody. There were probably somewhere between fifty and one hundred families in the greater Pigeon Forge area and Gatlinburg . I don't recall the exact law or its regulation of drivers, either underage or for those with driving permits, but it was very liberal as I remember. The unwritten law was "you can't drive on paved highway." That was pretty logical. Those were the days when government actually made logical sense.

Our area was ninety five percent farmland and most everybody farmed. As a result, most every youngster needed to drive farm equipment and the family truck around the farm and on the dusty lanes connecting farms. Law enforcement was very lenient. The highway patrol, I'm sure, had much higher priorities than stopping some farm youngster helping out the family farm. Even if you overstepped your boundaries, they'd usually get the word of caution back through someone indirectly.

Our whole county was a network of rough, unpaved roads, some graveled. Tourist traffic was still light and not problematic. In reality, a youngster in his teens or even twelve could navigate the countryside fairly freely if they drove responsibly. As a thirteen year old, many of my driving adventures began on this dusty, unpaved four-lane. Today, many of my friends and classmates would say the same.

A call from the front of the store released me from my bondage and set me free, "Ronny, we got a delivery over to Mill Creek to the Ledbetter's grandmother. Go ahead and take the Jeep." This always spelled an Uncle Remus day.

A sign here and there on the new construction directed any auto forced to drive on the unfinished highway to honor twenty-five mph. I started at twenty-five and was well intentioned. My eyes found the saucer shaped hole in the Jeep's floorboard on the passenger side. It was like a little window that allowed you to see the ground speed by. I always thought it was neat and sort of extra, like something nobody else had. For some reason, my dad didn't have the same attitude.

I caused the hole earlier that year by smashing over a pointed rock that hid in the shallows of Mill Creek. I tried to ford the stream on a grocery delivery. The rock was hidden, taller than the rest, and had no business being there. It was too tall, uneven, and not even level with the rest. Trying to see how high the water would splash, I guess I was going a little too fast. Well actually, I didn't even slow down. I really gunned it to make the biggest splash of the summer. My dad got right to the point when I blamed that big rock that got in the way.

He looked carefully over, under the jeep, stepped back, placed his hands on his hips, and said, "Son, I just want you to know, this makes me and your mother real proud. Today, you've made us really proud of you." And he turned and walked off. I felt bad. His Jeep was his pet.

Nevertheless, it was a great day that day. I was making a delivery and driving the Jeep. I might even sing "Oklahoma" again.

Like most grocers, my mother extended credit for groceries. The rural economy was cyclical and very dependent on weather, crops, and luck. A large black metal frame with heavy spring clips rested to the right of the cash register. The customer's charges were recorded on simple tickets with a customer's carbon copy. The original was placed behind the clip and awaited payment. When various crops went to market, the customer came in and settled up the account balance. While most folks were well intentioned and paid the balance as planned, some did not for a variety of reasons. Legal recourse was not really the custom in those days nor was it in the best spirit of community. When her grocer chapter finally closed after a decade or so, the total customer balance owed and unpaid was sizable. It neared six figures. Unlike autos and other tangible products, groceries were consumable and did not lend themselves to repossession.

Mom and Veryl were always on the lookout for new and interesting clothing, food, and other items. They wanted to stay abreast of the times and be first to provide the trend to the customer. This willingness was a delight to the salesmen and distributors. "I really like those, and I believe they'll really sell. Send us a couple dozen, and we'll see how they move," both Mom and Veryl were quick to say.

Now the two ladies were fairly well organized and the store was logically laid out and stocked fairly efficiently, but neither believed the old adage

THE BLUE MOUNTAINS SING
of rivers, old men, trails and trout

that "you can't put forty pounds of flour in a twenty pound bag." The store literally bulged at the seams and threatened to spill up into the library on the second floor. This led increasingly to the store " by-line " that both ladies used quite often. " Yes siree we've got it, and we'll be happy to sell to you— if we can just find it!"

An old mountain general store was probably the last of those places where one could always find a fair exchange of mind and heart. Today the building is one story, a leather and moccasin shop. Its character is gone along with the characters that called it home. The Lone Ranger, Johnny of Philip Morris, and the cute little blue-eyed, blonde girl proud of her ninety nine percent pure Ivory Soap are also gone, their fading delight resting somewhere in memory and age. Gone too, is its concrete landing with the overhanging porch. Now, no one pauses long enough to enjoy what the old store once offered. Only a few remember, but the colorful characters of the grocery store days still linger as unforgettable.

All three of the store ladies would retire in the late fifties leaving a hole in the town's delicate social fabric. It would be a community rend that was never quite made whole again. Until then, Miss Mildred's husband John Rellie used his own black four door sedan and served as our postal carrier. He drove the Star route to Sevierville, daily helping sort mail and hauling ours back at the end of each day. In those neighborly, laid back, un-politically correct days, if you needed a ride to the high school, to visit the doctor, or wanted to visit a Sevierville friend, John Rellie happily obliged. You were more than welcome as long as you could squeeze in between string bound bundles of Atchley's Funeral Home almanac calendars, Sears Roebuck and Montgomery Ward catalogs, postage stamped mail, packages, and twine bound stacks of the county paper, the Montgomery Vindicator, and an occasional wooden crate containing a tractor, thresher, auto, or truck metal part. With its back seat removed, his sedan was a self-modified station wagon; we just didn't know it.

You could see our home from the schoolyard. It was nearly a mile southeast, as the crow flies, on a ridge top that was taller than the one our elementary school perched on. Our home rose directly over downtown Pigeon Forge and on its clone and sister ridge top next door, north of us by about three hundred yards, was the Pigeon Forge Methodist Cemetery.

My brother Rick was five years younger than I. With similar interests and close enough in age, we enjoyed our mountain life and every opportunity for adventure. Our home was at ridge top surrounded by five acres. Our front yard was two flat grass covered acres filled with five or six large white and black oak trees, and a few small outbuildings that we added.

My Great Smoky Mountain Boyhood

After our first home burned in 1947, we rebuilt on the west end of our ridge. Site is now home to Whispering Pines Condominiums.
(Ron Rader family collection)

One was a chestnut log smoke house for my outdoor gear storage and a one room poplar log cabin with loft that served as Dads "playhouse," workshop, outdoor camp, and hideout. Dad purchased the cabin when the Park sold off some cabin inventory it no longer wanted to maintain. Dad, myself, and several of his friends labeled each log with East, West, North, and South and numbered each one. We dismantled it, trucked it to our backyard, and reassembled it a short privacy distance at the rear of our home. Marion Watson, son of Doc Watson, was a local master stone mason and neighbor, and he added a fine mountain stone fireplace and beautiful chimney to the cabin. Its draw was outstanding and always kept the cabin smoke free. The cabin was a treasure and used often.

Our view of the Smokies from both our front and back marble patios was spectacular. Our gaze paralleled US Highway 441 and was the same view the traveler saw on their drive to the Smokies. Our home literally hung out over downtown Pigeon Forge. Sitting on a grassy, flat ridge top, encircled by the gravel driveway, we had the back half of the property in a few hardwoods and mostly Virginia pines that provided a thicket screen of privacy at the rear on Duggan road. Our driveway bordered the front pasture and ended at the great white oak in our front yard. A large flat beneath the tree , large enough for four or five automobiles, was firm with fine gravel, intermeshed with fescue sod, and last year's acorns. This flat shelf joined the gentle slope of the rest of our front yard and served as a nice extension that served many purposes. My dad parked the family automobile there. Since it was just off our front patio , it made a great picnic table and lounge area, playground and trapeze arena, and met most any need for outdoor space. The canopy of the huge oak provided cooling shade that seemed unmatched especially since there was always a breeze at "Windswept." Our view was spectacular. You could see every movement in downtown Pigeon Forge.

THE BLUE MOUNTAINS SING
of rivers, old men, trails and trout

After our home burned in mid 1940s, we rebuilt further west about one hundred yards. The driveway was extended so that it encircled the entire ridge top and bordered the back patio of our new home. The homeplace landmark, the white oak, remained and continued to provide much enjoyment. As the years passed, its growth spurts made it seem monstrous in size. Our back neighbors were Bill and Mamie Duggan and their son Jack, he was my close friend and most every day playmate.

Our front acreage that faced Pigeon Forge was a gradual sloping pasture, entirely in grass and bounded by Ogle Road from the end of our circular driveway to the four lanes of US 441. The pasture itself was somewhat oval shaped, completely fenced with two barbed wire strands stretched atop the more animal friendly squares of page wire. The fence rows were overgrown, laced with blackberry briars, and mixed with wild flowers and vines that made the rows thick and deep. The wire sagged under the heavy matted weight of honeysuckle vines. This matted solitary stretch was home for most every small wild animal. Hornets, bumble bees, wasps, and yellow jackets also prized it as a best place for a nest. At the foot of the ragged fence row was a path, a red clay ribbon that stretched clear around the pasture. Animals tend to follow fencerows. It was easier than climbing straight up and down. The walk offered a gradual grade. It was smoother, sometimes softer, and it fit well in a routine.

Ever since my folks had moved to their hill top in the early thirties, they had a cow, chickens, a garden, and maybe a horse or two. Apparently when Rick and I came along we evidently trumped farm animals and poultry. We had a garden and fishpond until Rick turned four and wanted a pony. We soon had a pony in the front field. At the foot of the hill, we still had a cistern well and a concrete trough. After replacing some rubber gaskets and other repairs, we could pump water with the old metal pump and long handle. From this pump and trough, our fence continued about another thirty yards until it formed a corner of our pasture with the fence row of the adjoining pasture that belonged to our neighbor the Mel Lawson family.

Their large white two-story home was no more than forty yards away, and it fronted on the new highway at its intersect with Ogle Road. Their pasture was very steep. At this corner, our fence row turned and went straight up the hill to our corner white oak and front yard.

Lest you become bored with these details , believe me, this is important. This fence leg was perpendicular to the fence and road at the bottom. Here the only entry to our neighbors pasture was a poor man's cattle guard typical of that day. Two posts were set just wide enough for a man to squeeze through but too narrow for farm animals like a cow or horse to manage, except possibly the smaller animal determined to get to the neighbor's greener pasture. Each post was faced with a flat plank that made it appear like a doorway face. Our wire fence was continuous except for this break and two other drop-down wire gates that were just extensions of the page wire. This front pasture was home for Rick's pinto pony.

As far as horses went, ours were always family, friendly, and we thought nothing of riding with a minimum of gear. You need to understand that we seldom used a bridle with a bit and never a saddle on my uncle's farm horses. Typically, we'd get a saddle horse, work horse, or mule and take them out into a plowed field in case they threw us off. We'd find a short piece of plow line and fashion an Indian bridle. Ours consisted of a simple loop lightly slipped over the horse's nose followed by pulling the remainder over and behind the horses ears and threaded through the loop on the opposite side. The tag end was then attached to the opposite nose loop, and the rider had a bridle and rein. Sometimes if the horse was fairly well trained and ridden often, you could ride with no bridle. You could grasp the mane, use knee pressure, and with an occasional flick of a wispy, willow limb to the side of the horse's neck, a ride tuned to pleasure. Assessing and anticipating the horse's tameness level and deciding its disposition of the day were most important as far as we were concerned. Several times we learned the hard way that the mood of any horse, no matter how gentle or well trained in the past, can be unpredictable.

Ponies are another story. At times, I wondered if they really belonged to the same equine species as horses. They are as different as cats and dogs. In fact, they seem more like cats. They are stubborn, independent, self-centered, unpredictable, aloof, skittish, have a mind of their own, always have their own agenda, always focused on their own mission, and are rather devious and deceptive. At times they will bite you, kick you, and throw you at every opportunity.

One of my many summer jobs as a boy taught me some Jekyll–Hyde absolutes about that Tasmanian devil called a pony. If you saddle one for a child, the pony will take a deep breath right before you pull the saddle belly cinch and buckle it. You believe the saddle is snug and tight around the belly so you buckle it. The child mounts, the pony breathes out, and the six inches of slack quickly converts to a very loose saddle. As the pony gallops away on the pony ride that you promised the child would be wonderful , it occurs to you the screams you quickly hear are not screams of glee. They sound more like horror and fright. When you can finally peer through the startup dust, the youngster is not mounted upright as you had expected. No, he is hanging upside down, though perfectly straight, back unbent, his posture is one that would impress any instructor in horsemanship. Dust is blowing in his eyes, the wind is whipping through his hair, and the top of his head almost touches ground with each bound. By the time the pony stops and the child, unhurt, stops sobbing and the dust settles, you wait anxiously for some response.

Thanks to this solid proof of the unpredictability and unfathomable personality of a pony, you hear a child's screaming voice, "I thought you said a pony ride was fun. I'm never getting back on any horse—again—ever. In fact, I hate horses—I even hate people who like horses."

I've seen it happen a million times. The moral of the story: Knee a pony in the side if you don't want to wait an hour for him to breathe. He'll expel his breath and you can saddle him with a properly tightened belly strap. It's like a push to your stomach or solar plexus. You cannot hold your breath. This advice will probably inflame most of the animal rights groups, but it's true, effective, and harmless if used responsibly.

Normally, our own brown and white pinto pony was pretty good most times. His most notable and mischievous pranks happened once or twice a month during school. A summons for me to leave my classroom and go to the principal's office was always unpleasant. Sweaty and pale, I'd stand in front of his desk thinking the worst. "Ronny, Ricky's pinto pony followed you all to school again; he must have got out again about eleven o'clock. You can take him over across the field to Mrs. Mary Henry's house. I believe Ricky takes piano lessons from her. Just tie it up to that big maple tree out back. You all can get it after school, or Ricky can ride it home from his piano lessons. I believe he takes them on Tuesday afternoons after school. I don't want a pony left on school grounds cause all the kids will be trying to ride it, and we never will be able to round them up after lunch and recess and git'um back in class. I'll be bustin' tail all afternoon if you don't get that pony out of here. And bustin' tail is not what I have planned for my afternoon."

One lazy summer day I was bored and just roaming around near the pasture gate at our hilltop. I climbed through the three barbed wired strands and stood shirtless, barefooted, and wearing nothing else but worn shorts. I petted the little pinto lazily shading in the shadow of our big oak. It was a fine lazy summer day full of sunshine, June bugs, and all things summer. Bees were hard at work probing the yellow and white of field daisies that covered the field. School was out. I was free. Even the bugs of summer seemed happy as they buzzed in constant motion. This really was an Uncle Remus day. It was that kind of balmy summer morning that always made me want to sing "Oklahoma."

My Great Smoky Mountain Boyhood

The pony, tail-swishing some pesky horse flies , seemed content as he daydreamed and munched red clover. It seemed a perfect day for both of us. I absentmindedly rubbed his neck and wondered who would be in the river swimming hole at Broady's this afternoon. I dreamed of the rope swing. At the bottom of the hill, I could see my little brother, Rick. He was sitting on the concrete trough alongside another boy his age and size. I recognized him as one our neighbor friends who lived across Mill Creek about three miles back in the mountains. Both were almost nine and almost the same size.

Cappie was one of seven children and was dressed just like Rick and I. Our summer uniform of the year was shorts only, no underwear, unless your mother caught you, no shoes, no shirt, and no cap. The three or four cowlicks in Cappie's uncombed hair always added to his unkemptness. An image that suggested his last night sleep was restless and outdoors. His skin was berry brown from sun and his bony knees, wing bones, clavicles, and ribs gave him an undernourished look. His entire body was splotchy with cuts, scratches, mosquito and fly bites that had healed or were healing. His action badges were always white, untanned, and contrasted with the rest of a small bare body that looked roasted by summer sun.

That day, his legs, back, and face were dust caked. Sweat from the near noon sun slid rivulet trails of red dust down his cheeks and out of the curls at the nape of his neck. His only clean skin was from his feet to his knees. He usually waded Mill Creek at the ford rather than walk the extra quarter mile to the wooden bridge. The Lucky Strike cigarette he puffed as he talked suggested his was not the life typical of most eight year old boys. He was a good kid though, friendly, jovial, and laughed a lot, he acted as if his life could not be any better. Everbody in town liked him as far as I knew.

Bored from a no-excitement morning, I decided to ride the pony down, join the two at the bottom, and see if there was any news. I didn't have a bridle or even a rope. I knew I could ride with no bridle, and I sure didn't need a saddle. He was gentle. I'd just let him walk at his own pace around the clay trail to the far end of the hilltop pasture across from where our driveway, Ogle Road, and the road to the Pigeon Forge Methodist Cemetery met. In the curve of the path and fence row, the hill's slope lessened and grew flatter and flatter along the roadside ditch and fencerow as it descended to the bottom of the hill.

At the bottom, it soon became a grassy flat, or track, for about one hundred yards to where Rick and Cappie lounged on the concrete water trough. The cattle guard gate was some thirty yards past them. I was in no hurry, and figured we'd both enjoy the amble. So I climbed aboard like always in a friendly sort of way and clicked my usual "giddyup" sound—the one that's best for calling your dog, if he was close by, or your horse if you wanted to offer him a friendly, respectful request for a ride. The tone of this particular sound explicitly and gently requested that I'd like for the pony to carry me forward—if he didn't mind.

The pinto pony bolted like a football player being timed on the forty yard dash. He was on the path all right and going the way I planned. He was running so fast that the only way I could stay astride him was to grip his mane and lock my legs around his body. In the first fifty yards, I thought he'd tire and certainly could go no faster. I was wrong on both counts.

The sharp curve in the trail and fence row loomed closer and quicker, and his speed increased with every step. It was as if the Kentucky Derby gates were flung open, and those imaginary horses on both sides of us were trying to outrun him. I decided he'd either try to jump the fence and ditch and land in the gravel of Ogle Road, or he'd simply run headlong into the mass of fence and brush, or he'd turn the curve at lightning speed with centrifugal force that would launch me into the gravel road, alone and horseless. None of these options seemed particularly healthy. I was determined not to join the varmints I'd often seen in the fencerow. I quickly decided that where he went, I went.

I was already gripping him with every appendage of my body, so I raised up slightly, pried my fingers from his mane, its ends now whipping my face, and leaned forward as far as I could extend my arms and wrapped them around his neck as if I loved him dearly, which clearly at this time, I did not. I could not believe it; his speed still escalated.

We turned the curve, him in my clutches, or vice versa, and were in the flat stretch now. I could see two eight year olds standing on the concrete trough, hands at their brows shading their vision against the sun. They appeared a bit puzzled as they talked excitedly, one to another. Cappie kept pointing at me, at us, his head moving from us to Rick and back, all the while pointing and talking. Rick seemed to be trying to figure out this apparition that was fast approaching. He seemed to fidget and look around as if he really should try to get to even higher ground but was reluctant to leave the protection of the concrete.

Since I was wrapped around this pony like a rope, I think they were mesmerized in puzzled wonderment as they queried each other. They seemed to debate. Would I really try to make this pony jump over a five foot steel pump with extended handle, two four foot tall boys, now pasty faced, and a concrete trough that was roughly eight feet long, three feet wide, and three feet deep? The pony galloped faster. Then, screamed right by the trough and them.

My Great Smoky Mountain Boyhood

"Oh Lord," I said aloud hoping He heard, "he's still not through. This pony is gonna run right through that too-narrow slot of a cattle gate and try to run into the next pasture."

It did not take research calculations to decide that even if he did probably burst through, my body and leg wrap, that now felt part of him, would not follow. I sat up for the first time since we launched, only seconds remained for my decision; his speed slowed a bit as his head entered the gap. Still in an astride position, I shoved my body backward, hard. The palms of my hands and my extended forearms slapped the planks with a flat smack ,and my thighs did the same. Since his coat was now sweaty and slippery, he ran out from under me and shot through the gap at a dead run. I was left standing straight up against the wooden planks, my palms and thighs touching the roughness of the weathered oak, unhurt.

The silence was deafening, my knees were weak, and not a word was spoken, at least not by me. It was that familiar pregnant pause when things seem frozen in time. It was that familiar long eerie silence that time fills ever so slowly, the same one that trails things unnerving and unexpected. The same one where someone always shrieks the proverbial questions, "Are you hurt? Are you OK?"

I turned slightly to my left and looked back over my shoulder. They were still too far away for normal conversation, but I could see their facial expressions clearly. Cappie alternated between excited jumps, open mouth exclamations that were soundless, closing his mouth only long enough to take long pulls on his Lucky Strike cigarette. The smoke cloud revealed his animated excitement, and the smoke encircled Rick's head until I could no longer see his expression.

Occasionally, Cappie's head would appear above the smoke. His Zulu like jumps alternated from fawn fashion leaps to pogo stick bounces, still no sounds came from his open mouth. Cappie looked like he really needed to go pee and was bouncing while his teacher tried to decide whether or not to grant him permission to leave her room.

Acting as if he'd just seen the most exciting and amazing act of his first Barnum and Bailey circus, he screamed at Rick, "Gaaaaaaaawwwd daaaam!!! Your brother can really ride a horse. I ain't never seed nobody ride a horse like at! And to beat it all, he don't even have to have a bridle! Er a damn saddle. Why, I'd bet my ass nobody in any gawddamn circus can do that! Your brother is a damn 'tushhog' , I bet he ain't afeered of nuthin' 'ner nobody! If I wust tuh ever fight anybody, I'd sure as hell want him on my 'bygawd' side!"

I felt like I was about to vomit. I slumped down in the clover almost lifeless as Cappy ran over and started slapping me on the back. It was like I'd just run a one hundred yard touchdown for his team. He continued leaping around fawn fashion and, all the while, asking me if he brought all his buddies over from the poolroom would I do it again.

Tourism Changes Our Mountains

It had not been long since World War II ended. Now, from Pigeon Forge to Gatlinburg, infant tourism flickered. Cottage industries like weaving, woodworking, and crafts began to spring up. Along US 441, locals built small, wooden, open-air souvenir and craft stands, their open fronts facing the roadside traffic. Stretched to the left and right were taut clotheslines that held chenille bedspreads, colorful Indian blankets, and all manner of crafts. Forming the backbone of the local cottage industry, many women wove handbags, place mats, and other items on wooden looms placed in spare corners of their homes, their homemade crafts would soon end up in Gatlinburg shops or the roadside stands that dotted the area landscape. All these outlets were well stocked with authentic "Indian" feathered headdresses, toy bows and arrows, moccasins, and similar items, most imported from China. The craft of the day was anything loomed. Most popular were the place mats and handbags loomed in pastel colors of white, pink, baby blue, and seafoam green.

Overnight rentals consisted mainly of a few small cabins that many home owners built in their side and back yards. Tourist courts were synonymous with today's overnight rentals ,and the Pigeon Forge and Gatlinburg corridor saw many spring up.

My close teenage friend, Jim, and his family probably had the most creative and unusual tourist offering in Pigeon Forge at the time. Their small home faced the new construction of US 441 and was at the rear of Butler's Grocery store, which fronted south into Pigeon Forge's downtown commerce. The little, white, one-story bungalow sat somewhere around where Sue's Fashions is now located. Jim's father was probably the town's first jeweler and watch maker. Max, Jim's younger brother, was about the same age as my brother Rick and an elementary school classmate. They had moved here from Florida in the late 1940s, and his dad operated his business out of their home. They also were probably the first concrete yard statue retailer in town. They cast animals and fowl in rubber molds—from flamingos to rabbits and beyond. Painted or unpainted the figures were very popular.

In a side addition, they had a small photography development studio. In front of the home at roadside, they had two huge animals—stuffed—not live. One was a very large authentic, bucking bronco frozen in midair as if throwing a cowboy from its back. At its side stood a monstrous buffalo. Unlike his violent bronco pal, the buffalo stood placidly peering at the road seemingly chewing grass and watching the tourists pass by. The sign read : "Get your picture made astride a real bucking bronco or a fierce buffalo $ 1.00."

A family member, usually Jim, would greet the stopped visitors as they tumbled excitedly from their car, help them climb the step ladder and get astride their animal of choice, make their picture, retire to the photo room lab, develop the shot, return with the prized picture, and collect the money. The scene probably created the most tourism excitement in all of Pigeon Forge. Saturday and Sunday afternoons were filled with shouts, finger pointing, and autos coming to sudden screeching stops. For some reason, the animals and their enticing offers of a neat picture seemed to be a magnet for pretty teenage girls. Once Jim and I discovered that pattern, I felt it was my very Christian solemn and loyal duty to conscientiously help my good friend as often as possible. It was the least I could do for a good friend. We often argued who got to assist with the ladder and who got to take the picture.

Around 1950, Pigeon Forge probably got its first "not-from-here" artist. Ted traded New York for Pigeon Forge as his new hometown. A bachelor, Ted was a bright, intellectual sort, an excellent sketch and pastel artist, and he stood out like a shiny new penny among the locals. He soon ingratiated himself into the community and purchased a tiny parcel of riverfront land at the end of the Old Mill bridge that was directly across from Butler's Grocery Store and diagonally across from The Pigeon Forge Shopping Center, our store.

By midsummer of that year, Ted began his plan for a live-in art studio designed for the river's edge. He had a small flat space excavated and Ted, intending for the construction to go on at night as well as during the day, strung some light bulbs on a couple of poles at river's edge. As teens always looking for ways to make a few more dollars, Jim and I agreed to dig the footings at night when it was cooler and in afternoons after school. So with minimum wage in hand, we dug the footings over a few weeks. Soon, Ted moved into his two-story cinderblock studio. The street level space served as studio and gallery for his work, and the lower level served as his living quarters. A small open space, street side, almost touching the bridge rail served as an outdoor patio of sorts where Ted was visible to passing tourists and, especially at night, could sit outdoors and quickly sketch caricatures or serious pen and ink portraits of passersby.

THE BLUE MOUNTAINS SING
of rivers, old men, trails and trout

Early 1950s our store at bridge's end and Ted's art studio diagonally across on river.
(Pigeon Forge Library)

After a few years, he married a local beauty, Jane, the sister of one of my close friends and classmates from Pigeon Forge primary days. Ted died suddenly and unexpectedly a few years later while still a young man. He had become a comfortable fixture in this small mountain town where fitting in was not always easy, especially for an artist everyone expected to be eccentric. To his credit, he became a friend to many folks through the years. He was sorely missed by many locals saddened by his untimely death. In later years, Ted's property was sold and became The Jim Gray Gallery.

Memories are funny. They bubble up at the strangest times. Like black and white snap shots, the strangest things trigger them. Just a walk up river road sets them free. Mine are disconnected scenes and frozen highlights that tumble out in disarray and have no logical connection, one to another. They are still here. They will always remain here.

I still hear and see them in my thoughts on most any visit back home: Ricky, Herman Adams, and Bobby Quarrels riding and feeding the pinto pony, a Sunday touch football game with the Forge bunch in Alda Householder's side yard as each player reviewed yesterday 's Vols game. In the house to our left lived the best yellow cake with chocolate icing baker – Alda Householder – who often served us at halftime, and even better, one of Alda's four daughters, each of whom I planned to marry, often served the cake from time to time.

Jean Conner and her sister, Ruth, and sometimes their brother Jack, served as my sitter to help out my Mom while my Dad was overseas in WW II. Clara Quarrels, another of Stringtown's prized beauties, was slender, with porcelain skin, doe-like hazel green eyes, demure, gentle, with the most

46

serene demeanor of any young woman I ever remember.

The great memories of the thrill of birthdays up until about eight usually included good friends and classmates, Joe, Jerry, Joan Ogle, Charlotte "Annie" Seaton and Kenneth, Charles "Herky" Paine, Kay Henry, Barbara Lafollette, Jack Duggan, Wayne Dale and James David Ogle, Marion Temple Householder, Bobby and Clara Quarrels, Charlotte Ruth and Wanda Travena, and others.

How well I remember a star athlete in four sports, Earl Lawson, as he booted his sky high and too long punts that always seemed to land mid-river in the Little Pigeon. It always sent our team into a mad scramble to retrieve our ball before it floated over the milldam. Then, we'd often move the game from the Householders side lot—only after the cake—to the unfinished and dusty side of the new highway mostly to neutralize Earl's too-long punts.

Birthday at Windswept – Circa 1944

Back: Charlotte "Annie" Seaton, Kay Henry
Front: Me, Charles "Herky" Paine, Jerry "Pete" Ogle
(Ron Rader family archives)

There was the great fishing for smallmouth and redeye fish along Stringtown riverfront where France Whaley and Billy Allen always seemed to catch the biggest smallmouths. Charlie and Bessie King—perpetual party and picnic hosts to the Pigeon Forge First Methodist youth—held a quarterly picnic and wiener roast on their farm just past the current city hall. Bill Delozier, their nephew, now occupies in the big white farmhouse and is owner of the Three Bears Gifts shop in Pigeon Forge.

The daily Pigeon Forge filled my life in brief sketches.

I remember the chaos of the Pine Gove swimming hole filled with elementary and high schoolers as they stood waist deep and awestruck as Frank McCroskey launched his highest and hardest forty-foot dives from the cable swing. Laid-back Maurice "Mousey" Marshall watched, chuckled, and drank lemonade with the rest on the riverbank. Standing waist deep waiting a turn were Jim Cox, Bon Hicks and a dozen others. Bon stood out with sun reddened skin. Milling around playfully in deeper water were Jack Conner, Cotton Adams, Dale and Don Naugher, Dale Fox, three of the Householder beauties, several majorettes and cheerleaders at Sevier County

THE BLUE MOUNTAINS SING
of rivers, old men, trails and trout

High School, and a few dozen other local beauties and studs.

As a fourth grader, I watched three older and bigger boys bully Sammy Henry, a seventh grader. The four met in the middle of the Old Mill bridge. My dad urged me to go help Sammy. I resisted. Within minutes, Sammy whipped two to the ground as the third, bloody and screaming, ran towards Possum Holler.

Saturday nights we spent cruising by the Dairy Queen coupled with the 1950s version of every teenage boy's dream—the thrill and excitement of the latest style—see-through blouses. I always enjoyed the town's excited attitude toward winter ice, snow, and the many ways they found to enjoy it treating it as a gift.

Jack Henry and his cousin, Harold Butler, returning Korean War veterans, recruited a number of youngsters for the Civil Air Patrol Watch. The first Saturday each month our hilltop became a spotting and reporting station for potential enemy planes.

There were extreme Halloween pranks that saw farm wagons reassembled on rooftops, outhouses blown up or deposited in the bed of someone's dump truck, large animals left on rooftops, and farm wagon loads of harvested corn, horseless, and resting in someone's front yard.

We tried to suppress excitement at Midway Drive-In, our town's first, as we stuffed several friends in the trunk. Patience was waiting for the opening day thrill of any season—trout, trap, squirrel, quail, and rabbit.

The dread that came when we bought the new school year's stuff like brand new, stiff, denim overalls, yellow number two lead pencils, and Blue Horse notebook paper. The buying pleasures when we finally got bags of marbles, firecrackers, and Clove or Blackjack chewing gum. The pleasure buddies enjoyed as they ate Fudgcicles, Dreamcicles, in their hideout, or cherries, apples or pears while sitting on the tree's limb or lounging under it. The images that continue as does the dread of having to carry two one-gallon jars of fresh milk from Earl Lawson's house straight up our pasture to home at the top of "Windswept" hill. It was pre-teen bewilderment when we watched men cut off "chaw" from an Apple, Redman, or Days Work tobacco plug, and actually chew it. We pondered like young Einsteins, as we watched a hog eat coal.

Fun was loading pumpkins as you pulled the corn; disgust was farm machinery that always managed to breakdown midway through planting or harvest.

A daily challenge was trying to gather eggs from under a reluctant hen while trying to keep the rooster from flogging your back.

A real stomach knot came from that proverbial dare you had heard so many times before, "Betcha I can knock that hornet's nest down with this rock on the first throw and run so fast I'll never get stung—you believe me?"

Anxiety was real when you took an exhibit to school for your class "show and tell." It became your first and last when your green snake, stored safely in the corner of your classroom, went missing from its box. On a hot, humid, April day in your elementary school classroom, staying power was the ability to concentrate while the smell of ramps wafted from several classmates who had enjoyed a big "bait" of ramps with last night's supper.

Boredom and impatience triggered hitchhiking to get you most places. Most often, you hitchhiked to and from high school or ball practice. Spring excitement was joining friends, skipping school, stripping to your underwear or more, and swimming in the April ice of the Little Pigeon.

A knot in your stomach was seeing divers, jumpers, and swimmers compete for the title—bravest, as they plunged from the Old Mill bridge and the Old Mill dam.

Pigeon Forge Boys Elementary School Basketball Team
1951 – Sevier County Champions

Back: Doug Conner ,Jim Owens, Pat Whaley, Jack Duggan, Bob Proffit, Jim Trotter, Coach Frank Marshall
Front: Marion Householder, Max Trotter , James "Jesse" Whaley, Homer Henry, Ronny Rader, Charles Ray Lafollette
(Ron Rader family collection)

A thrill that no words could express was that of our greatest eighth grade basketball win. The Pigeon Forge Boys basketball team won the 1951 Sevier County Boys Championship. We won. Never had we been so jubilant. In later years, I was always glad to see so many of my teammates go on and later excel in high school and college sports. To name a few, there were Jim Trotter, Jim Richardson, Herbert Whaley, Doug Conner, Pat Whaley in SCHS basketball and Pat Whaley in SCHS football, along with several others. I always felt a close and special bond of kinship with them when I saw them excel. Their success somehow brightened my day, and I was happy for them.

The Old Mill – Its Life and Times

I passed by the old mill daily. Our store was on the corner diagonally across from her mill wheel. She had a colorful history before I came along and her history grew in Technicolor until I went off to college and beyond.

Although Pigeon Forge had a number of landmarks that were important to friends, our neighbors, and us, this particular landmark would later become an icon. To her credit, she survived when many of her sisters did not. The Old Mill had an exciting past. Its varied serial episodes and uses were as different as the people it served. It had housed a manufacturing company, though the business was short lived, it was the site of the first iron smelter on the banks of the Little Pigeon River, battling the years and struggling to survive. It had been partially destroyed more than once by flood and fire, and it had sat dormant then resuscitated several times.

The terrain and geography of the area surrounding the mill has an interesting and colorful history, also. Veta Wilson in her account of the history of *Pigeon Forge* pointed out that the land was used by the Cherokee for hundreds of years as a hunting ground because of its fertile valley coupled with a river on whose banks Pigeon Forge now stands. Named for its Little Pigeon River location, it was near the site of the current Old Mill. The valley with the river at its center was frequented by massive flocks of Passenger pigeons.

When you hear the early drama of the Passenger pigeon and its early impact on the area, it is quickly evident why the word pigeon was chosen as most descriptive of our town and the river that divided its center.

In 1700s and 1800s, they were estimated to total in the billions. The migratory birds sometimes streamed overhead for hours. Old timers and locals still regale stories from their grandparents and ancestors who told stories of the regal bird. It roosted and fed in the valley that surrounded Pigeon Forge and frequented the river valley. Experts estimate nine billion Passenger pigeons flew across the heartland of the US in 1850, according to Peter Bayne and John Lawson.

Descriptive stories of the massive flights of the pigeon and its impact locally are graphic. The bird was rumored to fly in such great numbers that they darkened the skies at mid- day, and the roaring sound of their wing rush in flight was so deafening and terrifying that grazing farm animals often stampeded from fear as well as deer and other wildlife. Stories passed down by Pigeon Forge family ancestors still linger. The birds were reported to have such voracious appetites and flew in such high numbered flocks that they could strip many acres of land of chestnuts, acorns, and other similar mast in just a few hours. At sunset or even on their arrival in an area during the day, their attempt to roost broke large limbs from trees and shredded smaller trees. The sheer weight of so many birds perching or roosting was very destructive to trees. Pigeon dung created by thousands of the birds in the area was reported to cover the ground several inches deep.

The valley welcomed the first Euro-American settlers' arrived on the Little Pigeon, and Pigeon Forge found its name around 1820. From his father-in-law's one hundred fifty one-acre land grant near the heart of what is now Pigeon Forge, Isaac Love, constructed the iron forge and half the city's eventual name. His complex had a furnace and water-powered trip hammer to smelt ore and mold iron bars.

Love erected the Pigeon Forge Mill in 1830, and eleven years later, William Love, his son, established a post office. In 1849, local businessman John Sevier Trotter purchased the mill and furnace and added a sawmill. The iron furnace was later sold and relocated in the 1880s.

According to Veta King, the Pigeon Forge Mill, usually called the "Old Mill" and has been placed on the National Register of Historic Places. The river still drives the water-powered gristmill's two stones and grain elevator. The massive flint granite stones, French Buhrs, are only the second set ever used in The Old Mill's one hundred seventy eight -year history. The millstones convert grain into about one thousand pounds per day. Its history of service is eclectic and varied. In a sense, it's once utilitarian uses trace mile markers across the face of Pigeon Forge's past. In addition to its earlier forge, smelting, and sawmill services, it once manufactured Union uniforms for a brief time, and later provided electricity to a small area of Pigeon Forge until 1935. Today it adds retail and restaurants to the eclectic list.

With that colorful history undergirding it, it's easy to see why the Old

THE BLUE MOUNTAINS SING
of rivers, old men, trails and trout

Mill is so special to those of us who were "born and raised here," who grew up here in The Forge, and even now, still call it home.

The Old Mill has always been special, a part of my childhood. Our homeplace perched on five acres of hilltop only a quarter mile to the southwest overlooked the mill and its pond. In the mid 1940's, I walked by this looming icon daily on my way to Pigeon Forge Elementary School. When you are belt high to most adults, the Old Mill seemed stately, mysterious, and somewhat overpowering. It served as the community's "all-purpose fun center" in every season, and its creaking, groaning, grinding sounds made it Halloween perfect. It stood directly across the millpond from my family's grocery store the Pigeon Forge Shopping Center.

The Old Mill was our neighbor, one whose persona and aura grew by the day. Since 1870, it had always anchored downtown Pigeon Forge. Probably its banks, concrete columns, river, and pond had hosted most every social activity imaginable—legal, illegal, and politically incorrect, but without a doubt—fun.

If Mayberry's Aunt Bea could have been a building, she would have been the Old Mill—solid, dependable, interesting, someone you could depend on —someone who was always there overseeing everyone's fun.

Bigger than anything else in town and perched astride the dam and the millpond alongside the rushing Little Pigeon River, the Old Mill's architecture, scale, location and size always suggested a battleship at anchor. That made it even easier to refer to it as "her." In the early 1950s, she always towered, looming above everything manmade. She seemed regal, aloof, and for me seemed like Pigeon Forge's own Statue of Liberty. She has probably been photographed as often as the New York icon.

Just like Aunt Bea, she always stood patiently, protective and watchful —watchful over most of the town's youngsters and many of the older "young at hearts" scurrying around her riverside skirts of water, rocks, and pastureland.

In summer, her millpond and rushing waterfall was a primitive version of today's waterpark but more fun with over the top risk. Youngsters swam and fished above and below the dam, several dared fate and raced for best time across the dam's narrow rim top, and even fewer jumped and dived from the bridge or the dam to join other swimmers below.

Underneath the Old Mill among the huge concrete support pillars, tired swimmers slid and leaped the rocks and chased each other in the game of the day. At night, well away from the mill, a bonfire would light up the night and like moths attracted to the flame, the "tall-tale tellers" would appear and drink "lemonade."

My Great Smoky Mountain Boyhood

Heavy rain or an occasional cloudburst high in the Smokies would often send a rushing wall and torrent of angry, red clay water that quickly leveled the dam's water area. Like the result of a master magician's act, the swirling, boiling water seemed directionless and threatened to swallow the bridge. Riding the water torrent from upstream came everything imaginable, anything that was unlucky enough to be in or too near the river's edge.

Fairly soon, cold, moonshine clear water from deep in the Smokies replaced the water's angriness. Its return to serenity also returned the waterfront back to normal. Its smooth calm always sent out a call for everything to return. Trustingly, the ducks were usually first. At the first sign of dangerous flood waters, they usually retired to several Stringtown yards. Once they reached safety, they lined up in random rows and nestled and chatted. To a passerby, they appeared like an audience comfortably enjoying a movie—the stormy flood. They were like barometers. When you saw them waddling back to their familiar water haunts, you could be assured that the worst danger had passed.

Winter was just as exciting. It often created a millpond iced over from the dam upstream to the First United Methodist Church. It became the town's quarter mile ice rink. People of all ages flocked to the ice. A lucky few who had ice skates wobbly showed the rest how to fall. Many slid on shoe soles, sleds, anything flat, or pushed others in wooden straight chairs and rocking chairs. Darkness and bonfires at bankside signaled the arrival of the skating night crew. That meant ladies from their river front homes brought out pimento cheese sandwiches, fried chicken, hot dogs, cake, and hot chocolate.

No matter what activity was happening around her skirts, the Old Mill—ever the old lady aunt—seemed to be rocking quietly on her river overlook porch, nodding approvingly, as her kids, neighbors, and friends played in her yard. Like the "always there" promise of the blue mountain haze behind her, she offered continual hope and promise. Yet, she remained unfathomable, stoic, unchanging, dependable, and she always loomed above the busyness of everything around her .

Thankfully, she is still alive and well, and her presence offers us sweet nostalgia. And for many of us, yet another anchor that keeps us grounded.

THE BLUE MOUNTAINS SING
of rivers, old men, trails and trout

From the old mill bridge looking south in 1940s, smoky haze veils the Smokies.
(Old Mill collection)

A 1940s' risk-taker about to enjoy the milldam pool's coolness or a surprise that may be -lurking from the last flood.
(The Mountain Press)

A frosted Little Pigeon River.
(Pigeon Forge Library)

My Great Smoky Mountain Boyhood

When one tugs at a single thing in nature, he finds it attached
to the rest of the world ... In every walk with nature, one receives
far more than he seeks ... Climb the mountains and get their good
tidings—John Muir

My Dad & Me

Orphaned and raised by grandparents and an aunt, "Aunt Ida," my dad Alvin Clarke Rader grew up in the Lincoln Heights area of Knoxville near Washington Pike. His father was killed on the railroad before his birth, and his mother died of influenza when he was three. A teenager during the Depression years, he grew up in a rough and tumble era. Men were still rowdy in the streets and fistfights were commonplace. Dad's Uncle Fred owned the Strand Theatre on Gay Street and hired him as a "jack of all movie theatre skills." He was a cleaner, popcorn maker, projectionist, ticket booth operator, and bouncer, and he was expected to master them all. Bands of young toughs would gang up, rush past the ticket booth, jump the turnstile, and plunge into the darkened theatre. Losing themselves in a darkness lit only by the screen flashes of Hollywood icon greats of the 1920s and 1930s, they were difficult to find. My dad was expected to drag the gatecrashers from the theatre and pummel them as he threw them into the streetcar tracks of Knoxville's Gay Street. He spent much of his free time working out in Knoxville's YMCA where he was very diligent in bodybuilding, sports, and his favorite competition, amateur boxing and the Golden Gloves. The Depression Era cast a pall of hopelessness over most youngsters, each hungrily searching for hope, a job, and a promising career.

Franklin D. Roosevelt became the messiah of hope for the country, especially for the South. He signed off and birthed the Civilian Conservation Corp, the CCC, and millions of hopeless young men found opportunity in their grasp. Very soon after, my Dad became a member of the 212 men at CCC's Sugarland's camp just outside Gatlinburg. Army officers first managed the camps, patterned after military boot camps. Conditioned and trained similar to army basic training, the young men lived in tented camps replete with cook shacks and all amenities of outdoor camping. Their days were spent in constructing most of the trails, bridges, tunnels, retaining walls, and later the Great Smoky Mountain National Park facilities that stand so prominently today. They cut and laid stone, felled trees, sawed

THE BLUE MOUNTAINS SING
of rivers, old men, trails and trout

Dad and squad members in mountains of Germany and Swiss Alps during WWII.
(Ron Rader family collection)

My dad ready to hike in CCC days.

lumber, and exercised every trade skill required of master carpenters, stone masons, excavators, and related trades. Even though many CCC boys were from cities, all became very knowledgeable in the ways of the woods and the water. Living outdoors in tents, working in the woods daily, and hiking to and from work honed them into top physical condition. Along the way, they became temporary specialists in botany, mammals, fishes and Park geography—self-taught naturalists.

For Dad, it was love at first sight after his first month in Sugarland's CCC camp. He came to love every aspect of the mountains. Despite the intense physical hardships of the earlier CCC days, he loved the mountains and streams. He often spoke of being awe struck as all things woods and waters unfolded. Later, the hands-on knowledge and practical skills expanded to include the science of the flora and fauna. He prided himself in learning all the constellations and all things astronomy. Daily deep woods hikes to and from a camp at work offered all the men the opportunity to learn the name and species of every tree, plant, flower, and every animal both large and small. They soon learned most inhabitants of the insect world. Dad would have made an outstanding naturalist. In fact, my ventures with Art Stupla amd John Morrell set in motion my early goal to become a naturalist.

The boys of the "tree army" swam in the icy, gin-clear streams, and competed against other camps in all sports. Leaning early on the real world skills of bouncing gatecrashers from his uncle's theatre, Dad quickly became the champion boxer in the welterweight class for all the Great Smoky Mountain CCC camps. He remained the champion and unbeaten when Congress disbanded the camps in May of 1942.

Dad and scores of other CCC boys joined the World War II effort. He was quickly processed, sent through basic training and entered additional training for combat engineers. After basic, he became a member of a combat engineer squad. Combat engineers attached to a combat unit served as engineer specialists. They were tasked with and expected to search out, sweep, locate, defuse and neutralize enemy mines, booby traps and to clear the path for the combat troops. Once there and true to their name, they were responsible for building pontoon bridges, clearing and building airfields, and filling a multitude of other engineering needs.

Dad, me, and Uncle John D. Ogle. Both were home on leave in WW II.
(Ron Rader family collection)

Dad's war journey throughout Europe paralleled Easy Company in Steven Spielberg's television series "Band of Brothers." Although he was never in Easy Company, his company may well have shared the same battalion, for he fought through the very same cities, towns, provinces, and countries. His squad was the first Combat Engineer squad to reach and enter the Wolf's Lair and Hitler's Eagles Nest.

Upon his return from WW II, he was invited to return to a job similar in many ways to that of his CCC days. Except now, the CCC efforts had evolved into something much greater with an even more noble and altruistic mission. The Great Smoky Mountains National Park had become a reality and it needed young men with passion for conservation, men who loved these mountains. They needed men who already knew the wilderness, men who believed that this wilderness must be protected, preserved, nurtured, and, especially, men who could help extend the park's recreational enjoyment commitment to the many. It would require a herculean administration effort to do it right. The Park was in an infant state. Dad was offered the General Supply clerk position. His role would be to survey, catalogue, record, and periodically inspect all Park equipment, ranger residences, cabins, trail shelters, fire towers, and other property on the Tennessee side. In addition, he was tasked with seeing that they were maintained, kept up, and repaired properly. If ever there was a dream job with a perfect fit for my Dad, this was it.

Herbert "Herby" Holt, Gatlinburg's first city manager and his wife Judy became almost surrogate parents to my Dad early in his CCC years. Dad's parents had died very early in his life, and I'm sure Herby graciously filled a father role model Dad needed but never had. Dad returned his love for Herby when he gave me Holt for my middle name. I know Herby and Judy were touched.

Soon after my birth in 1938 and his return from WWII, our family returned to normal. My younger brother Rick was born while Dad was in Europe. Dad got several two-week furloughs home while overseas, and I guess he made good use of at least one of them. My younger brother Rick probably thought so. Rick was two years old before Dad saw him for the first time. It took Rick several months to overcome his resentment toward this strange man in bed with our Mom.

Settling into his job, Dad was constantly in the woods visiting and evaluating the back country trail shelters, bath and rest facilities, storage areas, cabins, fire towers, and similar sites throughout the park. He was the liaison between maintenance and the ranger staff insuring maintenance groups did timely repair to the various sites.

Dad proclaimed me, as a four year old, his hiking partner, and I jumped at every opportunity to go. Many of his former CCC buddies were now rangers located at various ranger stations throughout the park, and we visited them often.

By this time, the Park staff, the rangers, and their wives and children formed a close, very tight knit community and socialized often. They stayed overnights with entire families at various ranger stations, played bridge, hiked, camped, trout fished, and the adults danced away the weekend nights at the Wonderland Hotel and the Appalachian Club at Elkmont.

The Gallery of Early Windswept and Pigeon Forge

Granny, Dad, Pop and Homer Ogle, then a teen, resting at my granddad's cabin on the hill in Pigeon Forge. Later, this would be my home.
(Ron Rader family collection)

Mom waves from our front porch overlooking Pigeon Forge. Landscaping was entirely of native shrubs. Later when I was born, my room was at the top of the stairs, and its view faced the mountains through those two windows. The room had a matching set on the other end.

Our garden with Pine Mountain in the background. The structure on the right would become a two story barn. Our car was garaged underneath; the other half was a tool shed and wood storage. Upstairs was open storage and a playroom on rainy days.

THE BLUE MOUNTAINS SING
of rivers, old men, trails and trout

Howard and Virginia Davenport
with me in the middle.

Dad , Ted Davenport, unidentified, Howard and I.

We were constantly outdoors.

My dad, mom and me at Savage
Gardens in Gatlinburg. Circa 1941.
(Ron Rader family collection)

Pop with me at age one at "
Windswept" our remodeled cabin and
home in Pigeon Forge. The pastureland
at mid left was our elementary school
ball diamond and now Patriot Park.

My Great Smoky Mountain Boyhood

Over the next seven or eight years, Dad and I hiked most every trail in the Park that had a fire tower, building, cabin, or trail shelter and many that did not. We made day visit round trips or just as often stayed overnight at the sites, and we hiked many, many more that did not have overnight shelter. He always enjoyed the evening and the nighttime skies and spent considerable time pointing out the various constellations by name and suggesting ways to find your direction without a compass. He really enjoyed the full moon nights and liked to be outdoors in the moonlight. It was then that he often spoke of his World War II experiences in Europe and of his favorite stories from his days with the Civilian Conservation Corps in the Sugarlands.

Even now, on full moon nights, I am often reminded of one story that always made him laugh each time he retold some version of it. In the CCC days, he often lived and camped in four-man, canvas wall tents. The tents were heavy canvas and bleached white like white muslin cloth, similar to the ones we often see now in western movies – white wall tents with front flaps that house the cavalry soldiers.

One particular night he was alone deep in the mountains and sleeping in one such tent. The moon was full and though tall trees of the deep woods surrounded him, the tent sat in a small open grassy patch that allowed the moonlight to fully bathe the small area and the tent. The full moon light literally transformed the white canvas tent into a white glowing blob in contrast to the darkness of the woods surrounding it. Dad said that he kept hearing periodic thumps on the sloped canvas roof. Since he was alone, the sounds took on a spookiness that unnerved him. It was if someone was throwing a small object on the tent, and it would slowly slide to the edge and roll off (he speculated) to the ground. It was summer, too early for acorns, hickory nuts or any other type of nut or fruit to be dropping to the wood's floor. Puzzled, he continually opened the flaps, looked all around, and finally walked all around the tent several times. There was nothing on the ground and no tree directly overhead. Time after time this thump and slide repeated itself. His imagination began to really play tricks on him. Finally, he stepped into the fullness of the moonlight that seemed like daylight and walked to the edge of the tree line just a few feet away and sat down against a large oak tree and waited. Within minutes, a small furry object sailed from the nearby tree canopy landed with a plop on the tent roof slid to the edge, jumped to the ground, and scampered back into the woods. Almost as quickly, another furry ball sailed through the air and repeated the same death-defying stunt.

"Boomers," my Dad said. "Can you believe that? Those little flying squirrels must have decided my tent was a good target, couldn't sleep with such a bright full moon, so they decided to play jump, sail and slide."

THE BLUE MOUNTAINS SING
of rivers, old men, trails and trout

Apparently, several boomers, like kids lined up at a swimming pool diving board, each awaiting a turn, figured out the moonlit tent was a perfect fun target. Finally freed of rattled nerves, Dad went back to bed and slept even though the flying squirrels played until sometime well into the night. His story still resurfaces when I see the cartoon character duo, Chip and Dale, as the two chipmunks scamper in their mischievous and ever-whimsical antics.

I am grateful for those quality father and son years. Dad was alive in the moment, in his element, inspired by the wilderness spirit he embodied and one that surrounded us constantly. He laughed a lot, joked often, and was the constant teacher seemingly anxious that he might not be able to pass along all that he wanted me to learn. I sensed that maybe, like all fathers, he felt there might not be enough time. His impatience showed when I didn't grasp the significance of the knowledge he wanted me to grasp and appreciate.

He had always been an avid reader, and I inherited that from him I guess. His thirst for knowledge was insatiable. He was curious about everything. He had me reading and enjoying Tom Sawyer , Huckleberry Finn, all of Mark Twain's works, Kit Carson among the many western heroes, Treasure Island, Daniel Boone, the Zane Grey novels, Jack London, Edgar Rice Burroughs , all the American Hero novels, and a wide variety of outdoor books in a wide range of subjects. He read everything he could lay his hands on including the latest rifle and ballistics magazines, men's magazines, Popular Mechanics, any and all outdoor works, including all of Horace Kepart' s works. From *Gibbon's Rise and Fall of Western Civilization* to the latest novels, he devoured them all.

Along with all the woods and waters lore, he, like most fathers, wanted to make certain he imparted all the "right stuff" I'd need on my journey to manhood. When you grew up in cities like Knoxville on the twenties and thirties streets, you had to be tough and street smart. When you are orphaned at three, never knew your mom or dad, were raised by an Aunt Bea- like aunt, it came easy to believe that it's you against the world with nothing in between. Dad had been a body builder and fitness freak way before it became fashionable. He lifted weights, trained, and boxed at the YMCA in between shot putting theatre interlopers into Knoxville streets. He never smoked or drank until he was forty. Since they don't give you an operations manual for parenthood, he searched for the best way to raise me. He felt that maybe the best model for a man should be one that exemplified the Boy Scout Creed: trustworthy, loyal, helpful, friendly, courteous, kind, obedient, cheerful, thrifty, brave, clean, and reverent. Probably like most fathers he projected his wants, desires, and dreams on his son. It was probably a good thing for me.

My Great Smoky Mountain Boyhood

I believe he thought that I earned passing or average grades on most of the Boy Scout creed, though he never said it. I guess the jury was still out on the brave part or probably better labeled, confidence. Since I was small for my age, had mastered grades one and two the first year in elementary school, I was a third grader at age seven. My second year in school meant I was trailing my classmates emotionally and physically. To compound the challenge , I was shorter in stature than many of the boys and most all of the girls. It did not get any better with age; it only got worse until high school. I decided very early that I was an equal. This generated a determined, never-give-up attitude that would have made Winston Churchill proud. Through the years , it served me well.

So when I reached the age of eight, my Dad, and a couple of other dads formed a boxing team at the American Legion Hut in Gatlinburg. Dad was insistent that I learn to defend myself, as did most other dads of the mid-forties. So we started to work on Dad's plan for the confidence-courage program aimed at me and included several other kids my age. I tolerated it. I really did not want to punch anybody in the nose, especially kids I knew.

The thirty-two ounce boxing gloves, one on each hand, looked like two large, five pound, thawed Thanksgiving turkeys. Once they were on, they really did feel just like you'd punched a large chunky leather covered turkey right in the butt all the way up to your elbows. Coupled with hands that had previously been tightly wrapped and taped, my arms could barely lift my encased fists.

The mark of a true boxer, I was to learn, was to dance to the center of the ring ever moving. And with the killer instinct of my Dad's hero, Jack Dempsey, you were to jab constantly with your left, protect your chin with your right, until such time as your opponent dropped his guard and gave you an opening. Once your opponent gave you an opening, you were to throw a fast one-two punch delivery-- a left jab followed by an exploding right to your opponent's chin. In theory, that really made sense.

In hindsight, I believe they forgot that an eight year old with a five pound turkey mitten on each hand might be lacking in lightning hand speed, no matter how much or often he'd punched the speed bag with no gloves. Three-minute rounds seemed like waiting on your birthday, Christmas, or pie to cool. Three rounds seemed like you'd likely be in the eighth grade before they ended, and you were only in the fifth grade. Never had I gasped like this for oxygen, oh precious oxygen. My lungs burned, sweat popped from every orifice in my body, and some came from places I didn't know I had. My burning tortured forearms and biceps felt heavy and strangely numb after round one.

THE BLUE MOUNTAINS SING
of rivers, old men, trails and trout

Between rounds, I was motivated professionally as I sat on my corner stool. My coach in my blue corner was called my "second" and was usually more experienced than I. To me, he was the guy who yelled and jabbered in my ear trying to make me hear his instructions over the noise of the crowd as he told me which punch combination to throw and in what order.

Apparently, most of the time he didn't speak loud enough because my gloves didn't listen. Putting my full weight and hips into a right cross or right upper cut sounded expert. I could do it. I knew I could. Dancing to the center of the ring and looking very much like a pair of giant boxing gloves wearing a boy was the easy part. Trying like Joe Louis to throw those lethal punches had its downside. For if my striking blow glanced or god forbid, missed, the pull of my concrete gloves hooked to my exhausted arms and body would simply launch me into and through the ropes or even worse, down in a flailing pancake dive to the canvas on my face. Never was I so glad that I had not invited Susan Laudermilk, the prettiest girl in the fifth grade, to see me box. I retired from boxing at age eleven after a long and illustrious three-year career.

When all of my one hundred eight pounds discovered Boy Scouts as the preferred road leading to manhood, I was ecstatic. Apparently, the annual Golden Gloves administration never missed a beat or missed me. In fact, they never even called to inquire about next year, and I'm sure my Dad was disappointed. My Dad was well intentioned and considered this a necessary part of my growing up. Actually, it was very good training for me. I learned how to put on my sports game face, become aggressive, and build a certain confidence that only one-on-one boxing provides. Knowing how to put on your game face served me well in high school football my freshman and sophomore years.

Since I was old enough for the Boy Scouts, my dad encouraged it, and I became a proud Tenderfoot. Relieved that I didn't have to box, I loved scouting, the outdoors, the camaraderie, and the fun. Driving me twelve miles round trip every Monday night to attend Boy Scout Troop 111 of Gatlinburg, my dad seemed to relax a bit. He was active in the parent support group and accompanied our troop on many hikes and campouts. I think I passed the courage test somewhere along the boxing way, and though he never mentioned it, I think he decided I'd accomplished what he set out to have me learn. Thanks to him, his chauffeuring, support, and perseverance, I earned the Eagle rank in scouting and became the second Eagle Scout in Sevier County in 1952. I missed becoming Sevier County's first Eagle Scout by six weeks bested by close friend and troop mate, Howard Davenport.

In fact, many of my friends from scouting still live in the greater Gatlinburg area. Over the years, we spent many fine times scouting and camping in the mountains, summers at Camp Pellisippi, quarterly Camporees, and many other activities. Each Monday night we met in the American Legion hut on Gatlinburg's Airport Road , we hiked and camped on overnight hikes two or three times each quarter.

Several names come to mind from those years; among them are Carl Newman, Ronnie King, Bruce Gorenflo, Jimmy Huff, Jack Arthur, Max Johnson, Jerry Ogle, Bud Lawson, Lynn Zoder, Eric Kron, Thorp Kron, Carl Wade, Tom Edwards, Billy Steele, Howard Davenport, Pete Koster, Bruce Gorenflo, Jerry Reagan, and a dozen more that my recall fails me on. Many youngsters were from park service or U.S. Bureau of Roads families. Their fathers often served as scout leaders.

Gatlinburg was like a second home for a few years. Boy Scout meetings, the subsequent group projects, camping trips, and overnight visits with my friends brought me to Gatlinburg often. As part time work on afternoons after school and on weekends, I'd bell hop at the New Gatlinburg Inn for Rel and Wilma Maples.

Both of my parents loved the mountains and the outdoors. They hiked and camped with friends often when I was young. The children were always included and many fine summer days and nights were spent camping and swimming in the rivers as a family. My mother was a fine cook and liked nothing better than cooking over a campfire. Bridge was probably her second love. As a couple they both looked for and captured the moment as they looked for any excitement outdoors. Many of their friends were other park service couples who shared common interests.

Community was real to us back then. People gathered often for any reason. Being social was big. For example, one winter in the late 1940s, Pigeon Forge and the mountains had quite a blizzard. The deep snow lasted for a week or more. It seemed to be about eighteen inches deep. Trees and bushes sagged and snapped and walking was difficult. The hill we lived on was next door to the United Methodist Cemetery hill. We were the next peak to the right toward the mountains, and our five acres was aptly named "Windswept." Whispering Pines condominiums now occupy the site. The front of our steep hill toward downtown was dormant pastureland had a swag in the middle and was covered with scores of small pine trees ranging from four feet to seven feet. Dad cut a path straight down the swag, slide shaped, center of the hill, all the way to the fence line, the ditch, and Ogle Road.

Word got out, and half the town kids already excited about the snow, came and joined us as we dragged the pine trees and piled them into a high thick windrow against the barbed wire fence at the bottom. Now we had a safety barrier for sledding. What could be more fun than sledding at top speed down the long, steep hill and crash into a pungent evergreen smell of young pine boughs?

The first afternoon of sledding went well into the night. Dad kept a large bonfire burning at the edge of our driveway at the very top. It served as a level, sled launch spot near the edge of our yard. Soon kids kept showing up one after another with sleds or anything that would serve as a sled. My mother, ever the hostess and cook, soon served her famous pimento cheese sandwiches, hot chocolate and coffee, hotdogs, and marshmallows for roasting in the bonfire, and later in the evening fried chicken. The following afternoon and night, more adults and more children joined the blizzard party. The mothers brought lots more food and several pies and cakes. Even smaller kids didn't lose their patience. To pull your sled back to the top after a fun ride was agony. Most everyone was dressed like the Pillsbury Doughboy. So the cold, the agony of the return climb to the top, and the mummified clothing layers set the stage for lots of potential discontent. But the thrill of this joyous hilltop in the snow adventure stifled any complaining or crying, lest your parents made you leave.

I believe the impromptu well into the night "town sledding festival" lasted about four or five nights with hardly a drop in attendance. For those of my era, this was a special time. The exhilaration, excitement, adventure, and closeness of our small community was one filled with salt of the earth, just plain folks. This togetherness as part of our community's tradition was an important quality of life that has all but disappeared. It was a spirit of dependable camaraderie and respect for others that has faded away. I believe it's at the core of what we miss most in all our communities. Those natural, small town virtues, the fruit of the spirit, were shared by all. We took them for granted fully expecting them to live on forever in our community. Unfortunately, they didn't. It underscores the truism: Big is not always better and more doesn't always lead to quality.

Memories wrapped around my hometown always leave me with a feeling of time well spent, daily experiences really savored, friendships long treasured, mentors still revered. They say we are composites; that we're made up of bits and pieces of all those folks who've touched our lives. To the many who helped shape me, from the heart I thank you. As a Forge boy, I hope I did my part to make you my friend and to make you proud that we were friends and neighbors.

My dad retired from the Park service after thirty-six years of service at the age of fifty-five. In November 1976, my dad died of colon cancer at age sixty-two. He was one of the group later labeled " The Greatest Generation." Recalling him, his friends, colleagues, and those who were such a significant part of my young life, they were—he was—part of that greatest generation.

Thanks for everything Dad. I'm sorry it took me so long to appreciate you and all that you did. Dad, you and the others of that era truly were the greatest generation, yet you never realized it. All of you just went on doing your job as best you could.

Grace Grossman, Mom, and Dad with John and Grace Morrell in rear.
Probably at Spence Field.
(Ron Rader family collection)

Retirement age meant riding instead of hiking. John and Grace Morrell in back, Grace Grossman, Mom and Dad in front, as they ascend somewhere off- road high in the Smokies. The Willis' Jeep was my dad's beloved WW II vehicle. The trapper pack basket was John's favorite, and one he always strapped on prior to any hike.

THE BLUE MOUNTAINS SING
of rivers, old men, trails and trout

> *Everybody needs beauty as well as bread, places to pray in, where nature may heal and cheer and give strength to body and soul alike.*—John Muir

Doc Ogle, Five Oaks and Me

Since I was his first grandson, and son of his only daughter, my physician grandfather made the most of our time together. I called him Pop, as did all of my future cousins. His small brick office next door to the sprawling Five Oaks farmhouse was busy and served as my nonexistent 1940s television and X Box. He was a country doctor, as most were then. Country doctors travelled by horse and buggy. The roads were rugged, unpaved, steep, often rutted, and either dusty or muddy. More folks required house calls back then, depending on the illness and the weather.

My granddad, Dr. John Willis Ogle, had varied interests and hobbies. Chief among them was his passion for horses. He bred, raised, and showed Tennessee Walking horses, and the changing numbers, colors, and sizes of the horses grazing his farm pastures were a testament to his equine passion. Sometimes there were more than two dozen horses of varying ages, and patterns frolicking there. In those early days of his medical practice, he usually rode horseback to make house calls throughout the mountains and foothills.

My grandmother often told of earlier days and harsh winter times when he rode horseback for house calls. She said that many times when he returned from a long day in the saddle fighting the snow and ice that it would be nearly dark. Astride his horse at the back door, his duster and leather chaps covered in snow and ice, he was often iced to the saddle and his medical saddlebags. Frozen to the leather, he was unable to dismount. Getting buckets of hot water from the kitchen wood stove reservoir, my grandmother poured it over his lap, the saddle's leather surfaces, the saddle skirts, his boots, and clothing, until she melted the ice enough to free him from the saddle. She said that he was always very relieved to return home and warm up from the icy grip of deep winter. He worried continually about the hardships that deep winter placed on his horse, yet he always went right back in response to the next plea for medical help. When she begged him to rest and wait for the weather to break, he would simply say, "I've got to go; I'm their doctor, and they need help."

My Great Smoky Mountain Boyhood

At back door of Five Oaks, Granny welcomes Pop home from house calls. Notice ice tongs on left wall and one of many cats lazily observing from its perch on right.
(Ron Rader family collection)

Picture believed to be first family picture after the war in summer 1945. I was seven years old. Pop died in October 1946. The Five Oaks family from L to R, front row: Joe, Jerry Joan Ogle, Kay Henry, Ronny Rader, and Ricky on Dad's arm. Back row: Harry Ogle, wife, Estalee Sims Ogle, Dr. John W. Ogle, wife, Blanche Wayland Ogle, Homer Ogle, wife, "Babe" Cardwell Ogle, Alvin Clarke Rader, wife, Louise Ogle Rader, Antoinette Ogle , husband, John D. Ogle.
(Ron Rader family collection)

THE BLUE MOUNTAINS SING
of rivers, old men, trails and trout

Granny said this was a very common occurrence from November through March. While he sometimes rode in his surrey or buggy, I think he preferred the adventure of horseback. His large leather saddlebags were special designs with hundreds of pockets and vial slots that made him a travelling surgeon and pharmacy.

His medical office was an adventure unto itself. The small brick building fifty feet from the Five Oaks homeplace was a very interesting showcase for all things medicine, especially to a youngster. It was surrounded with much more drama than the Ole MacDonald miniature golf amusement that now sits on that site.

Dozens of multicolored medicine bottles, decanters, and pill and liquid vials of all sizes lined his office and lab walls. The hundreds of multisized bottles of every color, especially cobalt blue shades, showered you in a kaleidoscope of colors. Their dazzle spun your mind like a sparkling ballroom ball. His was an office that could be as fascinating as a zoo. In bright sunlight that often streamed in, the bottles made your vision uncomfortable. It forced your mind into overload. Their explosive color mix, your rush of discomfort, and that doctor's office smell— a mix of the sterile, the medicinal, and the pharmaceutical—gave instant warning, the one that always tells a youngster, "Be anxious." Then your memory was the next to scream, "Run, run, you're about to get a shot," or worse, "Stitches!"

From the age of four on, I was his shadow in that office and his passenger in the passenger seat of his steel gray two door Pontiac coupe with two separate and tiny upholstered stools that served as a back seat. Folded up, they provided hauling room.

Pop on Maverick. Circa 1939
(Ron Rader family collection)

Pop and Granny enjoy the snow. Circa 1939
(Ron Rader family collection)

My Great Smoky Mountain Boyhood

Making house calls with Pop, I recall riding to patients' homes navigating muddy, rutted roads to, most often, a log cabin in a deep hollow. If the illness were not contagious, he would take me inside. He would visit with the healthy spouse, who often looked older beyond their years and kid around with the young kids playing jackrocks on the linoleum floor, most of whom he had probably delivered. Then, he would go to the back bedroom and reassure the patient, an ailing wife, grandparent, uncle, or extended relative. He teased, joked, laughed, and found humor in everything. His upbeat cheerfulness seemed to lift the pall of illness for the family, if only for a brief moment. I suppose the practice of medicine with its often unpredictable outcomes forced the practitioner to seek humor at every opportunity.

Usually, as was the mountain custom, they offered us pie, cake, and coffee as if this was a social visit, and most often Pop made it seem that way. Just as often, we would accept the pastry offer and stay, eat, and visit. In looking back, Pop was probably a "town crier" of sorts, bringing them his version of the latest Sevier County news. His office certainly was the crossroads for a diverse mix of information throughout the county. And most folks were as hungry for news, gossip, and current happenings as they were for medical care.

Back at Five Oaks, his office was also an exciting place filled with adventure, drama, healing, and less often, death. As those real life dramas unfolded, it made a real growing up place for any young boy. My eye level was just about six inches above the always icy cold stainless steel top of his Ritter examining table. If I tiptoed, I could see all of the tabletop action.

Our very existence was at the center of these foothills of the Smoky Mountains and its rural countryside. It was our life. Most of Sevier County's geography, spirit, and vitality existed in that mix of pastures, ridges, hollers, rivers, and creeks. Most important was the passionate stewardship of the farm families who nurtured them. As such, the injuries and ailments of Pop's patients were mostly the result of farming accidents or outdoor related injuries. The injuries consisted of all manner of broken limbs, crushed limbs from machinery, cut limbs and fingers from all manner of sharp tools, puncture wounds, injuries from larger animals, bites from smaller ones, and an infinite variety of other accidental injuries that only farm life in the forties seemed to generate.

While each patient office visit had its own special drama of excitement, fear, anxiety, and screaming script, many were routine and comfortable. If I were to recall a classic office visit for a patient, a single one that exemplified the many daily patient visits, the conversations, the ambience of the day, and the drama, it went pretty much like the anecdote that follows.

THE BLUE MOUNTAINS SING
of rivers, old men, trails and trout

The serenity of a perfect summer day in June right at midday is broken by a rapid knock on the frosted glass of Pop's empty office. From fifty feet away, a woman's voice calls out a welcome from next door at the Five Oaks Farm house. She stands in the half opened screen door of her kitchen, leaning half out so her visitor can see her.

Blanche, Dr. John's wife and my Granny, says in a very concerned and caring tone, "Woodrow, doctor is eating his dinner but finishing up right now. He'll be right there. Are you hurt bad?"

"I'm not sure."

"Well I hope not , let your kids go around to the front on the screened-in porch, and tell'em to play on the swing glider and chairs.

"Be sure and tell them if they play in the front yard not to cross the highway to try to pet our horses at the horse ring. This traffic is getting worse and worse. It's not even the weekend; it's just Wednesday. I bet there's already been one hundred cars going up to Pigeon Forge and Gatlinburg today. I don't know how John Rellie keeps carrying our mail and getting through this traffic all in the same day. I bet the rolling store ull' be late too. I wanted to sell them some chickens and get this week's *Montgomery Vindicator* paper so I can get it read before I have to start fixing supper. Wait, here's doctor coming out now."

Pop, speaking as he lit up a cigar, "Well, Woodrow, from the looks of that bloody rag on your right forearm, looks like you either cut it, or Sally finally tried to run you off. Is that your drinkin arm?"

Woodrow wincing, "Now, dammit Doc, you know I don't drink and don't never plan to take it up. I damn near cut my arm off on my hay rake. And here I stand bleeding bad with a near cut-off arm that's hurtin' like hell's fury and you're a jokin' and blackguardin' me. "

Pop patted the exam table, "Come on in and sit down there next to where Ronny's standing and lay your arm across that examining table. Let me see that 'nearly cut off arm' of yours. Where in the world did you find that matted old burlap sack you wrapped around your arm? I bet you put it under your John Deere tractor seat the last time you greased it two, maybe three, years ago."

Woodrow arched his back defensively, "Now, just where am I going to find a 'sturile' rag out there, a mile from the house , by myself, my arm half cut off, and me barely able to even drive myself here bleedin', lightheaded, and all? "

Pop, grew silent for a minute as he continued to touch, squeeze, and inspect the wound tenderly, and with utmost care. Finally he said, "Looks like you sliced her open pretty good. You didn't hit any major veins or arteries, and the metal missed the tendons. Fact is, you did a good job squeezing that long slice back together. Well, looks like I'll have to put about, let's see, twenty nine or maybe thirty stiches in, if you need one to grow on."

Woodrow almost apologetically said, "Dammit, Doc. I was greasing that hay rake and that jagged broke edge was sharp, and when it snapped down in place, it cut me good."

"I'll swab your whole arm down with Mercurochrome to kill the germs, numb it, and swab some iodine in the wound for double germ insurance, and stitch it. Here, Ronny hold this bottle while I swab. Woodrow, if your version of a Florence Nightingale's sorry burlap bandage didn't put too many varmints in your gash, it should just be plenty sore for a few days and nothing else. You'll have to watch about straining and lifting for two weeks. I'm sure Sally'll be glad to hear this. I guess this doubles her work for the next two weeks plus wet-nursing you."

Woodrow grimaced at the needle's sting as he searched for the Lidocaine's numbing relief. He wondered if Doc had started those first two stiches too soon, too far ahead of the Lidocaine's effect. He tried to get his mind off its pain track and searched for words of a more routine nature.

Trying to calm his nervous anxiety Woodrow said, "So is this your new doctor helper? How old are you son?"

I said, "Five."

Pop nodding approvingly, "Yeah, that's Louise's boy. He's my first grandson and my only daughter's first child. He and I travel and doctor together. He likes to ride my horses. And he's already a good rider. Moon Glow, my Tennessee Walking horse, is his favorite, but she's a little big for him right now. She looks like a big horse wearing a wisp of a boy when he's astride her. My yearling, Gloria, is more his size and safer." Pop started his thirteenth stitch. His horse tales were so distracting and rich with humor they bettered any anesthetic. He continued. "Last summer, he was parked on top of one of my smaller horses, holding the reins. She stretched her neck and dropped her head to chew some clover. It jerked Ronny from the saddle, headfirst, and broke his left forearm. His

Ronny, Moonglow, and her colt. Circa 1940
(Ron Rader family collection)

73

THE BLUE MOUNTAINS SING
of rivers, old men, trails and trout

Dad was really down and feeling real guilty, but it's just one of those things around horses. Even the gentle ones can bite or kick you at times. I got it set and got a cast on it, and he's good as new now, aren't you Ronny?"

Holding up my left arm bent at the elbow with my finger pointing skyward, I said, "Yes, see how straight it is?"

For weeks, my Dad had been secretly worried that my arm might mend back crooked leaving me handicapped, until finally, the cast was removed. I saw the color return to my Dad's face framed with a broad smile of relief.

"Ronnys' got the run of the farm, and he likes to stay close to the farmhands. They like having him with 'em and really protect him like mother hens. For a boy, this is a hard place not to like. I've got the pea granary where we shell all the peas we raise, eighty river-bottom acres of hay and corn that needs planting and harvesting. Little Pigeon river borders our farm, and its full of fish, wild ducks, and swimming holes.

"We've got cattle, hogs, sheep, and Blanche has chickens and seventeen peafowl. I raise and show Tennessee Walking horses all over Tennessee at the horse shows. Those two farm hands out there groom, train, and ride each horse every day over at that horse barn and at the training ring across Highway 441 in front of my house.

"And I've got three sons—the youngest is making a doctor and the other two are farming here and on their own farms. They haul Ronny around with them a lot, too. It's good when a boy can have three uncles and two of them doing farm life and a bunch of other outdoor things and always including him. Once he comes of age when he can be on his own, I figure Ronny will want to be here with us on the farm as much as he can. What boy wouldn't, not to mention his Granny's cooking and all her doting on him?"

Woodrow, appearing to forget why he was here, gazed off into space, "Ain't this county fine? Hit really is a great place to live in and grow up in ain't it, Doc?" Turning quickly to me he said, "So are you goin' to be a doctor like your papaw and your Uncle Homer?"

"Yes."

"Yeah , he's already decided to be a doctor after travelling all over the county with me and helping the sick people, and sewing up cut arms of the dumber ones. In fact, he's decided to specialize, haven't you, Ronny? Tell Woodrow what you're specializing in."

I said proudly, "Well, Pop says if I'm going to be a doctor and specialize I need to be the kind that has the most fun. So I'm going to only doctor women. Doctor all the women and nobody else." Both men broke into loud laughter. Now there seemed to be more meaning in what I'd said, and I sensed it even more in their glance exchange. It puzzled me as I tried to discern its exact meaning.

Woodrow, raising his good arm in proclamation, "Lord, son, if you can make all the womenfolk happy and content, my hat'll sure be off to you. Be sure and don't miss airy a day of medical school when they teach that part. And, when you get out, be sure and give me a call. Cause by then, your papaw will be so cantankerous I won't want to be around him, and you'll be 'uh knowin' a lot more'en him especially when it comes to doin' all that woman doctorin'."

"OK. I will. I don't think that will be for a long time, will it Pop?"

"It'll sure come sooner than we all like to think about, son."

"OK then Mr. Woodrow, my Granny and Pop's number here at Five Oaks is 2530. What's yours?"

Pop finished and said, "There you go Woodrow. Just like new. You watch that arm for heat and redness. I'll give you a bottle of iodine and one of mercurochrome. Swab the wound with each one three times a day to keep down any infection. If it looks funny or feels like it's getting infected, come back here quick, and don't put it off. I gave you a tetanus shot. You probably needed it anyway. How is Sally and the kids? Is Aunt Lizzie doing OK? Tell her I saw her digging the other day when Ronny and I went in the Ownby Holler above you. I know she thinks and acts like she's fifty, but she's not. Tell her not to be raising that fifty-pound miners pick over her head to dig that Bermuda grass out of her flowerbed. She's ninety-one not fifty! Next thing you know she'll be here in my office complaining of heart and chest pains and holding her hernia."

Woodrow shook his head, "You just better tell Ronny to hurry up and get to women doctoring, and let him deal with it. I ain't about to say nary a thang to er. She'd probably cut my cornbread off for a month.

"Doc, I can't pay for this til my terbacky money comes in. But if you need some pay right away, I could send you a couple lambs that'll be weaned in a couple of weeks. We just robbed some good honey from three beehives, or I could bring you over three or four Dominicker hens. They are skillet ready."

Pop gripped Woodrow's shoulder helping him out the door. "It doesn't matter Woodrow, you make it easy on yourself." Pop grinning, "Whatever suits you best, suits me. Stay with us Woodrow, don't rush off."

"Got to go doc. Missed getting that hay rake ready today, got to go. Oh, tell Blanche we really enjoyed that Angel Food cake and the blackberry jam she brought when Sally had her flu in February. Me, and the kids too, all of us, believe she really is an angel just like her cake."

Pop grinned, "I'll sure tell her Woodrow. Now don't be drinkin' and cut the other arm."

THE BLUE MOUNTAINS SING
of rivers, old men, trails and trout

Mothers. day 1937
In honor of a Woman
with, a. heart, as pure
as pure as gold -
a principle and
character as white
as snow - loved by
me better than any
other. She is my mother

Woodrow scowled, "Now dammit doc, confound you. I hope to the devil you don't ever say that in front of the other deacons. Anyhow, thank ye' though."

The country doctor's service, the type of medical care delivered, and the harshness of the land was captured recently by Florence Cope Bush. In an excerpt from her regional book, *Dorie*, she recounts those struggles her mother, a mountain settler, faced. Of particular interest to me was her description of some medical care my granddad provided to her family. She wrote:

"Our second son, Charles Edward was born December 29, 1922. Dr. John W. Ogle came to deliver him. He thought it was a false alarm, and remembering he had spent the night (with us) waiting for Edith to arrive, he went over the hill to visit his mother, Martha Jane Ogle. Her farm was the next one over from Pa's.

Mrs. Martha Ogle had been married to Ma's uncle, Samuel Maples. They had two children, Wesley and Lucinda. Cindy died when she was young. According to family lore, Uncle Sam had been killed while he was working in the cornfield. Some said he was shot in the back by snipers who thought he had caused their still to be discovered and destroyed. After he died, Aunt Martha married Isaac Ogle. They had five children, two sons, and three daughters. Both of their sons were doctors – Dr. John W. Ogle and Dr. Ashley Ogle (Ashley was the oldest by five years). Although not really related, we shared some relatives with Dr. John Ogle and felt he was part of the family. A few minutes after he left to visit his mother, Charles decided it was time to make his appearance in the world. Ma called the Ogles' to have the doctor return. By the time he came back, Charles had already been born. 'Dorie,' he said, 'I think you do this deliberately. I can't ever tell when you're ready nor how long it will take. Try to be on time next time, young lady.' 'I hope there won't be a next time,' Ma said. She let me know she thought my family was big enough now and that I should stop with this baby – my fourth."

From all accounts, this familiar episode unfolded often in the mountain life of a 1920's country doctor.

My Great Smoky Mountain Boyhood

Another insight into my granddad's persona came from a faded news clipping probably from the *Montgomery Vindicator*, one of Sevier County's earliest newspaper. A friend of his had written a brief acknowledgment of his birthday. A Tribute on Dr. Ogle's 37th birthday read:

"Sevier County is fortunate in claiming Dr. J. W. Ogle as her citizen. Besides being an active physician, he is also a servant of the people. He is public spirited and interested in all the people. He is a member of the Board of Trustees at Pigeon Forge Baptist Church; on the Board of Medical Examiners for the State of Tennessee; on the Board of Education for Sevier County; on the Committee of Reference for Pi Beta Phi Settlement School at Gatlinburg; a member of the Staff of Doctors in the hospital at Pi Beta Phi; and Director of the First National Bank in Sevierville. Dr. Ogle has a broad interest in his community, county, and state, and never allows the opportunity of serving to pass. Happy is the nation which produces such sons, and happy are all the people served by them."

As Pop and Granny's family matured, each one followed their heart. Harry moved to his own farm on Mill Creek in the early 1930s. Louise began college at Tennessee Wesleyan. John D. involved himself in the automobile business where he worked with "Cap" Paine's Chevrolet dealership in Sevierville until he entered the Army-Air Corp. Homer prepared to enter the University of Tennessee and planned to go to medical school at Memphis.

Although Uncle John D. , the middle son, was interested in the world of automobiles, farming was his primary calling. I would call it his first love but that was Antoinette Ogle. She was the daughter of Charlie and Hattie Ogle in Gatlinburg. Her siblings were Earl, Tom, and "Lib." The Gatlinburg Ogles were a different "set" of Ogles from Dr. Ogle's clan lest you wonder. Uncle John D., discriminating and eager, was more than smitten by this flaming redhead with porcelain skin who hailed from the south end of the county. According to Aunt Antoinette, with whom I recently spent some quality time, the two of them got serious quickly,

Aunt Antoinette chuckled, "Dr. Ogle had a lot of pride, and when he saw we were so serious and were spending so much time together, he went down to Bennett Jewelers and bought a ring. She speculated that her future father-in-law must have said, " Here John. Looks like it's time you gave her this." They were married in 1945. They later had four children: Gloria (deceased), "Jim," David, and Sarah. Following Uncle John's early death in the 1970s, his Phillips Sixty Six oil distributorship coupled with his tire dealership were closed . Fairfield Inn now exists on that site. The Five Oaks Farm, its roomy farmhouse, and the river bottom acreage became the site of Tanger-Five Oaks Outlet Mall. All three of Antoinette's children developed the outlet mall with David at the helm. Day to day, Jim manages most of the family's Gatlinburg businesses, and Sarah moves back and forth between the two. Sarah recently returned to college, earned her accounting degree, and is working toward her CPA license.

Aunt Antoinette, ninety-one is the only surviving member of Dr. Ogle's immediate family. All of his sons, daughter, and in-laws are deceased. Today, my favorite, redheaded aunt is alert, interested in everything around her, swims in her pool, and misses bridge with old friends no longer around. My aunt reminisced about her life with this other set of Ogles.

"I'm so glad I married John D. We had such a good time together and I so enjoyed the family. I used to go on house calls with Dr. Ogle, and it was so much fun. Your Granny was a wonderful cook and made the finest, fluffiest, lightest, golden brown biscuits. I never made biscuits. John D. kept trying to get me to make them, but I never did. So one day I came in from Sevierville and the kitchen was in shambles. Over time, John D. learned to make his mama's biscuits. He made them with breakfast quite often. Since he was an early riser because of the farm work, and I was not, I was often served breakfast in bed —-thanks to granny's biscuits."

Although I shadowed my uncles all over the farm through those years and they let me help, I remember once I may have almost been dropped from the ranks of Uncle John's nephew list. I was about four years old and just active enough to be on my own around the house—or so they thought. Arlie Matthews, a local painter from New Era community, had painted the house and sun porch for what seemed like days, and I had watched every stroke. Eventually, I leaned into his wet paint, and my right buttocks turned to a crème beige. After days of shadowing the painter, I guess I was intrigued with the process and frustrated at not getting to help. Pop's medical office had a two car garage. Parked in one side was the bright red convertible with shiny hubcaps that Uncle John drove. Apparently, I decided I wanted to paint something just like Arley. I searched for a painting need and found it. It was quite obvious the car's hubcaps did not match it's red finish. Where I found red paint and a brush, I'll never know, but at the end of an hour, the car's hubcaps pretty well matched its red finish. Well, matched may not be an accurate description, the hubcaps and car were red. I don't recall, and I've often wondered, if the car was a dealership demonstrator on loan or if Uncle John actually owned it.

My fondest memories of the Five Oaks Farm and its big room- filled house were those routine days on the farm, especially in the summer. The homeplace next door to his little brick medical office, was a large white, two-story farmhouse. The home of white, painted clapboard with every window framed in dark green shutters was stunning compared to most other homes. Its tin roof was the same dark green. The entire interior of the house was sealed in wormy chestnut.

It was a unique home and very special to me. I was born in the second story bedroom facing south, and my grandfather delivered me. One of my favorite places was the screened porch with the green canopy and the Five Oaks logo. The swings, chairs, and gliders were deep and wrapped you up when you sat on their leather pillows. We spent many late afternoons there talking, listening to the peacocks calling just before dusk, cicadas calling from the treetops, and watching the few dozen cars pass on the way to the mountains. Directly above us was another porch, identical in size except its three walls were glass enclosed. It overlooked the yard and the highway. Its second floor height mingled with several of the surrounding oak canopies and always gave me the illusion of a glass tree house.

Once you entered the front door, you stepped into the great room or formal living room. Immediately to your left were steps to the second and third levels. From the great room, a main hallway lead to the rear of the house. Immediately adjacent to the great room as you moved down the hall, a glassed sun porch on the right served as an office and the exit to the medical office next door. The hallway opened into a small dining room and the back door.

To the left, a door led to the kitchen. It was long and rectangular with a bank of windows facing north toward Sevierville and overlooking the Munsey Rambo farm. Completing the right side of the U shaped hallway was a passageway that exited the kitchen. It provided a narrow space that was used as a small sitting and sewing room and entry to the den or casual area. The large den had a fireplace, radio, and those amenities that created hominess. Granny often cooked soups and cornbread on the various metal contraptions built into its fireplace for some occasions. Cold weather and snow in those late 1930s and early 1940s often called for meals cooked in and over the den's fire. This room also had a front door, and it opened out on a marble patio. That area housed the well-house, the cistern that caught rainwater, and fronted the graveled, circular driveway. Most casual visitors parked at the patio edge, crossed the patio, and entered through this door rather than through the screened porch that led to the formal great room.

The stairs led to a landing that led toward the back of the house. A bedroom on the left was directly across from the bathroom. A second bedroom, on the right, shared a common wall with the bathroom. At hall's end, a large open space formed an L at the back of this area. It was mainly storage, and later served as a playhouse for me and my cousins, Joan , Jerry, and Joe Ogle. From the landing at the head of the steps, three more steps led to an upper open balcony area that housed a large closet, two bedrooms, and the glassed sun porch that was directly above the screened porch at ground level. Unchanged, my glass tree house is still visible from the highway as it overlooks rapid change. After many years of absence from the old homeplace place, I returned and there was only one difference— all the door knobs were much lower.

The Five Oaks Corporation, the current Ogle generation, completely remodeled the homeplace, swapped home fixtures for office décor, and transformed it into an upscale management center for their Five Oaks operation. With a fitting sensitivity and respect for family tradition and heritage, they maintained the integrity of the homeplace, refreshed much of it, kept the entire wormy chestnut internal skin, and created a unique business ambience. Now, when you enter, the chestnut wood still dims the brightness slightly, and the room still exudes a homey secure feeling. Just as it once did, the room welcomes you warmly, and I can't really explain why. I still expect to smell cigar smoke from my granddads HavaTampa cigar, hear the chime from the old grandfather clock that once reached the ceiling, and listen for Granny to call from the kitchen, "Honey, I just made you some egg custard and shortening bread."

As months passed , the Five Oaks summers became more memorable, filled with fun, and adventure. My summer free time was a time when planting, haying, threshing, and other summer farm work seemed busiest.

1940 at Pop's home. Me, Dad, Pop on Moonglow, and her colt at front. Uncle Homer standing on running board of car, Uncle Harry at far left.
(Ron Rader Family collection)

My brother and I sit with Pop and our mom. Dad, an Army Combat Engineer, was away in the European Campaign of WW II. Ricky, in Pop's lap, was one year old and I was six. Circa 1944
(Ron Rader family collection)

My Great Smoky Mountain Boyhood

Anytime there was hauling to be done, I got to drive the wagon and yell commands to the horses who, of course, paid very little attention to me. While awaiting their next wagon pull, the pasture clover they picked always trumped my commands and won out for most attention. Until Uncle Harry or Uncle John, who both had more testosterone in their voice, yelled at the horses, they seldom moved.

A tyical yard gathering at Five Oaks, family enjoy lunch at 1930 reunion.
(Ron Rader family collection)

As had long been the custom, since they first built the home, the Five Oaks lunch ritual continued. Somewhere around noon, my uncles, the farmhands, and I would head back to the front yards cool shade under the towering, green canopy of the five huge oaks. The breeze always seemed best there. The hedgeapple trees, their trunks freshly whitewashed encircled the yards perimeter and made the setting even more private and cooler. Granny always had long tables set up in the shade with tablecloths, ice, and food ready to come out. Mountain recipes were often passed down for generations. Most of our family used them and continued the cooking fame that went with them. Country cooking in the mountains was a cuisine unto itself, both gourmet and unique.

Those dinners at midday on the farm always seemed more like thanksgiving dinners or family reunions with large crowds. The food was varied and endless. Since most everything came from the garden, field, or the farm, it was a horn of plenty table. The meal was an endless procession of freshness. Daily vegetables were creamed corn, fried okra, green beans, green onions, sliced tomatoes, spinach, and "kilt" fresh lettuce (fresh lettuce, chopped green onions with sizzling hot bacon fat and vinegar poured over it). Entrees usually featured two or three meats like fried chicken, country ham, pork chops, or maybe fried cube steak. Always in plentiful supply was cornbread, country butter, whole milk, sweet ice tea with fresh lemon. Dessert varied. Granny's egg custard, short or raisin bread, fruit pies of every flavor, depending on the month, and sometimes-baked salt rising bread with butter and jelly to name a few.

Those shaded dinners never lacked laughter, joking, teasing, and debates. If only those remaining oaks could speak. Since we were sitting

THE BLUE MOUNTAINS SING
of rivers, old men, trails and trout

Summer at Five Oaks

Back: Kay Henry, Joan Ogle, Joe Ogle, Jerry Ogle Front: Me, Jack (collie), and Ricky

Circa 1945 (Ron Rader family collection)

probably forty yards from US 441, passers-by were locals, friends, and acquaintances, and they didn't hesitate to drop in and visit with their neighbors who filled the yard. A few always had the proverbial question, "Oh, Doc, I hate to bother you at dinner, but while I'm thinking about it, I've been hurtin right here. What do you think it is?"

The lofty canopies of the century-old oaks offered a cool shade that made leaving the outdoor table hard. But the right-on-time approach of an afternoon lightning storm was always reason enough for everybody to head back to the unfinished farm work that awaited them in the river bottom. All too well they knew the wisdom of completing the work in the fields before the wind, rain, and lightning made work dangerous and muddy, and the horses agitated and unpredictable.

Most of the farmhands were like uncles to me. Sam Stinnett was red haired, five feet two inches , stocky, laughed a lot, always busy, and could do most any task. Sam mostly worked with the horses and trained them. Newt and wife Rebecca "Becky" Reagan lived in the small farmhouse on the farm. Newt was like a brother to my uncles and helped the family farm the eighty plus acres. Becky was gentle, had beautiful red hair, porcelain

Bothers John D., Homer, and Harry Ogle with their favorite Tennessee walking horses at lower level of the Five Oaks barn. John D. the middle brother, Homer the youngest, and Harry the oldest.

(Ron Rader family collection)

skin, and I, at six, hoped to marry her one day. She made sure I was always fed a meal or dessert anytime I was within yelling distance of her house near the Little Pigeon River. She got lots of opportunity, since her house was wrapped by Five Oaks pastureland of corn, tobacco, pea, and other crops as well as the fields holding the sheep, horses, and cattle. Most farm activity was always nearby, or I found excuses to wander near.

A large barn, pea granary, wheat granary, corncrib, chicken house, hog lot, tractor and implement sheds, and a few smaller buildings such as a smokehouse for storing hams and pork made up the barnyard. The barn was split-level. The upper floor held a couple of smaller storage stalls on either side and most of the remaining space was open. It had an upper loft so the loose hay could be snatched from the hay wagon by rope and pulleys that controlled two large grabbing hooks. The hay from one entire wagon load could be snatched up, pulled high to the peak of the roof, and pulled the entire length of the barn, from front to back. When the release triggered, the jaws dropped the hay in a huge fluffy pile onto this half loft balcony area.

The hay drops were repeated until the loose hay almost reached the pigeons' roosting spot in the peak. In good hay years, the space under the loft balcony was filled with loose hay that often cascaded toward the front sliding doors. Still, only half the floor would be filled with loose hay. Stables occupied the ground level of the barn. Two open corralled spaces for calves, hogs, lambs, ill horses, and other smaller animals were located on either side of the ground entry area leading to the ground level stables. The left entry wall held all manner of horse saddles, harnesses, equine medicines, plow lines, and other necessary farm leather and implement needs.

Rainy days or slow boring days were perfect for creating excitement at the barn. The coiled plow lines stored neatly and hung on the storage wall on ground level made perfect Tarzan swings. The bad news was somebody had to climb high in the barn, walk the rafters used to hang tobacco, and tie off a knot that would hold the swinging weight of a small boy. We miscalculated the physics a few times. Whoever braved it got to be called Tarzan's son's name, "Boy," for the day. The other less courageous swinger earned the less prestigious name "Cheetah" named after Tarzan's chimpanzee. The rest of the day was spent climbing and swinging from every nook and cranny in the highest points in the barn.

The goal was to make a long sweeping swing from the highest possible perch the barn roof had to offer, and at the end of the arc drop into the fluffy, sweet softness of new mown hay. We never tired of the game as the excitement built. Each swinger tried to climb and swing higher and higher. We ended it for the day only when somebody mis-aimed or mis-swung and dropped, not

THE BLUE MOUNTAINS SING
of rivers, old men, trails and trout

in the hay, but instead into one of the corn chutes, much like the laundry chutes at the home of the wealthy . Hidden by the hay, anyone unable to avoid a hole in the floor earned a bone jarring surprise ride, as the victim sailed down thirty feet of dusty, cobwebbed, splintered, rough-cut oak square pipe that dumped feed, or, in our case, misaimed swingers directly into the hog lot.

Pop with new colt
(Ron Rader family collection)

Usually, a missed aim pretty well called for a scared, screaming run to the big house where the women could once again tell us, "I told you boys you'd get hurt at the barn, didn't I?"

A special treat for me and often my cousins was a fishing trip complete with a half mile walk through the river bottom pasture to the Little Pigeon River. I guess my love for fishing came from my mother. She loved to fish any place or anytime but especially on summer days. Even after we moved to our new home in Pigeon Forge, when she returned to visit her mother and her homeplace, she'd manage to take me fishing at the Little Pigeon, her backyard. I suppose our return visits to her birthplace stirred a yearning to somehow recapture joys from her childhood. She'd take me, and I'd dig red worms in several wet spots around the hog lot or other unnamed spots, drop them into two Prince Albert tobacco cans, and top them off with some rich dirt from Granny's flower garden.

Mom and I would walk about three quarters of a mile down the dusty wagon road between corn crops to the river and sit under a huge white oak tree. The riverbank was tangled and overgrown. It was waist deep with thick grass covered with wild flowers, blackberry briar, pasture clover, rabbit tobacco, and willow trees that made a perfect screen. Bluegills, small bass, and catfish were thick, and we always caught several.

Just above us, a swinging bridge connected Five Oaks with the Benny Carr farm and the J. Hugh Shults farm. J Hugh was a self-proclaimed veterinarian everyone called Doc. He always came to Five Oaks on short notice when sheep or cattle were giving birth or in trouble. I especially remember him coming over once, almost in the middle of the night. It seems I forgot to close the grainary door, and Granny's milk cow fed part of the day before on oats and wheat and foundered. They called Doc in the wee hours of the morning. He rushed to the side of the old Jersey lying on her side. I was scared and thought she'd surely die, and it would be my fault. Never had I ever seen such a sight, a cow bloated twice her normal size, no wonder she was lying on her side.

The only other time I'd seen something like this was in the Saturday cartoons at the Pine's theatre. I remembered that animal had expanded bigger and bigger until it burst, which is exactly what I thought this cow was going to do. She'd gotten a lot bigger in just a few hours. The pure grain she'd overeaten was fermenting. The rapidly fermenting gas was inflating her. Doc arrived; he and Pop shared mumbled short sentences out of my earshot. He knelt and rubbed around on "Old Jerses' "rib cage, feeling for ribs, which you could sure see clearly now. He took out a jackknife, opened the longest blade that I'd ever seen on a knife, and slipped it between two of the cow's ribs.

What happened next I'd only seen twice before, except that I only saw it happen to a truck tire and an overinflated balloon, not a cow. A mechanic had let the core slip from a heavy equipment inner tube. The core shot past my head, buried in the wall, and the tube dragged him all over the room as the air escaped. The big plastic WW II weather balloon that I stuck with an ice pick, accidentally, actually sailed out of Five Oaks yard over the Gatlinburg highway propelled by escaping air. I still don't know where it landed.

That's not what happened to the cow. There was a whoosh. I, unthinking and sorry for the pain I caused the cow, grabbed her tail just as a stream of fermenting gas, digested and undigested grain, and other unnamed stuff in a cow's intestines spewed from the pocketknife hole in her side. The fountain of bile lifted about ten feet in the air. Unfortunately, like the sprinkler head on granny's flower watering can , the vile smelling liquid rained in about a ten-foot circle covering every one but Doc and Pop, who had thoughtfully moved back just far enough. Thoroughly covered in pungent, brown bile, Tarzan and Cheetah gagged for a few long minutes before running for the horse's water trough for a swim.

The cow moaned, but this time it was more of a relieved sigh. She tried a few practice rolls, then got to her feet. Then, as if nothing had happened, she thirstily headed to the same water trough where we were washing up, thirsty for some much needed water. Fearful of her retribution, we quickly mounted the fence.

By the time I was nine or ten I could swim, so we were allowed to go fish alone at the river. Although I played with other boys, the times and distance did not always provide me with a friend my age or one who shared common outdoor interests. So I learned early in life to enjoy my own company and do my own thing. I soon found that solitude mixes well with the outdoors, and nature could conjure up some breathtaking experiences and sights. Although I welcomed company, the excited chatter of two boys grousing around unfocused and not paying attention to their surroundings, pretty much eliminated any chance of observing any special epiphany that nature was to offer us that day. Since I learned that lesson so early in life, I grew comfortable with my aloneness. The solitude earned me some of nature's best returns.

Farm life, though at times difficult and harsh, was probably somewhat like childbirth pains. We forgot its harshness by summer and into early fall. When alone on a farm, there was a certain poetry in its nature, be it a farmland pasture or the woods. For instance, my dusty midsummer walk through the Five Oaks bottoms to the river was filled with joyous activity that completely enveloped me. It elicited one wow after another. Redwing blackbirds chattered to other feathered buddies, each one hung, and then swayed on separate cattails in the bulrushes of the low marshy pasture. Their red-splotched shoulders always added to the tapestry of the day. The untilled, wild, and unplanted pasture stretched randomly in bits and pieces. Bounded by matted fencerows, some fields showed off field daisies abloom in a carpet that stretched as far as you could see. June bugs and curious mayflies followed me down the twin tracks of the wagon road. Its center filled with nettles and overgrown Bermuda grass. This open pathway was the only cleavage between the corn patches to my right and left, and it ended at the riverbank willows.

Their ranks evenly spaced. The corn stalks, tall, straight, and at attention, stood shoulder to shoulder watchfully guarding me as if they were British soldiers. They relaxed only long enough for their tassels to whisper to the swirling summer breeze. The river that lay just ahead promised me even more adventure. Wild ducks always courted would-be mates along the waterway in summer. Muskrats darted back and forth unsure of which green tidbit to sample among the many. Soft-shelled turtles sunned on every sun-lounge log or rock, and this year's crop of tiny rabbits tunneled playfully through the tall grass.

Ever watchful, a red fox, on the opposite bank, hopped high in the air indecisive in its stalk for a field mouse. A red tailed hawk, its talons outstretched and wings completing descent, landed and postured royally on the one remaining limb of a dead walnut tree; its darkened silhouette was haunting and stark, a study in contrast. Everything else around me was so alive, so green, and so vital. This living, breathing, moving summer tapestry was ever changing and ever exciting. The farm's freshness had a living vitality about it , one that sang in an unforgettable harmony that delighted my every sense. It was nature at its best.

Following a brief illness, Pop died in October 1946 at the age of fifty-nine. I was eight. I often think of the many new life advances he was able to enjoy given his birth year was 1887. My brief summers and too few years spent with him were idyllic. Although these fun years can't be recovered or relived, I still enjoy their recall.

Our Pigeon Forge home burned from an electrical wiring short on New Year's Day 1947. My granddad had passed away, six months earlier so we temporarily moved into Five Oaks homeplace with Granny, now alone. We lived there for nearly two years until we were able to rebuild further west on our hilltop at "Windswept" in Pigeon Forge. Our homeplace was demolished later in the mid-1990s to make way for the Whispering Pines Condominiums on Ogle Road.

In the 1950s, my grandmother would move back to Pigeon Forge on the river in the same house where she and Pop first started his medical practice. Granny was in good health and active except for a touch of arthritis. She seemed always to be in the kitchen cooking. She'd had plenty of practice. She had raised three sons, one daughter, scores of their friends, and only God knows how many tenant farmers, farmhands, and horse grooms and trainers she'd housed and fed. She lived to be one hundred three and died peacefully in July 1992. Before her death she still lived alone in her Pigeon Forge home overlooking the Little Pigeon river. Active in her late nineties, I can still see her walking the quarter mile up river road to choir practice or Sunday church at the Pigeon Forge Methodist church where she would once again sing her favorite hymn, "It is Well with My Soul."

Granny Ogle on her birthday, July 5, 1989 at age of one hundred. Uncle Homer, Louise, Mom, Granny, and Uncle Harry. Uncle John D. and my father Al were deceased.

(Ron Rader family collection)

Five Oaks Past

Ronny feeding Glory, Pop standing ready.
My seventh summer in 1945.
(Ron Rader family collection)

J. W. OGLE, M. D., OWNER
JOHN D. OGLE, OPERATOR

The Five Oaks logo on his envelopes
and stationery.
(Ron Rader family collection)

My granddad steadies Glory
for me at Five Oaks in 1945.
(Ron Rader family collection)

Early 1940 view of Five Oaks. Oak Tree Lodge now
sits on the site.
(Ron Rader family collection)

Jack, our Five Oaks collie, and I explore
on a hot August day. The area behind
the cattle is the site of the present day
Damon's Restaurant. The tree to the right
is near site of today's Oak Tree Lodge
and my granddad's horse training ring.
Approximately one hundred yards in front
of me is the entrance to the Five Oaks-
Tanger Mall complex.
(Ron Rader family collection)

CHAPTER TWO

Walk quietly in any direction and taste the freedom on the mountain. Climb the mountains and get their good tidings. Nature's peace will flow into you as sunshine flows into the trees. The winds will blow their own freshness into you and the storms their energy, while cares will drop off like autumn leaves.—John Muir

Summers ✦ Farm Life ✦ Zip-A-Dee-Doo-Dah
A Country Kaleidoscope filled withLife's Bits and Pieces

The families and way of life that surrounded me in these boyhood years were down home and salt of the earth. Summers seemed best. More outdoors meant more excitement. Nature's signs whetted my excitement of what comes next, whether it was the promises of the day ahead or what lies just around the next bend.

You tempered your plan for the day by many signs. The white faces of wind lifted leaves always watched an approaching summer storm. Gusts and black skies were quickly laced with chain lightening, backed by black thunderheads, and soon followed by steamy mud puddles. June bugs, chiggers, and yellow jackets filled blackberry-picking days. Blueberries, rhododendron whites and purples, and field daisies unfolded a countryside mural. Freshened and pristine, the green mountains were sunlit and seemed closer. Their summer veil of blue haze was absent and cleared by the rain, the mountain range stood in silhouette, sharp and three dimensional. Every glance revealed so many more faces of summer.

The ragged shoulders of those mountains always trigger fleeting graphic glimpses. Slices of fifteen plus Smoky Mountain summers come alive. No doubt, many of my friends and classmates remember our rural youth, those farm days, those treasured times we thought could never end. Like church and the county fair, they were icons we believed would always be there, unchanging.

Pigeon Forge was farmland. I was surrounded by everything rural. Home was these mountain foothills of hardwood ridges and pastureland, laced with springs feeding sparkling branches, creeks, and rivers. I never lived on a farm, but Harry Ogle, my uncle, did. It was an eighty plus acre Mill Creek farm, and as the crow flies, a one and a half mile walk south of my home.

The oldest of the four siblings, Uncle Harry left his Five Oaks farm homeplace, his dad and mom, Dr. John W. and Blanche Wayland Ogle, his brothers John D. and Homer, and sister Louise to start his own farm. He decided farming trumped college. His farm purchase included a white clapboard, two-story, farmhouse, and two barns. Mostly flat, it offered a creek surrounded by pasture, several hardwood covered ridges and wooded mountains laced with springs and branches.

His children were my three cousins, Joan, Jerry, and Joe. We were inseparable growing up. Uncle Harry was always glad to have the help of one more "half a farm hand," me. He opened up the world of all things planted, all things harvested, and every sacrifice it took to get there. From butchering hogs to tying tobacco for market, from gathering corn and wheat at the Five Oaks farm homeplace, to putting up hay, the days on a farm were often hot, hard , and long.

Kid's daily chores included egg gathering, fighting off the rooster who believed it was his chicken house, rounding up, feeding, and milking cows, trying to outsmart weasels and foxes that soon slid back in the henhouse, carrying milk to and from the spring, and scores of other "get in the way of fun" tasks. Along with the excitement, the unexpected, and outdoor fun came some graphic moments of drudgery, boredom, and frustration, especially for a kid.

One of those "oh gawd" chores that most farm kids will easily recall was cutting tobacco on a steamy dripping August late afternoon with two more long creek bottom rows to go and an end that was nowhere in sight. Throughout the day, Mill Creek's icy waters and the siren's call of our swimming hole, complete with a swing rope, called to us from less than fifty feet away. We knew all too well that a swim was available only at dusk when the day's work was finished. To further aggravate our stinging sunburned backs, a "pack saddle," the fat, green, pudgy little caterpillar with venom covered spines and with a sting that would make a wasp proud, would casually drop on some body part and remind us that this tobacco was their food. Just when we recovered and moved to the next chore, yellow jackets boiled from the ground or hornets or wasps attacked from above. They were always quick to show us we were not welcome on their turf.

Uncle Harry's huge creek-bottom garden had every vegetable known to mankind, and Aunt Estalee canned or cooked much of it. Joining my cousins, I remember helping hoe nearly every crop we ate and many we never ate.

Nineteen forties electricity had not yet reached many farmers on outlying farms .Only those nearest the heart of Pigeon Forge enjoyed the convenience Roosevelt had created. Summer evenings began with a fine supper of all things homegrown, all things fresh, all things homemade, and all things seasoned at Aunt Estalee's table. Meals were all cooked on a wood burning kitchen stove with a twenty-gallon side warm water reservoir for washing.

Beginning with all youngsters' nightly foot-washings to rid us of the days dirt, the Aladdin lamps were then lit, the battery powered radio turned on, and Aunt Estalee read the Adventures of Uncle Wiggly Rabbit aloud to us. This top hatted, British gentleman rabbit dressed in a long formal swallow-tailed coat was the subject of scores of morality tales and fables. Each story was designed to put our morals, manners, and us on the right track. They were accompanied, I'm sure, with a heavy dose of parental silent pleas and unspoken prayers asking that somehow we'd develop into OK young folks with "the right stuff."

In the background, the latest WW II news rose and ebbed in volume as the crackling radio voices of Edward R. Murrow and H.V. Kaltenborn told Uncle Harry of the U.S. and allied military advances against the Nazis with reminders that this, "The Greatest Generation," was defending us and were depending on us—the folks back home—to save tinfoil, ration sugar and gas, and keep tilling our Victory gardens. My Dad was there, somewhere. I wondered about him. With the exception of some two week furloughs, he'd been absent in our lives for three years.

I later realized that, however subtly, Uncle Harry taught me and my friends much about life, true values, and things that really mattered. Coupled with farm excitement and fun, he demonstrated self-sufficiency, good humor, how to roll and bend with life's flow and nature's life cycles. He was a master at neighbor to neighbor helpfulness, self-reliance, and optimism. He showed us how to really enjoy the outdoors and the many blessings farm life offered. Uncle Harry loved to hunt small game and always kept three or four hounds. We were filled with excitement when we could successfully sneak one or two hounds up to second floor bedrooms on icy nights.

Physically, Uncle Harry was lean, wiry, and laid back with pulse in the fifties, and like my grandmother Blanche, his mom, he never missed a chance to laugh. He was Bing Crosby's look-alike and my brother Rick and

THE BLUE MOUNTAINS SING
of rivers, old men, trails and trout

I were always waiting expectantly for him to suddenly break out in a song like "White Christmas" or " Bells of Saint Mary's."

Now, I realize that he was a Renaissance man, a farmer's farmer, and probably could have been the poster farmer of the century. His farm and service to others could have been a model for many others around the county. He was a valued friend to most of the county farmers and to just folks. People responded to his good nature and his willingness to help anyone in need. Neighbors reciprocated. They helped him with planting crops, harvesting, neighborly support, and he responded in kind. He remained tireless in his willingness to help his farmer neighbors, friends ,and often strangers. His skills at most things were superb, varied, and legion. He could envision a design for any need or any object, create it with torch and steel, and make it function.

The scriptures say we are all called to God's special plan, an individual gift for each of us. Well, Uncle Harry listened. He truly was a servant and God's man. You see, I saw him role model true unselfish servanthood hundreds of times. When a farmer's tractor or bailer broke down, the wait for a part was often three or four days, and he could be left at the mercy of the Trailways bus schedule. Following his own father's servanthood, the all-weather house calls of a country doctor, Uncle Harry would drop his own work, travel to the farmer in need, weld, repair, create, or remedy the situation.

Close friends from his childhood, Xan and Herman Davenport, once said, "Harry is a jack of all trades and master of many. If you can dream it , Harry can build it." Anyone who expressed a need for a new and improved sugar cane mill, apple cider press, hog butchering equipment, an exact part, a better tool, hitch, or anything constructed of metal, Uncle Harry was renowned for his creative ability to produce it. He truly was a humble, servant leader, and those are the best kind.

Uncle Harry was proud of his progeny and extended family. He married Estalee Sims, one of six equally beautiful sisters and their one brother, Bob. They had three children: Joan Ogle Hill(deceased) married to Jack Hill (deceased) was a registered nurse and formerly Director of UT-Knoxville's Cardiac Intensive Care Unit; Jerry W Ogle(deceased) married to Linda Nastasi Ogle was a Gatlinburg pharmacist-owner and successful hotel motel entrepreneur with multi properties; Joe D. Ogle married to Jane Whaley has an engineering degree and is a former hardware and retail owner, entrepreneur, and developer. I believe you find similar successes in the lives and careers of many of my classmates and friends who grew up on farms. Let's hear it for the quality of kids reared on a farm! Huh!

Much later in my life, a corporate CEO shared his successful recruiting requirements with me. We were building a trainee program for the company and seeking individuals who would excel. We sought to recruit bright, talented, capable, potential leaders. Among the many required traits for entry into the management training program, a potential trainee had to possess a strong work ethic.

The seasoned CEO said, " I have found that the individuals who will persevere and succeed in organizational settings must have certain key traits. Those individuals who can best overcome adversity and who will ultimately excel ,more often than not, I have found to be those young men and women who grew up on a farm, worked in a family dairy, or worked their way through school in a fast food operation."

Many of Uncle Harry's other nieces and nephews experienced this same type of farm life. They too enjoyed similar successes that would have delighted him. A Sims family nephew was one because of vocation. Jeff Sims, married to Nancy, is several times named Tractor Dealer of the Year, regionally and nationally. He is Sims Tractor and Implement owner, entrepreneur, local humorist, and sometimes pundit and politician behind the throne. Ken Seaton, also a nephew, built a corporate motel chain.

Uncle Harry's life was a life well lived. The world needs more people like him. My memories of his farmer era that he allowed me to enter and be a part of will always be treasured ones. I'm sure many of my friends, classmates, and folks of my generation have similar and equally rich memories of their own.

Uncle Harry left us all a great legacy. It was because of him and his family that I recently reminded my grandchildren and children, "The times you spend outdoors playing, working, and just having fun with your cousins will prove to be the most coveted childhood memories you'll ever experience. Make certain you create a lot of 'cousin time' and build some memories."

A wise man once declared, "If you don't set your own life's priorities, the world is going to set them for you."

What a legacy Uncle Harry so willingly created and shared so that others might see, learn, and grow. I can only hope that I can continue to model his lessons as well for those who will follow me.

And, as Uncle Wiggly would have me say, "Thanks Uncle Harry."

A young Uncle Harry proud of his hounds.

(Ron Rader family collection)

THE BLUE MOUNTAINS SING
of rivers, old men, trails and trout

The Then: Uncle Harry' Mill Creek farm before he began farming it. Circa 1928
(Ron Rader family collection)

Now, is the right time to pass out thanks to the many folks who were a part of so much opportunity, excitement, learning, and just downright fun. Maybe it will entertain you if I share my Top Ten or Eighteen Memories.

Of course, you do realize there are probably several thousand to choose from, so I'm doing my best. These are slices of my best of times and designed to prompt your recall. Hopefully you'll say, " Your words triggered this funny thing that happened to me as a youngster. It popped right into my head." If that happens, then my words fulfilled my intent, so please fill in your own storylines. Weave your own memories among my random sketches of our fun filled days. Remember, you have your own story —your own movie is in your head.

So let's begin with my *Remember When.*

Spring: The only ray of hope in the late winter's bleakness, trout season opened April 1 in The Great Smoky Mountain National Park. Late spring was dawn to dusk planting and hoeing nearly everything you'd eat, can, or sell the rest of the year.

Summer: June was great. July was a hot sweaty time of threshing wheat, putting up hay, hoeing tobacco, and everything green.

Best Feeling: The mountain cure-all was a twenty foot drop from the rope swing into Little Pigeon's ice slush at Pine Grove or from the rock at the Emert's Cove long river pool. The river's bend fronted the many bedroomed log cabin hideaway named *Non-Monotonous.*

Summers ◆ Farm Life ◆ Zip-A-Dee-Doo-Dah

The NOW: In the late 1940s after he had renovated and farmed for two decades. This view, from Mill Creek road, shows part of Uncle Harry's farm and surrounding woodlands, ridges, and upper pasture. His country lane drive way runs from the extreme right to left toward center of picture. Mill Creek borders this pasture and forms the top bar of a T with the driveway and the bridge at the front of his home.
(Ron Rader family collection)

Farm of the Century: In my mind at least, was Uncle Harry's Mill Creek farm. It came stocked with my three cousins. Summer there was strictly belly-down in Mill Creek, grannying and groping under every rock for fish or turtles. The plowed pastures were for riding any horse or mule or, for that matter, any available four-legged creature. We rode bareback, at top speed, with only a rope halter, and it lasted until the horse grew tired of our pestering and threw us off.

Most Fun: Seasonally, getting to work the farm and continually playing with my cousins, Joan, Jerry, and Joe Ogle.

Best Food: Breakfast on a school day in Aunt Estalee's' kitchen. A bowl of real homemade oatmeal, with a large glob of butter, fresh cream, a mountaintop of real sugar, and three jumbo homemade biscuits slathered in fresh butter. In addition to fresh sausage or pork tenderloin, sided with gravy and jumbo biscuits, topped off with a butter slathered hot biscuit heaped with fresh blackberry jam or molasses.

Hardest Morning Chore: Jumping up from that same breakfast table at the sound of the school bus horn and running across the Mill Creek bridge and out the gravel lane some two hundred yards to the "thank you Lord" mailbox/bus stop.

THE BLUE MOUNTAINS SING
of rivers, old men, trails and trout

Sports Country Style: We improved our times, our averages, and tallied our athletic statistics on something besides sports. Instead, the venues were planting tobacco, cutting tobacco, milking , gathering eggs, fighting the sitting hens, and quickly, her rooster, feeding everything it seemed that drew breath. For more sports, we climbed into the tobacco-hanging rafters and jumped to loose hay, those who advanced to the fearless level tied plow lines up higher and swung from the gabled pigeon and English sparrow roost.

Worst Feeling: There was a threshing machine chaff down your back mingled with sweat, yesterday's chiggers, and packsaddle stings. You stood under a bluebird, cloudless sky enveloped in one big humid drip. The land was ablaze with a midday sun at ninety-eight degrees.

Worst Reminder or Things You Never Wanted to Hear: "Who do you boys think had to climb to the top of the barn and untie my plow lines?" Or a middle of the night call from the foot of the steps after you are almost asleep – "Did you boys wash those dirty barnyard bare feet before you climbed into my fresh clean sheets?"

Scariest Challenge: Once we found the largest wasp nest around the farm, about the size of pie plate, we strategized on how to take it out, wasps, nest, and all. Uncle Harry covered his tobacco beds with white, gauzy type netting. We cut cape size pieces and tied them around our neck like Superman. When you ran, the cape streamed out behind you and made a perfect target for any angry wasp, hornet, or bee on the attack and faster than you. In theory, the attacker stung the trailing cloth first and not you. Next , we armed ourselves with both pine and cedar boughs , bushy and lengthy. You had to be able to swing them like tennis rackets very quickly. The final act was a humdinger. In our case, all four of us ran yelling and screaming directly at the nest and began threshing the nest along with the cascading and angry red or yellowish wasps. The Battle of Midway with its skies filled with Japanese planes could not have more fiercely fought. Later, soothing our stings by lying in the creek, we replayed the courageous acts of our little outnumbered band of Americans.

More Sporting Events : Tying Aunt Estalee's sewing thread to a June bug's leg and running behind a very alive mini-plane. Another sporting event was lifting the concrete lid on the spring, being careful not to knock over the milk or break the eggs, and gently finger strain the wet leaves, grabbing several unlucky salamanders as bait for tomorrow's river small mouths.

Most Creative Idea: Who to blame if milk got tipped over.

Fall: Was harvest, riding horse drawn wagons, pumpkin gathering, butchering hogs, and hunting , often in an icy coldness. It was wood smoke, apples, hay, and drying tobacco.

Coldest Hands: The below freezing sting of pumpkin juice, eight arms elbow deep as seven pumpkins were carved.

Second Coldest Hands: Think of the coldest, rainiest day, when rain turns to sleet. This is the day the Lord always decided to put my uncle's tobacco in case. Leaves were pliable, wouldn't crumble, and could be tied into " hands," knotted and packed for market. Standing in the open barn passageway, the whole family tied tobacco until it was finished. Like butchering hogs, the process had only a beginning, never an end. Gloved hands could not tie tobacco. With a stiff breeze blowing and the temperature well below freezing, it quickly dawned on several of us that farming lasted all year long, not just in the summer fun times.

At the end of that week, *Lesson Learned that Taught Me to Pray:* Thank you God! And please, I don't EVER want to have to do this farm work for a living every minute of every day or work in a dairy! And while you are at it, please don't ever call me to be a missionary. The last thing I ever want to do is have to paddle a dugout canoe down the Amazon River through those jungles. I know I'd be wearing sweaty clothes like Humphrey Bogart and be all covered with those gnats, mosquitoes, leeches, and especially those black swamp flies .

Lord, I can see it now. There I'd be , screaming and running from naked people with nose bones who'd be doing their best to catch me and eat me. And I'd be yelling back over my shoulder trying to tell them that YOU told me to come there. And I don't believe I'd ever get them to understand that all I was trying to do is give them this Bible and tell them about it and You— *No Sir!*—I just wouldn't be any good at that.

And Lord while I'm asking, I wouldn't even make a good door knocking Seventh Day Adventist even in a white shirt, black tie, and black pants. No sir, I just don't believe I have it in me to knock on doors. Try to find me something I'm good at. Anyway, Ms. Shultz told us in Sunday School, that You knew each of us personally, and You had a special plan for each of us, and You'd see to it we prospered. So could you please prosper me in something I'm good at ?

Biggest Scare: With almost frozen pumpkin-cleaning hands, four young butcher knife searchers run frantically and aimlessly into the night. They are barely ahead of the willow switch and very afraid that they can't find the family butcher knife. This would be the same knife they were warned not to use because they might lose it. That was just right before a finger was sliced. The slicee screamed, threw the knife into the darkness, and ran for bandage help.

Most Politically Incorrect Fun: In the early darkness of a freezing and windy

THE BLUE MOUNTAINS SING
of rivers, old men, trails and trout

winter night it was hog killing time. Daylong fire coals were rekindled and leaping flames highlighted the final butchering scene of chitlin making and lots of stirrin'. A huge pile of red-hot coals, rejuvenated, never failed to trigger the buried creative bent in kids near and far. You could tell right off the kid that was most likely to be an artist. As we grabbed hardwood sticks, plunged them into the fire, and with flaming, sharpened hardwood shafts, we ran wildly through the night whipping the glowing ends and painting the entire sky with a creative certainty, each outlining our own imaginary animal, a glowing silhouetted picture outlined in flame .

Other slices of growing up in the country come to mind in fragments and pieces, unattached . Bits and pieces of a lifetime that were thoroughly enjoyed, sorely missed, and never forgotten. They were profound and pure things that had their rightful place and gave me a sense of comfort and belonging.

Even the serenity of the porch was special. The front porch swings for swinging, rocking chairs for relaxing rhythms, a porch was designed for pondering life, the lost art of dozing outside after Sunday dinner, a porch was a place to watch grasshoppers, bees, and butterflies play tag in the yard.

Summer was the feel of fresh green grass on bare feet; it was the pastel pink, green, yellow, and orange of Easter's candy; it was an hour long search at finding four leaf clovers and turning on your back trying to decide which animal the billowy white clouds shaped. It was eating a tomato off the vine in the field; it was the crack of summer's first watermelon and the feel of its icy roughness on your tongue. It was the rhythmic dance of two hummingbirds.

It was the way young life should be lived.

It was river baptisms at a tiny sandy spot at banks' edge. It was lying on your stomach to drink icy cold, clear spring water. It was night delight, lying on your back to ponder the full moon and the stars , and run barefoot through dew soaked bluegrass. It was that feeling of freedom that came with a chance to catch lightening bugs in an empty peanut butter jar. It was discovering but not understanding the melancholy feeling that came over you as the aching beauty of Amazing Grace spilled from open windows of a country church. It was being swung ever higher in the tire swing. It was the smell and sound of the makin's of Sunday's dinner when a splattering sizzle announced raw chicken just hit fiery, smoking grease. It was the pompous prancing, the proud and rhythmic gait of my granddad's Tennessee Walking Horse as both horse and rider enjoyed an afternoon ride to the river.

Then there was our music; from the hills, hollers, and mountains came our music.

Summers ♦ Farm Life ♦ Zip-A-Dee-Doo-Dah

It grew from the dulcimer, banjo, mandolin, guitar, and others. There was that pure sweetness in the musical language of the dulcimer. It spoke in a special way to each of us. Its strains touched our heart, our very soul. At times, its voice was melancholy. The words told of hardships, harsh winters, summer droughts, infant deaths, war, and epidemics. More often, its voice was serene, prayerful, and celebratory of life's gifts, those good things in life. At times, you felt its festive strains like those of the fiddle, and you wanted to dance in the woods.

Many old-timers, the mountain souls, said that the dulcimer sounded best when played on the porch. They swore that the guitar, mandolin, and banjo, when played together, sound best under the big oak tree in the front yard. They say the fiddle needs more space. Most agreed that once "The Great Speckled Bird" began everybody had to dance. Our mountain music, mountain born, always had to be played out in the open where it remained wild, untamed, and free. Outside is where the Bible should be read aloud. Poetry, too, takes on a whole new meaning when it's read aloud outside in the woods. Some folks say the spoons and the washboard should only be played in a crowd.

Our other music came from South and West of the mountains. Mountain folks swayed in time with our music's many diverse strains. It was energy laden true country music. The real "pickin', grinnin', and fiddlin' "of hillbilly music spilled from the radio airwaves. WROL and WNOX , Knoxville's earliest radio stations, always come to mind. On WNOX, Lowell Blanchard introduced the "Midday Merry Go Round." The earthy twang of transitioning true mountain music soon took on the hillbilly tones of the 1940s and 1950s.

In my youth, there was little entertainment or little to do inside the home. Card games along with Monopoly, Checkers and Dominoes were popular. Listening to the "78" record player, reading or listening to the radio were about the only forms of entertainment. Hillbilly music strains from the radio permeated my being and surrounded me everywhere.

Often around noon, Lowell Blanchard , a WNOX icon and MC of his Midday Merry-Go-Round variety show, would begin introducing the country music singers and picker performers that day. Almost as quickly, the entire group would burst into song and sound. Wild, raucous, stringed instrument music loudly blared out hillbilly style. Most folks lived in farmhouses, kept their windows raised, prayed for a summer breeze , and tried to cool the house while cooking on wood burning stoves.

No matter where you were in the neighborhood, the wafting music of radio always disclosed much of summer days. It was dinnertime(lunch),

THE BLUE MOUNTAINS SING
of rivers, old men, trails and trout

and the minute we stepped into the edge of a friend's yard, several things happened at once. I smelled pinto beans simmering, cornbread baking , a hint of onions being peeled somewhere, and Lowell Blanchard's faint voice somewhere behind the rising pitch of Bill Monroe and the boys playing and shouting the words to the *Great Speckled Bird*. When our group played from yard to yard, the music and a similar lunchtime fragrance met us in each yard. We had background music throughout most of our summer days, and it was easy to tell when it was dinner time by the WNOX music strains wafting through the air.

To this day, when I smell similar country cooking around noon, my mind wanders back to the Midday-Merry- Go- Round, and I yearn to hear it.

The Cas Walker Music Hour and Porter Waggoner Show would launch many local entertainers. It spawned stars like Roy Acuff to Homer and Jethro and Patsy Cline to Dolly Parton. Many of our local entertainers would soon become icons in Nashville and beyond.

When asked by others, what it was really like in the mountains in those days, I didn't really know how to answer. It is subjective and hard to describe. We each had our own perception. I guess I could recount one of my typical grocery delivery trips. It was one that was routine and that maybe might paint a word picture, a portrait of mountain contentment found so often in those days. This trip was special and one of my favorites.

As I drove the Jeep on a grocery delivery, I was absent-mindedly enjoying the countryside. It was only two bags , but it would be good to visit with Ms. Delilah. I hummed and sung parts of "Oklahoma," and those backwoods of summer made me sing louder. Nobody was around. I thought of a story line someone should write sometime to describe a grocery jaunt like this back in these hills. I tried to mentally capture everything around me. My story opened with once upon a time. That seemed like a good start. If I wrote it, I knew who I'd write about. I'd probably start like this , I imagined.

Once upon a time, in those years and in that place, where time seemed to stand still, a country road wound to and fro. A road unpaved and rutted in winter but not in summer. And it was summer. Faces of summer gazed up from every angle. The roadside's shoulder matted with tangled weeds and grass nearly hid wild strawberries. Daisies stood boldly nearby, Queen Anne's lace, wild violets, brown eyed Susan's, were framed by the taller orange, purple, and white mosaic of wildflowers called Yarrow, or as the old timers called it, "Yerah." The sudden crunch of wet sand and creek pea gravel jerked me from my reverie. I slammed the brakes and ground into reverse, as I backed the front wheels, now rim deep in Mill Creek, back up the bank's slope.

Summers ♦ Farm Life ♦ Zip-A-Dee-Doo-Dah

Most often, a double rut track of our country roads ended at a creek. These rocky, shallow, watery flats always begged, "Ford me." Pondering whether to wade, ford, or walk, I decided to take the well-worn path to my left that led upstream. Partially hidden in the honeysuckle, it led to small footbridge further upstream. Across the creek, at bridge's end, a yard nestled a small log cabin. More often than not, it could have been a two story white clapboard house with wrap around front porch so common to the mountains. Its walls of chestnut logs were neatly chinked hiding its age. Two mountain stone chimneys, one at either end of the house, were solid and well laid. The proverbial front porch had a swing and two rocking chairs. True to the mountains, they were cane bottomed and their runners were of worn hickory.

Tulip poplars, sycamores at creek side, and mountain laurel on the slope behind the cabin spoke of wildness uncultivated. The fragrance from tangles of honeysuckle filled the yard. Honeysuckle fragrance always spoke in different languages to each of us. Even its dialects were special at times. Honeysuckle always spoke of earlier times well spent, of humid summer nights, full moons that offered near daylight brightness. It spoke of majestic views of the valley from hovering ridge tops above. It spoke of young love and the anticipation and mystique of life unfolding.

This yard was green and inviting. Nearest the front steps bloomed day lilies and zinnias. They were the signatures of this household matriarch , a surprising youthful woman with sun bleached hair, who planted and tended them. Spent jonquils, yellowed blooms faded, surrounded by dried crocuses told of spring long past. Dogwood and redbud two months beyond their blooms now sported leaves only and dotted the landscape. Two months earlier, their blooms had signaled spring's return and the promise of summer, a season so welcomed by most mountain dwellers.

Sitting alone on the porch in one rocker, a middle-aged lady rested with her dulcimer in her lap. Her long yellow hair was wrapped neatly at the back of her head. She was different from most mountain women I was accustomed to. Her blonde hair was twisted into an unusual swirl more on top of her head than the usual bun style of most countrywomen. Somehow, her appearance was one of a sophisticate. Her skin was deeply tanned; slight wrinkles circled by laugh lines framed an earthy, open face. Here features formed a profile any artist would prize. Her eyes were an emerald green, the same color as the Caribbean sea that I'd often seen in National Geographic. A closer look suggested she has spent more time outside facing the elements than inside away from them.

Her demeanor and stately bearing were quite the contrast to her surroundings. Her clothing was never heavy or homespun but was of loosely fitting silky type cloth that adorned her. Her blouses and dresses of thin chemise and cheerful colors seemed to enhance her coolness. She never perspired even on the hottest and most humid days. She seemed self-contained and above anything external. She always seemed at ease, comfortable with her body, and with other people. She found reason to smile and laugh often. I wondered if she had once been a princess in a foreign land before coming to the mountains. I was enthralled with this woman.

By all outward and physical appearances, she always seemed out of place here. Her posture was too aristocratic; her movement was too graceful. She seemed a reminder of some lost, forgotten lineage of nobility. Her body was full, lithe, and athletic. Her fingers moved gracefully and gently over the dulcimer strings. Her eyes were closed. Her body swayed gently to the time and beat of her dulcimer music. She was somewhere else. The smell of honeysuckle seemed fog like; its fragrance deepened and grew stronger as I neared her.

I knew where she was in the moment. This was her time. For soon, she'll have to start supper for her family as they come in from the hillside fields. But for her, for now, this peaceful and serene mountain aura enveloped her, her music, a balm for her soul. She could feel it. She could breathe it in. It even transcended prayer. It was peace, contentment, serenity. Nothing had ever matched this daily renewal of her spirit, her quiet place. *It* could only be found here in this place and in this time.

"Ms. Delilah, I brought your groceries. I hope you're getting along OK."

Still nodding in time with the strains, "How're your mother and grandmother?"

"Everybody's gettin along just fine. New baby in the family, Uncle Homer's new daughter, and the business at the store has really picked up," I said.

I always wanted to see her, to visit with her, but I couldn't think of anything else to say, for some reason. Sometimes, I wondered if I hurried over to play with Caleb or to visit her.

"I always wonder how you are doing. Every time I think of Caleb, I think about you. I always hope you're OK. Where is Caleb?"

"He's helping his dad in the tobacco up on the hill. You boys going fishing tomorrow I understand?"

"Yes ma'am and I can't wait. Trout season has been a long time comin'. Well, tell Caleb we need to leave from the store porch before dawn, about five, I guess. Dad is gonna drive us up to Little River and come back and get us about dusk."

Summers ♦ Farm Life ♦ Zip-A-Dee-Doo-Dah

"I'll tell him and, honey, you boys be careful up climbing those river rocks. The copperheads will be coming down to the water's cool places in the rocks for sure, even if it is just late May. It's a hot May already. You all watch where you put your hands and your feet."

"We will Ms. Delilah. Don't worry. Remember, we're in the eighth grade, so we are pretty well grown. We're pretty much men now, I guess. I mean don't you think so?"

She smiled and nodded. The dulcimer sounds that followed me to the bridge seemed to grow more mournful, more melancholy. I cussed myself for letting my imagination take over once again. Still, I couldn't help wondering if she was as sorry to see me leave as I was to go.

I never understood why I was so drawn to Ms. Delilah more than other older women. There was a mystique about her that escaped me. Years later, in a high school English class our topic of study was the mythical female character Aphrodite. Ms. Shultz used a phrase that, at first, felt like electric shock then turned into a light bulb then became an "aha" for me. The descriptive word phrase was "...her innate beauty..." That was it. That was why I was so drawn to Caleb's mother. The longer she described Aphrodite's appearance and attractive qualities, the more the image of Ms. Delilah began to take shape.

No wonder I so wanted to be around her, to visit, to find excuses to be near her, yet because it was her, my words would never come out easily if at all. As I struggled for conversation with her, my sentences were awkward and filled with word stammers and stumbles only to finally tumble out almost as babble. That was it, I was smitten by her innate beauty, a trait I had never experienced in any other older woman, certainly not to that degree.

As my life episodes grew more exciting, so did those characters that surrounded me. I was living in an ongoing movie filled with highlighted, real, Technicolor adventures that filled my days. I still enjoy the recall of many episodes with their racing excitement. Many remain alive in the hallways of my mind.

Uncle Harry enjoys the days end and a cigarette.

Uncle Harry plowing while his dad observes.

Farm Fun in the 1940s

Ogle Farm

Ogle Homeplace

Cousins and friends enjoy birthday with Ogle children. Circa 1950
L-R: Third Row: Joan Ogle, Charlotte Ann Seaton, Ronny Rader, Howard Davenport, unk, Teddy Campbell
Second Row: Charlotte Ruth Travena, unk, unk.
First Row: Wanda Trevena, Jerry Ogle, Ricky Rader, Joe Ogle, James Delozier, C.L. Sutton
(Harry Ogle family collection)

Ronny, Joan, Jerry—a bath at days end. Circa 1942

(Pictures courtesy of Harry Ogle family collection)

The Harry Ogle family at Mill Creek farm. Circa 1952
Row 1: Jerry, Joe Row 2: Estalee, Joan, Harry
(Harry Ogle Family collection)

My Knoxville Summers of the 1950s

A highlight for me each summer began around 1944. I was six and I was allowed to go alone— only big boys did that. The two week visits with relatives in Knoxville continued until my early teen years.

Culturally, Knoxville and Sevierville were light years apart. US Highway 441, locally known as Chapman Highway, was two lanes and the only major link between the two cities. The ultimate destination for most visitors lay another thirteen miles south— the Great Smoky Mountains and Gatlinburg. The asphalt ribbon wound through forty plus miles of sprawling countryside broken only by open untilled farmland, occasional buildings, and fenced pastures. The highway linked two polar extremes. Sevierville, Sevier County's seat, was rural and had a couple of thousand residents; Knoxville, Knox County's seat, was urban with a total population that probably exceeded Sevierville's numbers times twelve to fifteen. In short, they were city folks with all the glitter and bright lights.

My aunt Josie Adcock lived in North Knoxville with her daughter Ruth and son-in-law, Bill Stone. Josie was a sister to my grandfather, Dr. John of Five Oaks farm in Sevierville. Josie lost her husband early in life but not before she bore a son, Stuart "Dick" Adcock. The entire side of her family remained close to my folks, and we exchanged visits often. Ruth and Bill were childless and were especially fond of me. They always invited me to spend a couple of weeks with them at their Knoxville home each summer, and from the age of six until I became a teen-ager, I jumped at the chance. They always made it an exciting adventure. In addition, the bustling energy and glitter of Knoxville surpassed anything New York could possibly offer, at least in the imagination conjured up by a rural preteen boy. The city never failed me; it came through in high style every summer.

The Stone's home was at 1638 North Hills Boulevard. I remember the address to this day. It was part of the only commandment ever handed down to me by Aunt Josie and the Stones. It and their telephone number were insurance in case I got lost. They went to great lengths to make sure I was entertained each hour I was there. They doted on me profusely, and I loved every minute of the special attention. Summer days there were almost magical. I was accustomed to the average comfort of our rural "horn of plenty" middle class life, and I knew little of life that was ostentatious and ornately luxurious. In Pigeon Forge our nearest neighbors were half mile away and lived in farmhouses. North Hills

105

had large, roomy two story homes of varied and interesting architecture with large yards that linked the homes. Most of these homes had acreage, were neatly and tastefully landscaped, and were surrounded by large hardwood trees. The Stone's home had an in-ground pool, a three-car garage, and a circular driveway firmly compacted with crushed oyster shells.

A once-a-week black gardener maintained the grounds and the flowerbeds that interlaced the acreage. He had been with them for a number of years, until he discovered a black snake in the armload of weeds and branches he held tightly to his chest. I watched as he threw everything in the air and ran screaming down the boulevard.

Aunt Josie, Pop's sister. Sister to Anah Seaton of Pigeon Forge. Circa 1940
(Ron Rader family collection)

Ruth eagerly watched for his return for several days. He never ever returned to get his pay. The next summer a new face was there weeding away. He was grey at the temples, muscular, laughed all the time, and answered to Clypeus. His female counterpart was Serena, the maid and housekeeper. Serena had been with Ruth and Bill for several years. Riding the bus to the last North Hill's stop, she walked the last few blocks to show up promptly dressed in her neat grey and white uniform. She came three or four days each week to clean and to do various chores. Always upbeat, smiling, and her interest focused on me, she surreptitiously made me feel important. I grew to adore her as another favorite "aunt."

Bill owned Stone Produce on Market Square in the city. His chicken farms at Concord generated eggs, which he sold, but his core business was poultry sales—freshly killed chickens, plucked, dressed, and sold across the counter. He later added the slaughter of swine for pork sales. An industrious and successful business owner, Bill was short in stature, muscular, congenial, and well liked. His thinning brown hair was medium length and, after a touch of Wildroot Crème oil, combed straight back Valentino style. Usually dressed in a short sleeved, crinkled-crepe, baby blue nylon shirt, and khakis, he moved effortlessly back and forth from the front office dealing with the customer to helping process the live chickens back in the slaughter plant.

I am sure a great deal of his business success was due to his ability to play several roles really well. Customers and business colleagues enjoyed his congenial rapport and integrity; his employees revered him due to his willingness to work alongside them as a peer and "one of the boys." Based on his always consistent and casual demeanor, I could never detect when he was the owner and when he was the employee. A cigarette usually dangled from his lips. He smoked two packs of Lucky Strikes each day and reserved his pipe smoking for evenings at home when we listened to Kaltenborn's evening news and Bob Hope, Kate Smith, Fibber Magee, and Jack Benny.

These things framed my summer visits. Aunt Josie, then in her seventies, volunteered to host me during the day, and she carried out her mission masterfully and with flair. Aunt Josie was a lot like my grandmother, Blanche, her sister-in-law. She laughed, chuckled, and found humor in everything. Unlike my grandmother, she was mischievous, whimsical, and adventurous. She managed to create situations during my visit that would capture the heart and imagination of any youngster. Ruth was a gourmet cook, knew what I liked, and made certain my every meal was splendid. On the days when Aunt Josie and I weren't on an adventure in downtown Knoxville or swimming at Whittle Spring's pool, Ruth made certain my lunch was my favorite. I considered it gourmet: Whole wheat bread, spicy mustard, mayonnaise, lettuce, tomato, purple onion slice, a slice of bone-in, baked picnic ham, all layered into a sandwich. Her special sides were whole sweet pickles, potato chips, ice-cold applesauce, kidney beans, and a large glass of ice-cold whole milk. Dessert, cooked that morning, was vanilla custard.

Aunt Josie, leader of our joint escapades, made certain we visited downtown Knoxville several times during my visits. On rainy days, her agenda planning for me turned mischievous. On one such day, in my eighth summer, Ruth was out for her bridge day, and we were alone and plotting. Aunt Josie suggested that since Ruth loved to cook, we should secretly punch holes into one of her saucepans, preferably one she used most often. We would convert the pan into a surprise colander of sorts. Since Ruth used it each morning to soft boil eggs for breakfast, her attempt to fill it with water the next would be a shocker. I really liked the way Aunt Josie thought. She quickly found a hammer and a large nail and soon the pan bottom looked more like a cheese grater. I could hardly go to sleep that night as I tried to picture Ruth's morning surprise; however, overnight, I completely forgot our trap.

It wasn't until lunch and my second bite into my ham sandwich that Ruth exclaimed loudly, "How in the world did holes get in my favorite pan? Who in the world sneaked in here and did this? Why I tried to fix breakfast eggs this morning, my pan refused to fill up! Instead, water poured through a dozen tiny holes! What in the world is going on?" A seventy-year-old matron and the seven-year- old boy sniggered, exchanged knowing glances, their pursed lips framed "Who? Me? "expressions.

June sunshine and low humidity were sure signals that we'd probably go into downtown Knoxville. A few blocks from the end of North Hills Boulevard, Ruth dropped us at the North Knoxville's last bus stop. A city bus took us to the nearest streetcar stop, and we rode the rest of the way into the heart of the city. We'd exit the streetcar on Gay Street at Miller's Department store near the Riviera Theater and the S&W Cafeteria.

If there had been a dog-named Toto at my side, here is where I would have reminded us both that we were not in Pigeon Forge anymore. The street excitement was frantic filled with hurrying people and kaleidoscopic storefronts. It overwhelmed the senses. Like the three rings of the circus, it was hard to take it all in or even to focus on any one thing. Gay Street storefronts offered almost every retail choice imaginable and most had three or four levels. I was in a canyon of color and motion.

We entered Millers, went straight to the elevator, and waited to enter the latticed, metal door. The black man dressed in a grey uniform bordered with a burgundy stripe nodded to Aunt Josie, closed the grating like door, slid the lever, and began reciting upcoming floor levels and floor contents as we rose skyward. His ho-hum, emotionless drone of floor numbers and descriptions reminded me of a Trailways bus driver once on our way to Virginia. The bus driver wearily shouted the names of cities we could expect to pass through "Hiiiiickiiiry, Charrrrrlotte, Weeeeenstn Salum, Outuh Bannnnks, Cheeessssapeeek, Suuufffaaawfuk, Naaaaahhhhfuk, and Riiiiiiichmaawn". Back to reality in Millers and right after women's' lingerie, we stopped on the third floor—boys clothes and bicycles.

Our next stop was the S&W cafeteria across the street. A Knoxville dining icon since the 1920s, the cafeteria offered several dozen entrees, farm fresh vegetables, and succulent "homemade" desserts by southern pastry chefs. A uniformed waiter, usually an elderly black man, in white jacket, black trousers, and shiny patent leather shoes, would graciously greet us, carry our trays, and seat us. Often, he and Aunt Josie would acknowledge each other by name.

After lunch, we'd go to a movie at either the Riviera or the Tennessee Theatre. The Tennessee was my favorite. The moment you entered, you felt like you had entered a coliseum like structure. The lobby was marble throughout, its floor sloped and divided with brass rails. Ornate decorative carvings were everywhere and were silhouetted and highlighted with indirect lighting. Thick Persian appearing carpeting began at the end of the lobby and continued throughout. The restrooms on the basement level had elegant sitting rooms with eighteenth century style formal couches and chairs with heavy lamps atop end tables. Surrounded by granite stone, Italian marble and deep carpet, it appeared as if you were entering a private gentleman's club in England. A black, shoeshine valet was available and inside the restroom, another uniformed valet offered you a linen hand towel. The theater auditorium was equally magnificent, and I always wondered if New York and Broadway could really be any better than this.

After the movie, we'd always visit Woolworth's Five and Ten. I usually came away with comic books, a game, and a plastic gun.

Some days our visit down town was more educational and social—my education and her social. Fronting Gay Street was radio station WROL. Aunt Josie's son, Stuart Adcock or "Dick," was the owner of WROL. We'd go by his office where I learned to joke with the employees and Dick and learn radio. One particular executive was Alan Stout. I remembered him as very personable, well liked, and a friend of the family who remained close to all of us through the years. I did not realize until many years later that Stuart Adcock was a 1927 pioneer in radio. At sixteen years of age, he went on the air and launched what was probably the first Knoxville radio station. He later bought, developed, and later sold two stations, one of which belonged to the Baptist Church of Knoxville. He changed the call letters of the last station toward the end of the thirties to WROL. Many radio historians say he started the Grand Ole Opry. Many of those same musicians of 1930s and 1940s later became stars. They moved back and forth between radio stations, and Stuart's station sponsored many of them at one time or another. It was the era of Lowell Blanchard and the Midday Merry Go Round and the Farm and Home Hour. With the eventual birth and growth of WNOX, it was not long before WROL had a strong competitor and soon both were battling head to head.

Leaving Stuart's office, we'd walk a couple blocks to Market Square. "We better see Billy while we're here," Aunt Josie would always say.

Stone Produce was next door to the Market House. The long rectangular stone building with skylights nearly filled the entire block. It was open, airy, and open stalls on each side were filled with dozens of vehicles loaded with fresh produce. Farmers sold from the back and side of their trucks

Stuart "Dick" Adcock founded and owned WROL radio station in Knoxville. Aunt Josie, his mother, was Dr. John W. Ogle's sister and my great aunt.
(Ron Rader Family collection)

THE BLUE MOUNTAINS SING
of rivers, old men, trails and trout

Mother's Day at Five Oaks, 1937 The Stones and Adcocks attended. *See names in Appendix 1*
(Ron Rader Family collection)

with barely enough room for a chair and front counter. Inside, the ceiling appeared to reach sixty feet and gave it the appearance of an old European train station. Counters, end to end, reached the length of the building with a wide walkway through the center. Displayed on the counters were fresh meats of every variety, cheeses from only God knew where, fresh farm produce, dressed fowl, beef, lamb, and pork either hung from wire over the counter or were in cooled display cases. Each counter belonged to a particular vendor who was often surrounded by the entire family. The noise and chatter of vendors bargaining with customers was deafening. Honey, fresh fruit, shelled and unshelled nuts, and flowers added to the produce mix. The smells of freshly slaughtered meat mixed with the entire aliveness and ambience of the marketplace was unique. Cigar, pipe, and cigarette smoke hung heavy and fog like as it rose and fell at the mercy of the humidity. This was not Pigeon Forge.

Stone Produce was next door and pretty much ran the length of the block. Compared to the Market House it was a long, narrow, white building, probably eighty feet wide, with a small front office at street side and the rest of the block long space devoted to chicken and pig slather and processing.

Bill was in the front office, and I could always tell he was glad we came by. "Ronny, come on back, and I'll show you where your fried chicken and your bacon and sausage comes from."

We went through the front and entered the slaughterhouse. Now I'd been raised on and around farms all my life. I'd seen women wring and chop live chickens' necks. I knew the drill that led to the Sunday's fried chicken I ate. My mother and grandmother had rung live chickens' necks as far back as I could remember. I learned to rationalize the sudden death of a chicken. From a chicken's viewpoint, I figured a quick end was far better than that of the chicken unlucky enough to wander too close to the hog lot where I'd seen them snatched through the fence and eaten alive, on the spot, by a large sow or boar hog. Yet I had never seen animals slaughtered production line style. I suppose I thought each animal was killed and prepared one at a time by somebody's grandma.

It was June, already hot at midday, and the humidity was unseasonably high for early summer. Dressed in white shorts, white summer shirt, and white tennis shoes, I was dressed just right for any youngster of the day going to the Tennessee Theatre. As I stepped through the door, the steamy stench of scalded chicken feathers and the odor of blood and feces of slaughtered chickens and hogs met me. A metal rail pen enclosure, four rails high, ran the length of the building. It was equally divided inside by two narrow open rail chutes. They ended directly in front of me. I climbed to the second rail of the outer enclosure and rested my chin on the third rail. A large black man straddled the smaller chute to my left. He was shirtless, sweaty, and muscular. He wore a large worn leather apron that hid his pants and shoes. He looked naked except for the apron that dangled from his neck.

He grinned at me, winked, and with a kind smile full of pearly white teeth said, "I'm Amos. You Mr. Stone's kin ain't ye?"

I nodded, "Yes."

"Glad to have you visit us," he said warmly as if he truly wanted me to feel welcome.

Before I could say thanks, emptying from a large truck at the side door, a flock of white fully-grown chickens started running down the runway that Amos straddled. Amos snatched the first one then another. The first flopping, flailing chicken squawked only once. Amos clasped the chicken body between his thighs, stretched its head with his left hand, and with the sharp curved knife in his right hand, he severed the chickens head, and tossed it in a fifty-five gallon drum at his side. He hung the still flailing chicken neck down on a hook attached to a moving cable just above his head. Almost before I could blink, he had slaughtered six chickens and sent them on their way to the scalding room where they would be plucked, disemboweled, and readied for market. Chicken after chicken flopped from their hook on the conveyer spraying blood in an ever-widening circle. A mosaic pattern of dried spray that somehow was missed at the end of each day clean up chronicled the history of the building and gave testament to the nature of the business.

Somebody yelled and gave some kind of order or signal and another black man climbed astride the chute to my right. He looked like a bookend to Amos. Were they brothers? He nodded at me and then focused as the squealing, pushing, excited pigs trotted down the larger chute toward us. The aproned black man gripped the wooden handle of a sledgehammer and waited. The hogs were of medium size, maybe one hundred to one hundred fifty pounds, and as they neared from behind the black man, the chute narrowed. It forced them single file into a tight neat orderly line. The man struck the first pig between the eyes. Almost as soon as the hog dropped, two men snatched the hog from under the rail, hung it on the moving metal hooks overhead, and slit its throat. The hooks were expertly placed through the hind leg tendons at the ankle. Its blood drained quickly and ran off into the concrete gutter. The next stop was the scalding room where swine were scalded, scraped, disemboweled, butchered, and readied for market.

Much earlier, farm life had desensitized me to the necessity of the life and death of animals. I understood the life cycle and the importance of preparing farm animals and wild game for food. However, I'd never seen production line slaughter where people waded ankle deep in blood and killed animal after animal in just a few minutes. I was accustomed to one large hog, usually walking around like king of the hog lot for a year or two, being killed, scalded, scraped, and followed by the daylong process to convert it into sausage, pork chops, and ham.

How could several black men do this day in and day out? The smell, the fight, the death, the gore, the routine—how did they face this each day? My ten-year-old mind could not wrap around this. I knew it was necessary; I understood. Still, how could they do it? Did they have to do it to live? Did they hate it? Why did they stay? I wanted to ask someone, but I was afraid to ask Bill. It was his business. He was a good and responsible person. He was proud of his people and his successful business. I thought to myself that this is something I'll learn the answer to later. I'm just not old enough. I 'm sure there is a good and right reason for this.

I'd had enough. I stepped from the rail and dropped to the concrete. Ten feet away Big Amos held another flopping and bloody hen which only moments before had been a pure white chicken. I entered the small front office. Aunt Josie and Bill were in deep conversation.

Summers ♦ Farm Life ♦ Zip-A-Dee-Doo-Dah

Aunt Josie paused, "Lordy, child, I didn't mean for you to help the boys back there. You've got red bloody specks all over your shirt, pants, and face. Don't think I ever saw anybody with red measles on their shirt and pants too. Let's get a wet rag and try to get' em off so they'll let us in at Woolworths."

What great memories my Knoxville summers hold for me. The contrast of the urban with the rural introduced me to a culture filled with a certain elegance, city urgency, merchandise galore, and the rich and varied life styles of a people born to second and third generation Knoxville families and who were a quite wealthy class of individuals.

CHAPTER THREE

*In God's wildness lies the hope of the world–the great, fresh, unblighted, unredeemed wilderness...There is a love of wild nature in everybody, an ancient mother-love showing itself whether recognized or not, and however covered by cares and duties—*John Muir

The Park

My Memories of The Park and of its Rivers

My first and earliest memory of the national park has remained the same, a single impression unchanged, repeated countless times, and still an exciting experience. My first visit touched every sense at once. That memory has remained consistent. A mountain visit can only be anticipated, savored, and revisited. Its recall is sweet. There is a sameness about the mountains. A constant that defies the change all around it. There is little in life that remains constant, unchanging. I guess that's what I value most about this wilderness.

I always looked forward to the sameness. It excited me. As we'd drove through the entrance at Gatlinburg's south end, I knew we'd just traded civilization for wildness. The first twenty yards were magical. June's midday heat, the concrete, visitors on foot, retail, and traffic noise evaporated. Instead, a blast of cool, fresh, almost biting, pure, moist air, a river laden mist enveloped us in greetings. The fragrance was a unique blend of a century old forest floor and pure mountain breath. Within the first hundred yards, all vestiges of the modern world had disappeared. Up ahead, only the faint outline of the park headquarters roof glimmered through the heavy leaf canopy gave away the myth. One thing I always knew for certain, a mystical journey was about to begin, for here, I could smell the sunshine. I knew the journey's milestones would be filled with excitement.

My dad's office was in there. It was an island surrounded by rangers, biologists, stuffed animals, naturalists, biological specimens, maps, two way radio chatter, drama, and conversations centered on managing visitors, bears, and the park.

Once our car left headquarters behind, we were thrust in a world of green foliage, generations old trees, dozens of shrub species, flocks of birds enjoying this wildness and their freedom. They displayed their joy by their incessant patterns of flight, all the while calling, diving, chasing, perching.

Granite slopes to either side, were moist and moss covered. Occasionally, a hillside brook slid down the slope and splashed onto the road's edge. If you stopped and moved a few yards off the road, the sameness returned in a rush of remembrance. The silence was deafening, save for the rushing and gurgle and occasional roar of the river. The woods were silent, almost deathly still. Although unseen, they busily went about their life giving exchange. The dynamics hidden in their aliveness. A few yards at the foot of the slope below, the grey boulders at midstream split the continuous rush of icy water. Their skin worn smooth first by glaciers and then by generations of this water's rush. The rocks and the waters sung endlessly of solidarity, dependability, and everlasting hope.

In my Smokies boyhood, rivers and water in general played quite a major role for all of us whether trout fishing, swimming, or family weekends as we picnicked alongside and swam in it. Wild waters were important to the entire county. The various swimming holes served as weekend social gathering spots for folks throughout our three villages, if not the county. Our then small populations contributed to leisurely, uncrowded swim fun. The warm darkness of summer nights redressed the swimming holes with a different aura and an age-old ritual. Watery nights were soon filled with drama, laughter, and were cloaked in a hidden veil of mystique that only stars, the moon, and heat of summer nights can meld. River nights seemed special, cloaked in mystery, reserved for youth.

The sweltering heat and humidity of summer days in the mountains is not a new phenomenon, but In the early post-war days, your choices for cooling off were limited and very different. Those pre-air conditioning times offered two escapes—sit on the porch around sundown, or head to your favorite swimming hole. A few motels had postage stamp sized swimming pools but were off limits to non-guests. Unless you knew the family owner, you had to splash with those pretty local and tourist girls in the local swimming holes, if they dared, you know, with all the imaginary snakes, bears, alligators, and sharks that inhabited the Little Pigeon River.

The Park

In those surrounding lands that make up the greater national park area, its neighboring streams were a vital part of its watershed system of rivers and recreation.

The Little Pigeon River's three prongs, East, West, and Middle, and most creeks sported several deep sandy pools that became local favorites and were named. The Little Pigeon of the 1940s and 1950s was refreshingly clear, relatively cold, and relatively clean. They at least had a much lower level of today's e-coli.

The Park made Gatlinburg's swimming holes unique. Two rather long pools in the riverbed were just inside the park boundary as you head south and leave Gatlinburg. Located behind the old Burning Bush Restaurant about one hundred yards upstream, the Abernocker Hole was first, and fifty yards further up was the Brownlee Hole. Clones of each other, they offered icy water and fun-filled days of summer splash fun in our era and only a hundred yards from civilization. Later, the Park's liability was reported to be the reason the pools were filled, shallowed, and swimming discouraged.

If you were a Forge boy during the Truman and Eisenhower times, the two Pigeon Forge local favorites were Broady's Hole, replete with the roped one hundred foot Sycamore tree bankside across the river and behind Joe Carr's motel. Complete with a sixty-foot rope, you could leave the bank just above Broady's Dairy farm bridge and swing skyward toward today's Dixie Stampede. Your landing was in a deep pool with a sandy bottom.

The second favorite was the Old Mill dam. It was not for the faint of heart. You proved your alpha male or tush-hog level by racing through the swift current across the dam ledge or jumping from the bridge or the dam. The pool below the dam had rock ledges extending from the bank and required unshaken aim. Earlier roaring flash floods always left some jolting surprises for jumpers and divers. They ranged from entire trees to old refrigerators, from drowned cattle or other livestock, to the farm wagon full of harvested corn deposited from last Halloween's prank gone awry.

Located just below the Old Mill bridge about a hundred yards downstream was a long, quiet secluded pool with a jutting, flat rock at its edge. Hidden by trees, vines, and weeds, it became a secret hidden spot set apart from the others. It evolved into a boy's only retreat and appropriately became known as the Jaybird Hole. If you didn't have your swim trunks handy, that was the place to go. The French Riviera had nothing that could top this place. Often peeking from the thick brush lined riverbank, giggling girls thought it was hilarious and never once filed suit for discrimination.

Further downstream toward Sevierville, was the river bottom farm of the Hatcher family. Pine Grove swimming hole seemed to be the largest, most enjoyable, and most popular. Two hundred yards upriver from the mouth of Walden's Creek the river pool was wide, sandy, and deep. At river's edge, two utility poles formed an inverted V with an eighty-foot steel cable and knotted rope at the end. Further up the bank, a square wooden platform with several steps led up from the concreted base. Not unlike the circus trapeze artists, the swinger climbed up the steps and eventually climbed onto the platform as the distance from the river greatly increased. At the end of the swing's arc, the force could hurl the swimmer kamikaze style thirty to forty feet airborne.

Sevierville's swim holes usually seemed to be near a swinging bridge. The Middle prong, about a mile from its junction with its sister, formed the Reno Hole. It was about a half mile as the crow flies upriver from Postmaster Murphy's home and farm. Red Bank road sported two swimming holes. From Pitman Center Road turn left onto Redbank Road. The Shinbone swimming hole was in the first river bend to the right. It offered a rocky cliff for jumping, a tree rope, and a large sandy bottomed pool for swimming. Due to development, silt, and nature, many river pool favorites have disappeared, yet young teens still jump from Shin Bone's rocky face on Sunday afternoons, only the faces are different.

Upriver, above Mitchell Bottoms at the end of Red Bank Road, the Long Ford pool offered a quiet, long, and tranquil swim. Nearer the mountains the water was colder, clearer and offered the same features. There as was Long Ford's sister pool the Richardson's Cove swimming hole near the bridge.

Emert's Cove's "Non Monotonous" cabin was the landmark for a fine swimming hole approximately one quarter mile downstream from Flintrock. It was a deep pool in the river bend replete with banks of sloping, granite stone, icy mountain water, and located about a mile from the Park. It fronted the Wade cabin. This favorite is one that conjures up many memories even winter ones for those who fondly remember. Further upstream, Flintrock's summer delicious waters and large pool still attract river lovers and campers. It is nearest the Park boundary and probably has the coldest water.

My favorite was the lake at Elkmont. Directly across from the Wonderland hotel, the river had been partially diverted to form a lake. The body of icy water was approximately one hundred yards long and about seventy five yards across. Its small dam was coupled with an electricity generator plant that provided electricity to a small group of users including the Wonderland hotel, the Appalachian club with its cluster of cabins and houses, and the Camp LeConte for Boys.

The lake had a ten man WWII rubber raft bottom-side up anchored at midlake. It served as a lounging, sunning platform, and diving or jumping spot. Also the camp had constructed a multi-level wooden diving platform and a board walk at the lower end near the generation plant at the lake's deepest point. On a one to ten scale, with ten rated the coldest, I would rate its icy waters at a twelve no matter the time of day or degree of sun.

In later years, the mid-fifties, Gatlinburg's developers, the Maples twins Ralph and Roy, built their Maples pool, which served as a municipal swimming pool at the upper end of Airport Road.

Convenience, nature, development, and other changes caused swimming hole interest to fade and folks to drift to other venues. Time left only nostalgic memories of swim filled summer days in our favorite river spots.

Those better days of summer are still treasured by most who remember. Those were growing up days that created a sense of time and place in all of us. Times that instilled an unfading appreciation in each of us. Everything about that era reminded us of whom we were and to whom we belonged. The waters and woods offered us a unique quality of life, they allowed us to become a part of their wildness and to romp in their untamed freedom. The mountain shared their gifts with us; gifts possessed only by them. Little did we realize that their gift would be a onetime offering, one that would never be continued, replaced, or recaptured, only remembered.

A Band of Brothers

Our Appalachian mountains, now the Great Smoky Mountains National Park (the Park), in their once natural, unbridled sweep were slowly being corralled in the mid-1940s and early to mid-1950s. Visitor growth called for more regulation and administration more than ever before . It was 1950. My Dad was a career Park employee, and I was a twelve year old Pigeon Forge native. As a result of his job and his other outdoor interests, I was allowed to hike with him and many other park employees. It was pretty close to heaven for any outdoor loving teen. In those early years of the park's life, that group of its employees shared a special bond.

In fact, that special bond occurred to me recently as I watched an episode of a current WWII television series. Steven Spielberg may not have been the first to coin the phrase—"Band of Brothers." I believe one special band of brothers was born in those early days of the Park's infancy, the 1936 – 1955 era here in the Smokies.

I often had the good fortune to be in the company of park service rangers, resource specialists, staffers, engineering staff and trail, vehicle, and maintenance folks. As a group, they shared a special spirit and were bonded by a traditional set of strong core beliefs. These were the same beliefs that you'd welcome today into your grandchildren's world as the "right stuff." Though their grousing and macho dialogue was often pretty salty and expletive laden, they none the less, spoke the well intentioned truth with each other and others. You could quickly discern the true character of each man fairly soon when you sifted through the dialogue of their public persona.

Most of this brotherly band had come over from the Civilian Conservation Corp camps. Most were grateful for a CCC job opportunity in one of Roosevelt's depression busting work programs, most served in World War II, and few had more than a high school diploma. The most important trait they possessed—each shared a strong passion and love for the mountains and their outdoors.

So it was a natural move and a windfall for them to move from the CCC over to this new park. For most, it was a labor of love. As CCC crews, they had already spent two or three years devoted to bridge, trail, shelter, and park facility construction. To a man, they were determined to continue to manage, protect, and nurture the park and its outreaches.

If there was any discontent, the park's growing pains probably did create some floating anger, resentment, and frustration. This original band chafed under the cascading new government policies. True to form, as bureaucracies often do, they issued policy directives continually from Washington on how best to manage their Smokies—*their own personal mountains!*

Socially, they were close friends, who often visited, fished, hunted, hiked, and camped together. Their wives and families were close and picnicked and visited just as often. The Wonderland Hotel with its southern meals and its evening socials—bridge and dances—was one of their very popular gathering spots. A short walk from the Wonderland's porch were the icy waters of Elkmont's small lake. It provided a unique swimming and sunning pool and fed a small spillway and power generating dam. Several natural river swimming holes, near deserted CCC camps, were very popular for many park families and locals.

Ten or twelve of those interesting and colorful park service characters I grew to know very well. Each in their own way unknowingly "role-modeled" and sort of raised me. Their ranger green-grey uniform with sidearm loomed larger than life to a teenager.

Fifty years later, a few men that come quickly to mind were rangers Mel Price at the Sugarlands and Elkmont, Audley Whaley at Cosby and Deep Creek, Mark Hannah at Cataloochee, Frank Oliver at Hazel Creek, "Swede"

The Park

Hunting buddies; Mel Price, leaning against tree, unknown, Audley Whaley, Homer Smith, unknown, and Al Rader.

Ownby, the first ranger at Elkmont, Tom Edwards , and of course, John Morrell (who wore most every Park title during his career), Moody Fox, Bill Cron, and several others escape my fifty year recall.

While in the midst of the band, you'd sometimes get glimpses of cowboy actors, their look-a-likes. They shared traits that were remindful of their western movie counterparts with names like Joel McCrea, Glenn Ford, Jimmy Stewart, Randolph Scott, Ben Johnson, John Wayne, Clark Gable , Roy Rogers, Alan Ladd, William Elliott, and later on James Arness, Robert Duvall, and Sam Elliott. I could often match each with his " look- a-like" or "act- a-like" western counterpart.

John Morrell, park attorney, ranger, early property acquisition officer, and surveyor, was one of my father's closest friends. They hiked and camped often, and together our two families spent many fine days in the mountains, hiking, swimming, and camping. His wife, Grace, and their two daughters, Mary and Ann, loved the mountains as much as he did. When

An afternoon camp at the river's edge. Ruth Ferguson (Doug), Ruth Galbraith(Dave), Louise and Al Rader.

THE BLUE MOUNTAINS SING
of rivers, old men, trails and trout

Dear Ronnie
and
Rickey:-

In World War II your Father served with Valor and distinction in some very bitter fighting.

He brought home some very valuable and interesting souvenirs of his Campaigns, which, through no fault of his own, were lost.

I want you boys to remember the Service which your Father rendered his Country; and to that end, I am sending you with this letter some mementos of World War II which were given to me by your Father, Sergeant Roden, and by T/s Earl Franklin, who is also a Combat Veteran.

These trophies are very valuable to me; but as the years go by, they will be more and more precious to you boys.

John O. Morrell.
Christmas 1950.

our Pigeon Forge home burned in 1947, John returned many World War II German mementoes, Nazi spoils of war, that Dad had given him. He gifted them to me. I always thought of him as a walking Boy Scout creed, and I mean that in the very best sense of his image. He was the walking model for integrity, and everything true, honest, authentic.

The other brothers were every bit as colorful and varied. They were the Park staff individuals cast from one time only molds. Homer Smith was the dispatcher and operator of Elkmont dam's power generator that provided Elkmont's electricity. Art Stupka was a world renowned naturalist who fueled my interest in everything biological and wild. Thanks to his guidance, I had planned early on to become a naturalist. John Morrell served as surveyor, attorney, park ranger, hiking mentor , surrogate uncle, and family friend. He, along with my Dad, taught me the world of guns—rifle, pistol, marksmanship, ballistics, and the art of loading your own brass. John constructed his own shooting range near his home on Gnatty Branch.

Moody Fox and "Nub" Vance helped fill the annual deer hunting slots and kept everyone laughing. Ted Davenport was known as a civic enthusiast, sports lover, and was the father of a lifelong friend of mine, Howard. There were many more. Their inclusion is limited only by lack of space, but their families will know who they are. A few of the "sisters" in this early family were Ruby Webb, Mary Ruth Chiles, and Wilma Miller Maples (Mrs. Rel Maples),and later, Mary Ruth Cate Cutshaw.

Glimpses of their wartime experiences surfaced if you spent any time among this group. Words of war bubbled to the surface in their conversations. Names like the Battle of the Bulge, Normandy, Belgium, Swiss Alps, Argonne Forest, Berchtesgaden, Eagle's Nest, Luxemburg, Wolf's Lair, Berlin, Holland, Rheine River, France, and the English Channel were common.

The Park

Moody Fox and Homer Smith in rear; Al Rader and Audley Whaley kneeling in front. Circa 1949
(Ron Rader family collection)

More hiking in 1930s. Circa 1938 Park employees and wives.
(Howard Davenport family collection)

Ted Davenport, Swede Ownby, Al Rader and Mel Price. Note the CCC truck tag.
(Howard Davenport family collection)

THE BLUE MOUNTAINS SING
of rivers, old men, trails and trout

Sugarlands CCC swimming hole.
(Smoky Mountain Historical Society Journal)

Their gaze often turned distant as they unfolded their personal memory slices of the major battles linked to each name.

In those days, few of the Park service rangers ever moved .They spent their entire career in the Great Smokies. The world was a simpler place. Visitors were much fewer. Each ranger and many staff were intimately knowledgeable of the entire park. Where to enter any stream for best trout, the shortest and best route on any hiking trail, which flowers were blooming where, each "band brother" could answer most queries with ease and depth.

Their law enforcement was very just. Justice for poachers and other offenses was dispensed fairly, even handedly, tempered, and balanced. They knew the families that bordered the park, the individuals most likely to poach and could seemingly anticipate trouble. They were stealthy, spent many hours in the woods undercover patrolling and frequently checking the status and condition of *their* mountains. At times, enforcement was probably akin to Mayberry justice with a moral lesson.

The ranger world of the 1940s and 1950s was pretty much black and white, but they were book ends to a wide range of shades of gray. As visitors and traffic quadrupled in their mountains, the ranger focus and daily demands were changing. Most complained in later years that they were becoming the Tennessee Highway Patrol for the Park, work they felt they never signed up for.

Today's ranger must be Mr. or Ms. 911. Now, nearly ten million year round visitors have raised the demands on a ranger's time and effectiveness. The early ranger only wanted to be in the woods protecting and nurturing. Contrast that with the demands the ranger of today faces. They must be prepared to respond to any emergency a visitor faces. They must also serve as and perform highway patrolman duties just like their civilian state trooper counterparts. Their responsibilities have expanded greatly, from river rescue, to lost hikers, from public relations, to high speed pursuit, and from fighting fires as the result of careless campers, to protecting and nurturing wildlife and plants. In addition, they must care for injured wildlife and eradicate exotic plants. Maintaining and nurturing the natural balance of animal, plant, and aquatic life is a daunting responsibility. Their challenges range from trail, road, and campground maintenance to political correctness, from group seminar resource to public relations delivery.

Today's ranger is expected to be more than all things to all people. Dwindling Park funds and salaries have placed them in the ranks occupied by teachers and other underpaid professionals. Most are folks who are working longer hours only to see more job responsibilities continually cascade down. Their only increase seems to be in risk, the danger level, and the demands. They'd have to love it. They must feel called to the job or more attractive pay and pressures would drive them away. Maybe, like teaching, it is a calling, a ministry.

Most of this special group from that era never left for more money. I'm sure the lure of Gatlinburg less than two miles from park headquarters seemed like a siren's call. Motel, restaurant, and craft shop ownership was thriving. Local small business owner life styles seemed grand, and Gatlinburg's hospitality industry seemed prosperous and idyllic by comparison. Gatlinburg's business owners spent seven months of demanding summer work followed by a November through April period of empty streets, empty sheets and closed, almost deserted, businesses. For many an owner, it became a five month season of downtime that many filled by playing bridge and travelling to Florida.

I remember this special brotherly band as one bound together by and living out many of those same virtues we, as Americans, sing about, pledge to our flag, and pray about. I remember them as sharing a part of themselves and stopping to become important in the life of a boy. I, or my peers, could not have asked for better role models.

Despite their crustiness, macho posturing pride, salty talk, "keep a stiff upper lip" attitude, and pride as curmudgeons, most all were little boys with big hearts playing in the mountains at a life they loved and held sacred.

A part of who I am is because of their willingness to pause, to befriend, to coach, and to share themselves and their life experiences with me and many of my teenage friends. Several of the Park staff were very involved with the local Boy Scout Troop 111. Many of them accompanied us on overnight hikes and extended campouts.

I truly enjoyed their company. I feel l was honored to have known them. I respected them and their outlook on life. I cherish the values they taught me and others my age. I'll never forget this very special breed of men.

Looking back, the community probably owes them a debt of gratitude for their contribution to our greater Smoky mountain area. They truly were pioneers in the finest sense of the word. We need to recognize them as such.

Even now I ponder. How can you characterize the Park? What is an all-encompassing word picture you could paint that best depicts our Great Smoky Mountain National Park? This wilderness description seems to defy anything in our language. Maybe its strengths and its uniqueness are best found within questions. Where else can you experience such an offer of unmatched diversity of all things wild ? Where can you match this terrain, woodland, and waters with its solitude, excitement, sanctuary, recreation, economic outreach, and peace? Is there another place that offers inspiration, exercise, rushing streams, entertainment, and mountain views? Does there exist anyplace else that contains the diversity of natural features, flora-fauna species, wildlife, and pristineness? Where else can heritage, uniqueness, renewal, and hints of the eternal be found? Most importantly, where in this entire land can you find such promise of *HOPE?*

The brotherly band, unknowingly, stood in the wings of the nation's delivery waiting room. They eagerly moved to the bedside during the birth of the park. Then, as surrogate fathers and uncles, they took on the critical job of raising and nurturing the park for its first twenty years of life. They and those who followed nurtured it through its recent seventy-fifth birthday.

And what a magnificent, fascinating, unique, many faceted, priceless, middle aged jewel they've reared—our very own hometown wilderness icon and national treasure—the Great Smoky Mountains National Park.

Elkmont

A highlighted memory that will stay with me long after the others may fade came only at Elkmont at dusk. The boy's camp playing field was just below the main buildings and downstream a few hundred yards. It paralleled the highway, a sprawling, and open meadow across the river, and it began at the end of the wooden bridge. The meadow served as a grassy sports' field for most of their outdoor events and recreation activities. The field was flat, level, and covered in lush green grass. It evidently was seeded, fertilized, and nurtured because it always looked like a well-maintained lawn. Usually the thick grass stood at about ankle height. This thick grass along the river's side always seemed more heavily dew soaked. It developed a watery dampness much earlier in the evening. At that same hour of day, you could walk through much of Elkmont that was still sunny, hot, and dry. It was all due to terrain and the sun's path.

The Park

I remember many evenings we hiked the river trail back upriver from either trout fishing or tubing and hoped to make it to Sonny's home before dark. Abruptly, both the dense woods and trail ended, and you walked into this five acre field of lush, wet, green grass—the down river end of the sports' field. By then the setting sun's rays were filtered then blocked by tall mountains on either side. As a result, the field was already dark and damp, the heavy dew felt like a wade rather than a walk. Then it happened. Pinpoints of light literally exploded all over the field. We were totally alone and immersed in silence broken only by the faint rush of the stream. Lightening bugs offered their nightly ritual of light. It always seemed like millions. We felt as if we stood in a misty fog , a fine talcum storm, a tapestry of pinpointed lights. I used to imagine them as miniature merchants blinking the tiniest of neon signs as they tried to attract customers. If ever the mountains offered a nature epiphany, this had to be it—the dance of light. It always left us awestruck.

Today, thousands of people enjoy the lightening bug show at Elkmont. Because it has become so popular, the Park service is forced to control the crowds by tickets, reservations, shuttle busses, and scheduled times. I'm not certain the performers can be managed as well, but at least with an observed seventy-four years of dependable punctuality, lightning bugs continue to show up.

I have mentioned Elkmont here and there earlier, but these brief slices don't do it justice. Elkmont had an intense and colorful history, one that spoke of logging, a railroad, people settlement in temporary movable small shacks, all at the intersection of two or three creeks that formed the head waters of Little River and other such settler history. A recent and very definitive Park study revealed a face of Elkmont of which I was unaware. The Landscape Assessment for Elkmont Development was formulated by the Park over several years. It described the Elkmont eras in great detail. Like a four act play, Elkmont's life was defined in four distinct ten year eras: 1901–1942.

During the first ten years, Elkmont was logged throughout, even into Jake's Creek . A train offered daily excursions. A company store and post office opened; timber production peaked; Wonderland Park Hotel opened, and Appalachian Club built a playground and later dammed Little river for a swimming hole. Some comfort and leisure was beginning to arrive in contrast to harshness of life of loggers and their families.

Elkmont's beginnings were as harsh and turbulent as the mountains that encircled the attempt at civilizing nature. First, Little River Logging Company began logging on then the West Fork of Little River in 1901. It brought loggers, families, rails, mobile shacks, as it denuded the ridges. By 1910 it deeded fifty acres at Elkmont to a group of prominent Knoxvillians for a hunting and fishing club – The Appalachian Club. Soon after, it leased a forty thousand acre tract just south of Elkmont to the same group. The group built a clubhouse and several cabins as a getaway. The next year, the logging company sold sixty acres to the Carter brothers for the Wonderland Park Development. Two years later, a Knoxville group bought it from the Carters and renamed it – the Wonderland Club.

Growth and tourism triggered quick rapid expansion of Elkmont. Cabins were built at both locations. Appalachian Club soon expanded into three sections as new dwellings sprung up. *Daisy Town* was south of *Society Hill* and both communities were built nearer the rail and trail due to narrow topography. Along Little River, the land was more plentiful, less steep, and nearest the water, and it became the *Millionaire Row* section.

The second phase saw the Wonderland Club formed, and the Boy Scout *Camp Helpful* was built across the road. More dwellings sprung up in Appalachian Club and around the Wonderland Hotel as more and more people learned Elkmont was the finest of mountain escapes.

The third phase saw big changes. Logging in Elkmont gradually diminished and ceased in 1926. The logging company removed the rails, and it left behind a ribbon of road bed that was soon converted to gravel roads and trails. Now many more could visit. The State of Tennessee finally linked Little River Road from Townsend to Elkmont on the old railway bed. Now people west of the Park could get to Elkmont.

The fourth phase was one of growth in Elkmont's visitation, development, and accessibility. According to the Park documents, the newly formed CCCs built six hundred miles of trails, including seventy miles of the Appalachian Trail, six fire towers, and three hundred miles of roads and tourist highways. They cleaned up debris , began reforestation, initiated erosion control, and installed telephone lines throughout. In addition, they served as always–on-call fire fighters.

According to the publication, *Civilian Conservation Corp in the Smokies*, approximately seventeen CCC camps soon located in the soon to be park— Elkmont's camp was the twelfth camp. Four thousand three hundred fifty CCC enrollees, "the tree boys," worked in the park. This phase saw CCC build the Little River stone bridge in Elkmont. The Baptist Church was moved to Wears Valley and renamed Valley View. At phase end in September1940 Roosevelt dedicated the park, and two years later in 1943, the CCC operation was terminated and all the camps closed.

I guess my own journey entered into the call of Elkmont around 1940.

The Park

Probably my most active years at Elkmont were from 1944, at age six, through the mid to late 1950s.

These were Elkmont's visitor heydays, years when I spent the most time there. The Wonderland Hotel was bustling with visitors, offered fine mountain meals, and offered continual social activities. My parents, along with other Park service couples, their Sevierville, Gatlinburg, and Pigeon Forge friends, were there almost weekly for dances, bridges, and meals. The Appalachian Club hosted similar activities and often included folks that were not part of its membership. The Appalachian Village and its loosely formed homeowner's organization had fashioned their own natural swimming spot in the icy waters of Little River pretty much at the Village's front door. It was inviting, comfortable, natural, and private.

I remembered the summer homes there ranged from quite elegant to comfortable low maintenance cabins similar to ones you might find at a summer camp with few conveniences and an ambience that allowed the outdoors in. Several dozen cabins were sprinkled throughout the Appalachian Village and the main clubhouse for all social activities was almost at its center. Other than wildflowers and natural stone here and there, and except for the gravel road, you were surrounded by the trees. Their thick canopy shaded nearly everything. The forest floor was primarily moss, some wild shrubs, and last decade's leaves and needles. Most members were prominent families from Knoxville and the surrounding area. Numbered among them were the usual bankers, attorneys, businessmen, physicians, sports celebrities, and other professionals.

One thing I distinctly remember, people absolutely worshiped Elkmont. So did I. Its mystique provided them escape from the modernity and grind of their responsibility back home. Their praise for this mountain landscape was obvious. The body language and dialogue of any of Elkmont's temporary residents or visitors was filled with joy and exhilaration. Exuberance radiated in the ambience of any group. And why not, an hour away from their home stood this mecca. Elkmont's magic drew them like swallows. Many folks drove back and forth during the week and others waited until the weekend to return.

Camp LeConte for Boys was directly across the road from the Wonderland Hotel. Behind the camp, the river, partially diverted, formed the lake and the powerhouse. Upstream, just above the bridge, the diverted water along with floods had created a small island. It and a concrete raceway directed part of the river into a bowl-shaped lake bed. The lake water rejoined the river but only after it first turned the large steel dynamo in the powerhouse and produced electricity for Elkmont.

THE BLUE MOUNTAINS SING
of rivers, old men, trails and trout

The lake was about one hundred fifty yards long and at least fifty yards wide near the lower end nearest the dam and powerhouse, thus satisfying the camp Red Cross lifesaving requirements. Built to provide the boy's camp, a location for their swimming, and recreation activities, it also became a novel getaway swim for Wonderland Hotel visitors many of whom had only swam in public pools in the larger cities. A few locals often sought its iciness to thwart the heat and summer sun.

I had continual access to the lake. My Dad and Homer Smith were Park employees and good friends. Homer and his wife Veryl, son Sonny, who was my age, and daughter Mary Lou, lived in park ranger housing on the ridge overlooking the lake. Swimming in the lake or fishing in Little River was only a forty yard stumble and slide down the rough hillside from their home to the diving platform and the powerhouse. Homer was the park liaison with the Elkmont community. He oversaw the smooth operation of all things water and electric and served as radio dispatcher at park headquarters where my Dad also worked as General Supply officer.

There were few summer and fall weeks or days that I was not mingling at Elkmont and staying with the Smith family. My folks were there almost every weekend enjoying food and social activity at Wonderland Hotel and visiting with friends in the Appalachian Club.

Sonny and I made new friends and swam with many of the campers and counselors at the boy's camp. Most were from Knoxville and beyond. Most were from prominent Knoxville families, and many of the campers' parents were Appalachian Club members with summer homes at Elkmont.

Years later, watching the new television program *Northern Exposures* I recognized John Cullum in a lead part. John was a Camp LeConte camper and counselor during the late 1940s , and, I believe, got his start at the University of Tennessee's Carousel theatre where he majored in drama. He's had quite a distinguished acting career thus far and can often be seen in a variety of television roles. In fact, through the years, I've recognized names of many of the campers as they moved through the professional ranks, including names like Burckhardt, Gardner, Faust, Overholt, and Cullum.

The Appalachian Club was colorful and a favorite spot for visiting dignitaries, politicians, university coaches, and star football players. Herman Hickman was a constant with a home at Elkmont. A bit before my Elkmont time, General Bob Neyland visited there and usually was accompanied by several of his All American squad.

Swede Owenby, the first ranger at Elkmont, was reported to have made a deal with General Neyland. Since his five sons were a bit secluded in Elkmont, Swede brokered a fine athletic program for his sons. In those days

The Park

a ranger had more available time to devote to visitor service. They strived to be neighborly which made them very customer and service oriented with little or no threat of liability. So they often picked up any hiking fisherman along the road and hauled them in their Park truck as far as they wished to go above the gate. The fisherman was then assured of virgin, likely unfished, trout waters. Usually, the ranger would make a return run late in the afternoon, meet the fisherman hiking out, and give the tired sportsman a return lift to their car at the gated road's parking area.

According to Swede's sons, I think it was sort of a barter agreement: fishing trips in exchange for coaching and "sandlot" games with UT athletes, when they were there visiting. Swede told General Neyland that he'd take the coach trout fishing on his visits if he'd encourage his athletes, who often accompanied him, to share their football, baseball, and basketball skills with his sons. It turned out to be a fine training opportunity for the five boys. They learned to punt, pass, kick, block, and tackle from the best that the University of Tennessee had under Neyland. For several years, Swede's sons played ball with and were skill coached by the UT all- American stars like Hank Lauricella, Herky Payne, and others of that era. It must have worked. All of Swede Owenby's sons went on to athletic stardom.

Time has a way of generating change. I was eleven years old in 1948. Elkmont soon became my enchanting place of woods 'n waters, trout, colorful characters, summer families of summer friends, camping, lightening bugs, Little River swims, and lake lounging midlake on the anchored WWII rubber raft turned upside down.

It was dusk visits by bears following the wafting smell of grilling steaks. They usually only watched. It was seeing Homer rob his six beehives of

Lake at Elkmont and Camp LeConte for Boys in 1935
(Smoky Mountain Historical Society Journal)

blossom honey, spin it from the combs, and can it. It was eating at Wonderland hotel on weeknights and Sunday dinner, and tubing Little River all day long. It was passing football in October on Camp LeConte's fields, the buildings empty, deserted, boyish laughter and grousing silenced, and campers long since returned home.

Many Elkmont nights were nights you laid in wait expectantly. A trout fishing trip was to begin the next morning. Next day at dawn we'd pile in the official ranger green pickup truck and drive to Cosby Ranger station to trout fish Big Creek or Walnut Bottoms. Homer, Dad, Sonny, and I would jostle and jolt as the truck navigated the bumpy, curvy, gravel road. At the Cosby ranger station, which was really the ranger's home, we met Sonny's uncle, Audley Whaley, chief ranger of the Cosby district. From there, Audley would drive us deep into the mountains. We'd partner up in twos, choose our streams, and fish until late afternoon. Audley would pick us up just before dark.

A special meal highlight occurred most often at Elkmont. The day's catch of rainbow trout were butterflied, dredged in spice laden meal and flour mix, and fried until crisp. Only the intestines were absent. The entire trout was served with head, eyes, and fins intact. The moist flesh of the native brook and rainbow trout was unbeatable.

Elkmont still triggers memory wisps of youthful summer days that could enchant you, hold you spellbound. Like no other place I have known , it offered escape from that boredom and sameness that often appears to most all of us after several straight days of nothing but woods without people. I miss the lightening bugs and the come and go of interesting and colorful new friends and old acquaintances. I miss my "golly gee" insight into the apparent elegant daily life styles of the Appalachian Club members and the sure to be interesting parade of new and old faces of this year's campers at Camp LeConte. I miss the unique, relaxed charm ,and grandeur of the Wonderland Hotel, its food, and front porch. I miss icy swims early morning and late afternoon, tubing Little River at midday, and trout fishing all day. I miss secluded camping at the then primitive Elkmont campground with my folks and at other times with Uncle Dave or my friends. I still enjoy occasionally noting the name of a former Camp LeConte camper or counselor who grew to become quite the successful professional.

I miss the Elkmont solitude. I miss that silence of the woods after the tourists were long gone. I miss the fall and winter faces of that deserted village. I miss Elkmont's special gift—the perpetual roar and smell of the Little River—in that place where you could always smell the sunshine and in that place when time stood still.

CHAPTER FOUR

"But you, my beloved, are not in the darkness...for you are sons of the light; sons of the day..."

1 Thessalonians 5: 4

Adventures for Boys
Or
"Run fast boys cause they're ridin Shetland ponies"

Today I discovered a new plant , I sat down beside it for a minute or a day, to make its acquaintance and hear what it had to tell...I asked the boulders I met , whence they came and whither they are going.—John Muir

Discovering the Often Unseen

Most of the time my hometown friends unknowingly set the stage for most of my adventures. There were eccentric relatives, old timers, moonshine makers, WW II vets, hovering, possessive, and anxious mothers and aunts. There were family members who always drank, family members who never drank, uncles just out of prison, uncles about to go to prison, uncles who only fished, drank and played sports, and uncles who coached sports and did little else. These life sketches streamed on like a Saturday movie serial.

For instance, another close boyhood friend, Luke, had an American Indian relative. Like a mixed feral breed, a mutt of a dog from the shelter, his grandfather was a strange mix of tribal DNA. He seemed to be an eccentric, a hermit, and led a gypsyesque existence, never staying long in any one place. He reminded me of a wolf. He reappeared every several months as if nothing had happened in between. He knew the answers to everything that mattered. For two twelve year old boys, he was exciting, mysterious, and seemed not of this world. I remember the first time I met him.

THE BLUE MOUNTAINS SING
of rivers, old men, trails and trout

Taking twice as long to complete our after school jaunt home, Luke, also twelve and nearly my best friend, said, "As we go by the store, ask your mom and see if you can come over and play at my house this afternoon."

"I knew we'd find one sooner or later," he said. He crawled up out of a honeysuckle choked ditch with an old Prince Albert tobacco tin with a flap lid. He poked it high in the air like a newly won prize and said, "Now we both got one. Did you dump your red worms out yesterday? You better have cause I forgot mine Friday and Ma threw mine away, can and all. She said next time I left mine in my overalls and the washing machine found 'em first, it would be the last time you and me would redeye fish ever again."

Jumping to a more fun subject he continued, "Oh, did you know old man Clancy is starting his spring plowing in his Mill Creek bottom today? I saw him gittin' the mule's ready early this morning when I left for school. You want to hunt arrow heads on the way to my house, we'll have two or three hours before dark? Man, them plowed ruts are black as tar and deep. We'll have to foller his mule cause them plow ruts are knee high, and if we try to walk crossways over 'em we'll be uh mountain climbin, and I ain't for any mountain climbin today. Maybe we ort to wait a day or two though cause it's not gonna rain, and the ground will dry out enough to turn sortie tan like, and you can see them black arrowheads better. Right now, they'd be same color as them black ruts."

"Suits me. Thursday maybe if it's not rainin'." I quickly slid my words in edgewise.

Luke's home was on a ridge top about a mile from our house, and as one of my nearest next door neighbors, we played, fished, camped, BB gunned rabbits, smoked rabbit tobacco, and played together as far back as I could remember.

"We're nearly there," Luke said, stopping as if to emphasize his next words. "I wanted you to meet my granddad. Never know when he's going to be here. He lives way back up in the mountains and just shows up sudden like. Stays awhile and then takes off."

"What's he do?" I asked.

Luke shook his head. "I don't know, nothing really. Lives off the land er somthin', I guess. He used to be some kinda guide way back in them Indian days. He's really old but spry. My mom says he's part Cherokee and part Comanche and that I am too.

With a rising pitch, I asked, "So if he's some kinda Indian hermit, does he know a lotta stuff about animals 'n trackin' and woods stuff?"

Luke said proudly, "Best I ever seen; you'll see."

Leaving the road, we rounded a slight bend in the trail that led to their house. Hunched on the front steps of the cabin was a strange apparition. An old man sat silent and very still, his back rigidly straight. He was perched wooden-like on the porch floor's edge, knees bent, his feet braced flat on the third step of the nine leading up to the wooden porch. His chin rested in his clasped hands, his fingers laced and intertwined, his elbows rested on his thighs. His gaze never wavered from his spot of focus in the woods at our back. And we walked right through that focus, never breaking his spell.

"Esau, this is my best buddy, Ronny." The old guide's head nodded, and he turned ever so slightly and focused his steely, all-knowing gaze on me. I shifted from foot to foot, uneasy.

"Pleased to meet you sir, er uh, Mr. Esau." I didn't really know what to call him, and besides, his gaze made me really nervous. Esau's studying focus seemed to reach out and inspect every pore of my being, inside and out. His gaze made me feel a little sweaty and lightheaded. It seemed like a long time before he broke the silence.

Esau's pondering stare never left me , until Luke queried, "Esau, can you teach us some of that Indian stuff about the woods and animals?"

I, choking a bit, finally remembered to breathe. I wondered why I was holding my breath. Returning Esau's gaze , but much more weakly, I couldn't take my eyes off this squat, stocky, white-haired old man with furrowed, leathery skin. Something about him seemed ageless. Powerful shoulders and arms and large hands with long, delicate pianist fingers all created a contrast, a puzzling image of incompatibility, a mix of both strength and sensitivity.

There was a strange sort of delicateness about him as he spoke with his grandson. He was not a man you could size up quickly, put a label on, and treat accordingly. My mind raced and was soon lost in my own puzzlement. I heard little of the give and take conversation beside me, only the singsong murmuring as their words rose and fell.

I had never seen a man who exuded more mystique. His agile gestures, alertness, quickness, and animation seemed no more than that of a forty year old. Yet his appearance, coupled with Luke's stories about his adventures, made him seem, to my twelve-year-old mind, like forty years plus a century. He seemed interesting and at the same time frightening.

My palms were sweaty. Did Easau know some of my secrets? How could he know Luke and I sneaked two big watermelons and three ripe cantaloupes out of Mr. Casey's creek bottom under last week's full moon and ate every blessed bit? Nobody could know that . I knew we were skilled enough in any woods to avoid being seen. Why, not even God could see us sometimes when we were really wily and sneaking up on a deer. Well, maybe God could see us a little bit, but not very good, cause we blended pretty durn good with the woods when we set our minds to it.

Esau startled me when he stood up, turned abruptly, and said to both of us, "Follow me into the back yard here near that tree line. Ok , let's see if you've learned anything yet about the woods."

Luke quickly reminded him, " We ain't just a pair of little boy paintywaists. Why, we both been running the woods and mountains and chasing stuff probably a month after we 'uz born."

Esau said," Well now, that's a pretty tall feat, I say, for anybody, much less you two seasoned, veteran wood rats. Lay down there in the grass and those leaves at the edge of the woods and just look close; I'll be back in a little while, and you can tell me what all is going on in this twenty-foot circle."
"Why, I can tell you right now they ain't nothin' in that grassy spot in them leaves," said Luke. "I can see from here—why, my little brother is four, and he'd tell you that without even looking—why, if you wust to say that to my squirrel feist, Deacon, he'd look back at you over his shoulder with a wondering look on his face. Specially if you wust to sic him on a twenty-foot nothin' happening circle like that, he'd known in a heartbeat, just like my little brother would, that there ain't nothin' there."

Esau's lips held back a slight *we'll see* smile. "Listen, If you want to learn woods lore, you follow my lead in everything, in every way that I say, and for as long as I say. Otherwise, you just run on back to the school and pull that little redheaded girl's pigtails some more and stay citified like some peckerheaded , goober of a dude."

"Ok, Ok Esau, but I don't see how this is doing us any good." Luke shook his head forlornly.

"You can question me when I say you can and not before", said Esau," but you haven't reached that level yet, especially after only five minutes of empty jawin' before you've even done what I instructed you both to do."

We both fell to the ground on our stomachs, and Luke said, "Ok, what do we do?"

Esau said, "Life is all around you , in various stages and cycles. I want you to be quiet, no talk, and I want you to focus very intensely on every blade of grass, every leaf, every rock, every stick, every flower, every tree, every limb, every bird, everythin' alive or dead, and tell me what is going on and what is living there. This is all about intense focus, concentration, and searchin' with your eyes , ears, nose, and sometimes even your mouth. I'll be back soon, and you'll tell me everythin' you noticed, what was happenin', why it happened, and what the natural process was that was takin' place as you observed it."

Luke looked at me, sighed, and said, "Oh, God" as he dropped his gaze to the ground.

Esau said, "All right, that's better; I'll be back when that shadow there reaches the first step on the porch."

This time Luke dragged out an even longer "Oh Lord" sigh. His second one.

Esau, sensing our impatience, took the lesson to another plane. It was one we were afraid not to honor and respect. He stood behind us and hovered over us. I wondered if this was the way you felt if God showed up and you were scared, unsure, and really nervous.

"The Indians understood all this, and you'd be wise to heed their stories. Many scoffers call them myths, but they are universal truths.

Esau continued, "At first, man could talk to the animals, to everythin' that lived wild, and they could talk to him. They understood each other and lived in peace and harmony. But Man disobeyed the Great Spirit, disappointed him, and rebelled against his wishes. The Great Spirit punished Man by takin' away his ability to understand the language of animals and everything wild. This made life and hard times for Man in a lot of ways. Confused, he misunderstood the will of every wild thing in his path. He was alone, and he felt forsaken. Things between man and wild animals never went well after that. The Great Spirit never returned things as they once were.

Esau stood quietly staring at us. Taking a deep breath, he reassured us, "To a degree, you can restore that trust and understandin' with those things wild in the forest. If you're patient and honest, wild things will trust you, even speak to you in ways that are strange. You can uncover that brotherhood that was lost. In my life, birds, deer, beaver, and others have approached me and eaten from my outstretched hands. I have been warned when danger approached and have learned to be led to food and water when I watched them closely. Patience and commitment will help you build friendship with wild things. But first you gotta want it and be willin' to pay the price." Then he walked into the woods.

We scratched and waited. Finally, the oak's shadow reached the top step. Suddenly, he spoke from behind us sending a shiver through us both. Luke and I looked at each other. How did he get there.

"OK, one at a time tell me what you saw."

Luke went first, "Well, summer ain't over, and its hot down here. I've scratched and smacked gnats and about a million skeeters and..."

Esau interrupted, "I didn't ask how you feel—*what did you see*?"

Luke said, " I saw all them things I scratched, a wren sat about twenty feet away and looked at me, and old Rascal crawled up purring and laid right in the middle of my back. Do you know how hard it is to concentrate with a big, six pound, orange calico cat laying smack dab on your back and it ninety damn degrees in the shade." I don't know if Esau smiled or was mad. He still stood behind and hovered.

"Ronny , did you see anything while Luke scratched chiggers and played with the cat?"

"Well, sir , er uh , Mr. Esau, I saw the same wren. There was a rabbit in the edge of the woods and a mockingbird sung so loud I couldn't hear myself think. I guess that's about it. "

"Boys, boys," his voice implying he was talking to babies, " the reason I put you in the grass at woods edge was so that you'd have grass and leaves and all the life that goes with them. You apparently didn't even move a stick, or a leaf, or a rock. Life was there right under your nose."

He moved quickly in front of us and turned over a small thick limb and a couple of large leaves—they were almost between us.

" Look here. Ants, and every insect you might expect, are busy just working away not two feet from your noses. There's a grub worm, a red worm ,and these little critters that curl up when you touch them. And right here is a centipede. While you boys laid here waiting on a black bear, mountain lion, an eagle, or a deer , life was going on all around you. Important life.

"Lesson learned: Don't wait and look for the obvious. You've got to treat it all as one big world. Everything in it has a purpose, and you've got to learn to be in tune with it all. Now go on back to your Moms and help with the chores. Next week, I'll see if you've pondered and practiced on what I've said."

Now I was really anxious and a little scared. Esau sure didn't talk like he looked. It made me nervous. I couldn't figure him out.

"Luke, how come he doesn't talk like a real Indian? From what you said and from what I saw at first, I thought he'd talk like a real Indian."

"Like who," Luke asked as if he had me. "Which Indian do you know?"

"I mean , you know , I don't know any other one but him. But I thought he'd be more like those in a Red Ryder movie or maybe talk like a chief when he cuts his hand to become a blood brother to John Wayne or Alan Ladd."

"No, he shore don't talk like them movie injuns. You're right about that."

"You know what," I said, "he sounds more like that doctor guy, you know that TVA guy, the one that came to our class and talked to us about dams, and fish, and conservation. He talks a lot like him. Actually, he really sounds like that college professor that's married to our school nurse. Why do you think he'd rather talk like some professor instead of an Indian?"

Luke shook his head as if the puzzle was not unfathomable but serious and troubling, " I don't know."

"Well, I think I like him, but if I was an Indian, I'd want to talk Indian talk," I said.

Thursday of the next week finally came. We were back in the same spot in Luke's yard.

"What do you think he'll have us do today, Ronny?"

"I dunno, but I'm really nervous."

"Yeah, me too."

"OK boys. Let's move to the backyard."

His OK sent a shiver, and we both leaped and whirled around to face him. Where had he come from. We had been alert and were both tryin' for a glimpse of him. Last week had not been a total waste.

"See these two shallow trenches. They're grassy and blend with the rest of the yard. They are hollowed out just enough to make your bodies level with the rest of the yard. I want you to lie on your back today. I'm going to cover you with a light cover of leaves and grass so you'll blend with the yard —camouflage—is what they call it. You'll be side by side. See what you can discover today. Same orders as before."

For some reason, looking at the sky seemed more interesting. You could turn your head and your view included woods along with the sky. We lay quieter this time. The leaf covering made a game of it. We both believed we might lie still enough to attract an unsuspecting animal or bird.

We had made a pact earlier in the week to make mental notes of every sighting and to be keen observers of anything and everything. In fact , we laid awake one night almost all night pooling our knowledge and making our plan. And then we practiced hard. We wanted a big list to impress Esau.

Time passed more quickly. We worked hard at using all five senses that Esau favored. This time we heard his approach, although it was slight.

"Times up, mountain scouts. What did you sense?"

Luke asked, " Can I go first?" Esau nodded. "Well, an eagle circled for a while. Earlier a buzzard rode the updrafts for a longtime; it seemed to play like it was riding ocean waves. Behind it the sky was blue with big white billowy clouds. One of 'em looked exactly like a buffalo. Must a been about an hour later, another one drifted right over us, and it looked just like a naked woman, and she was really pretty too. A peckerwood hammered on that dead walnut tree looking for worms I guess. It would hammer and quit, hammer and quit, till I was plumb sick of the noise. Every time it hammered our cat jumped five feet cause it was tryin to creep up on a field mouse beside the smokehouse. A skunk skedaddled all around and under that rotten log again. He found right many grub worms. It must be near four o'clock cause smoke started coming from our cook stove chimney, mama always starts supper at four. Two wrens hopped all around my head and arms, one came back two or three times and got grass and twigs off my chest and flew into that cedar tree, I believe they are building a nest. I bet they would have eat out of my hand if I'd had some seeds in my hand, kept still, and laid it flat. That's about all. "

"That's way better than last week, you did good. Keep it up. Ronny, you see anything different?"

"Yeah, I saw those circling birds like Luke. The skunk was out of my sight. A red tailed hawk circled a while, then dived and knocked feathers out of a mourning dove over there to my right in the edge of the woods. I couldn't tell if he got a meal or not. On my side toward the west, the clouds darkened up and got gray and layered. The smoke from the kitchen is dropping, not going up, and it's hanging around the house and staying close in the yard. I think those signs together mean a front is moving in with maybe some rain. I thought that cloud looked more like a rhinoceros. But Luke's right about that naked woman, she was really pretty. Lordy what a body.

"I heard a weasel trying to get to the chickens, I guess it could have been a fox, whatever it was that squawking hen wasn't just saying, 'Look I laid an egg.' That orange tomcat caught a field mouse on my side over next to the house. Two little fawns walked right to the edge of the yard, and when the cat jumped the mouse, they ran back into the woods a ways and turned and looked at the cat. A dove waddled right up and ate grass seed all around on my left side. He might of over fed, got overload, and got popped by that hawk. Couldn't tell if it was the same one or not. A black snake slithered and circled us quite a few times. I didn't know if he wanted to hide in our leaves or beat the cat to that mouse. He left quick when that second hawk sailed over.

"Those same wrens walked all over my chest, inspected my leaves and stuff but never took any. I believe a hoot owl was eyein' that same mouse or maybe that snake. He sat stone still on that third limb in that hickory tree and never moved nothing but his head. I was hid really good, and I believe he stayed about an hour. He never made a try for bird, snake, or mouse, just watched. Then he flew in a northerly direction through the woods." I paused tryin' to think of more.

"You both did really well. If you are quiet, the more eyes the better. You all keep practicing this week, and we'll meet here next Thursday. Maybe that naked lady in the clouds will be back."

Although we changed locations often, Esau never stopped the challenge or lowered the bar. He stretched our endurance and skill levels a bit more each time we met. His demands for perfection were endless. Week after week month after month , he drilled us. It became fun and the excitement grew due to his management and creativity. Everything we did had a purpose.

Esau taught us patience, observation, stealth, and a desire to be an integral part of nature.

He insisted, "No matter wherever you find yourself, no matter the situation, you can learn to survive."

He instilled a knowledge of the symbiotic relationship of everything in nature. He made us understand that from the tiniest insect to the largest animal— all are a part of a chain— each has a significance and value to the entire cycle. He made us understand that to interrupt or destroy one part affects many other living things so vital to nature's balance. He stressed that we must first become one with nature, that the small birds like the chickadee will actually eat seed from your hand once you master your part in the harmony of the woods. These trials and many more like them consumed our ever-waking moments.

He was determined to exercise our outdoor skills at every turn. Every move was developmental for us. Envisioning ourselves as Apaches in every Old West movie or radio program we'd ever seen, heard, or read about, made every lesson and every task exciting and increasingly adrenaline laced. Although our few summer and fall seasons probably did not quite hone us into outdoor scout models or finely skilled master musicians in the harmonic symphony of the woods, we, nevertheless, developed an heightened awareness. In the end, we stood awed by the complexity of nature's contributions and the interaction and interdependence of her many parts.

It was about October I guess. Esau sat down with us and for a long time said nothing. We waited expecting our next survival training installment. We thought he was trying to out-wait us, to have us speak first.

Just as our minds were about to wander, he spoke. "I can't spend more time with you. I 've gotta leave and go back into the mountains. You both have learned much. The basics skills that can take you where you can become one with nature are there. It's time you begin your own journey alone. You gotta find your own life's special place. Let your heart lead you. It is the one thing you must do alone. I believe in you, both of you. You will find your way. These thoughts are special. Remember them. They are not just words. I leave 'em with you. They'll guide you. Never, never, give up. Practice this, and you will succeed."

These parting words were his last, at least, his last words to me. He got up and walked toward the mountains , and except for the one day that he took us to the place of silence, I never saw him again. After that day, Luke never spoke of seeing him again either. I always wondered if he searched for poachers in the park as maybe a shadow agent for the rangers.

THE BLUE MOUNTAINS SING
of rivers, old men, trails and trout

I'll have to say his lessons served us well

I recall that Esau taught us to revere harvest time. Summer's fruits and grains reward the diligence of nature's preparation. He spoke often of the mystique of the season , of the hunters' moon, the meaning and ritual in nature's harvest. He spoke of the age old reverence his people celebrated in thankfulness to the supreme maker for all the gifts nature bestowed.

His October insights always made my Octobers more meaningful. It recalled old time ways. The rituals are still with most of us every fall , as folks revisit, celebrate, and remember as they seek their past. Because of Esau , my fall thoughts replay in neon and Technicolor.

October conjures up all sorts of images. It signals summers final curtain call, and with it comes all the sights, sounds, and fragrances. The last of summer's sweetness is a preview of the harvest to come. My thoughts from somewhere in my October's past are images of small game animals, summer fattened awaiting the chase, frequent nightly possum and coon hunts, icy spews of ground that crunched underfoot after dark, trees that crackled as the cold chased summer's sap away. There were icy mornings in the deer stand where delicate sounds in the leaves made your pounding heart the only sound. In that moment wood sounds quicken until they become deafening. There were fall mornings with wafting, hovering wood smoke that wouldn't leave the yard because the moon's halo said rain, a signal of trouble for tomorrow's plans. Less frequently now, I wonder, would this be a good night to join the dogs for a hunt, but I know I won't.

In falls past, a full moon encouraged gane and fish to feed all night. There were hunts in a moonlit world that drowned out the kerosene lantern's bouncing glow. Sweaty and steaming in the biting chill, we ran our stumbling chase toward yelping, jumping hounds treed and impatient. They say it's the journey that's more important than the journey's end. Seeing the treed coon was enough. We counted coup with the spotlight, reassured he was there, and we called off the dogs. Hiking the dogs well away from the scent of this leg of the hunt, we urged them on to find another. A call from the wild would set us on yet another wild and joyous run though luminous moonlit woods.

Most any full moon, but especially the Hunter's moon, signals somewhat of a holiday for animals. Having fed all night in the light of its fullness , most animals, even the deer, sleep late the next day, and don't stir sometimes till noon. Their stubborn behavior is brazenly inconsiderate of the waiting hunter. I believe the animals know it and snicker and maybe even slap their thighs in peals of hee-haw laughter, much like a *Far Side* cartoon.

My October memory string featured a time of drying apples moved to the attic alongside ginseng, red peppers, and old quilts strung on an old clothesline. October spoke of sorghum molasses, Indian corn, spicy smells of autumn –the heavy sugary sweetness of the last mown grass of summer and the fragrant muskiness of sun starved leaves. Each leaf color owned its own distinct spicy fragrance.

There was smokehouse dampness that smelled of pork, salt, and musty smoke as country hams swung or laid waiting in bins ready to accompany redeye gravy. Well away from the barnyard, a late night bonfire blazed both for warmth and for the final rendering of this morning's butchered sow. Black kettles bubbled lye soap and others bubbled the sweet smells of apple butter. The stirrers were rewarded with sampling warm cracklings left over from earlier in the day. Irish potatoes, rows of whole apples, and Vidalia onions were spread out to breathe all winter in the steady coolness of the root cellar.

This tenth month is always magnificent and is a reoccurring reminder of our legacy passed along by the mountain settlers. It encourages us to revisit, savor, remember, and celebrate our unique mountain heritage. Native or not, we each have that special place in the heart that draws us to these mountains and keeps us here. The legacy we enjoy is unique, personal, and continuing. It shapes our values, our life style, and ultimately, how we respect and treat each other and the land.

THE BLUE MOUNTAINS SING
of rivers, old men, trails and trout

Here is calm so deep, grasses cease waiting...wonderful how completely everything in wild nature fits into us, as if part and parent of us. The sun shines not on us, but in us. The rivers flow not passed, but through us, thrilling, tingling, vibrating every fiber and cell and substance of our bodies, making them to glide and sing. There is a love of wild nature in everybody, an ancient mother-love showing itself whether recognized or not, and however covered by cares and duties... Wilderness is not only a haven for native plants and animals but it is also a refuge from society. It's a place to go hear the wind and little else, see the stars and galaxies, smell the pine trees, feel the cold water, touch the sky and the ground at the same time.—John Muir

A Mountain Legacy

The fall following my summer with the Luke and Esau adventures, I was introduced to another outdoor icon. It happened quite by accident. Yet it launched me on an exciting four year outdoor odyssey and gave me a mentoring partner.

I'd have to say it was a few trout seasons back, and I believe it was my thirteenth winter. Little did I know it was to fill my next few years with a legacy of memories. The rest of our little mountain town called him "Uncle Dave," so I did too.

He stood silently behind me on the bank of Mill Creek. His feist squirrel dog stood quietly, frozen at his side, her head in a puzzled tilt that dogs get when they are unsure of what's ahead. Hip-booted in knee deep icy water, I gingerly placed a number two steel trap onto a slight mud shelf in the steep creek bank. Gliding soundlessly from a grove of hickory trees to my right, the old man eased upstream toward me. He moved soundlessly even though wafting November leaves carpeted his path in winter's corn stubble. The old relic, nearer now, watched as I carefully covered the trap-jaws with a mud-soaked sycamore leaf that completely covered the trap pan.

Dressed in faded blue-gray bib overalls over a worn flannel red checkered shirt, he had a used look. A stooped slight frame supported his perfectly round head. Except for a few long wisps of white angel hair at the sides above his ears, he was completely bald. His sallow freckled skin showed an occasional liver splotched spot on his cheeks and the back of his hands. His faded denim jacket, worn in places with ragtag raveled spots, was probably aged by decades of farm. It framed the weathered look of one certain to have spent most of his years outdoors. In places, his freckled skin looked like a rabbit beagle's belly. His baggy overalls fell from his sparse frame as if he'd lost a great deal of weight. Large prominent ears and a wide grin framed the crinkled corners of his widely set, twinkling blue eyes. A large perfect set of false teeth completed this image of a seventy-eight year-old overgrown leprechaun. He could have just stepped right out of the hills of the early 1800s—the last of the mountain men probably, the Smoky Mountains anyway.

"Doing any good?" he grinned knowingly.

"Nah, I'm just re-layin' some," I said tentatively. Our word exchange had reassured the black and white squirrel dog who now instantly accepted me, wagged her whole rump and stubby tail, and moved as close to water as possible in her welcome. She almost fell into the water as she tried to lick my hand. I struggled against the current of the now thigh deep icy, coffee colored water as I tried to set the last dozen of my mink and muskrat traps, wondering if this ghostlike old man could really be a part of this blustery Thanksgiving Day. For a thirteen-year-old boy trying to earn Christmas money, I must have been living right on that dreary day. In less than two hours, Uncle and I had struck up a friendship as Uncle helped me reset the rest of the traps properly. Unknowingly, I had just launched a friendship that would ultimately teach me the " ways of the woods and the waters" from a mentor who had both lived and crafted many of them.

That afternoon I learned much of the art of trapping the wild mink and muskrat. But more importantly, I got my first informal lecture on natural laws that govern the balance of nature—conservation of next year's crop. Though I was unaware of it then, this was to be the first of my many outdoor lessons and many life lessons on my way to manhood. The common thread of instruction encouraged me to become one with the woods, mountains, and rivers. Later I would recall, "I guess we helped each other through our childhoods, Uncle Dave and I, me through my first and him through his second. "

For the remainder of the day, he walked the riverbank above, as I waded midstream, resetting and emptying traps. Both of us talked and laughed at the same time, like a couple of excited youngsters who discovered a common thread that excited them – the outdoors and all it offered. Our words spilled out and overlapped. Our excited exclamations caused our sentences to bump and over run each other. All the while, he was laughing and coaching as we quickly were getting acquainted. It was as if we'd known each other always. Occasionally, Uncle Dave would step to the water and skillfully hide a trap that he felt I had mis-set. I learned this was his river bottom farm. Those plowed creek bottoms where 1 last year had hunted arrowheads were his. Trailing behind the plower, evidently some of his kin, and looking for flint chards , I'd seen the big, white, two story house on the creek in the middle of an apple orchard. He and wife Molly had raised their six children there.

He only had to offer stack cake and a crackling fire at his house once, and I was off behind him. Hobbling behind him on numbed feet, I followed that bobbing head with elfin ears across the pasture to their tin-roofed farmhouse. It stood snug with large maples, hickories, and oaks in front and the orchard to the back against the foot of Flanders Mountain.

As soon as we stepped into the living room from the front porch, he stoked up the fireplace with two chunks of dry hickory. The heat poured from the coals then burst into flames. The fireplace's chimney stones, laid correctly long ago, provided smokeless heat. Faint mist rose from my wet feet and socks. A calico tomcat was curled on the hearth. It slept peacefully and contentedly, until now. He jumped to his feet, stretched, and then moved to a far darkened corner. He recurled on a bare spot that had a large piece of linoleum missing. Before he laid down on the cool subfloor, he looked all around the room and then at me. His demeanor was one of disgust, disappointment, and disapproval. Somehow he reminded me of a person who, upon entering church, finds his pew seat occupied by a total stranger. I started to get up from my rocking chair and move from his space, but Ms. Molly called us to the kitchen.

She served me fresh cow's milk and Uncle Dave scalding coffee. We both gobbled or at least I did, giant slices of applesauce stack cake with peppermint crumbled throughout. I learned that the two had moved out of the "Big Tops" of the Smokies to this fifty acre farm. For him, it began in 1938, my birth year. I soon learned their settler traits like self-reliance, survival, and independence came alive in Technicolor. Their motto should have been, "If you can't grow it or hunt it or catch it you probably don't need it." Their daily routine ranged from butchering hogs, canning sausage, making chitins, drying apples, making apple butter for stack cakes, to hunting small game, catching trout, searching for ginseng, trapping mink, and muskrats. The list was endless. Other than a few staples like coffee, salt, kerosene, shot gun shells ,and squares of Days Work chewing tobacco or snuff, they needed little else. There was an occasional need for one of them to board the rolling store, a school bus converted to a grocery store, to sell a few eggs or chickens. They continued to rear it, make it, plant and harvest it ,or butcher it. I remembered another old-timer who once said, "All you ever need to get by is some land, a little apple orchard, and a battery powered radio."

One afternoon, while I waited on Uncle Dave to get back from the barn, I sat with Miss Molliein her kitchen starting to eat her fresh baked pie. I inquired, What kind of pie is this? It's really good?"

"It's chess pie," she said. "My great, great , great grandmothers' recipe, and it's real easy. People in the mountains always made do with what they had. Corn meal, flour, butter, sugar, buttermilk, and lard, made up everything they cooked or baked. It all was purty much some version of those things. That's all in that pie. I just added a little vanilla extract."

In later years I learned that some folks say the name came from mountain women apologetically explaining their use of such simple ingredients. "Oh, it's jess (just) pie."

For many of my era , this was a fine time to live in the countryside of the Southern Appalachians. My uncle's farm was about another mile up Mill Creek. Farm life afforded many youngsters an adventurous mountain playground. The times when my dad's work schedule kept him from our own outdoor times, I filled in my outdoor time with Uncle Dave. His name was fondly bestowed on him by the whole town. Based on conversations of other families displaced by the new national park, I'd have to say Uncle Dave could have been the poster child for all those families who were so traumatically uprooted from the Smokies; he was the Everyman of the settler's relocation journey. Each family had its own Smoky mountain exodus story, its own trail of tears, and each had its own poignant drama.

Prodded by a love of nature and a matching five million dollar donation from John D, Rockefeller, Jr., President Franklin D. Roosevelt set about the task of creating a national park in the Appalachian range. According to Uncle Dave, the government sent surveyors and land buyers to begin acquiring some six thousand plus parcels of privately owned land. The purchase included several large timber holdings and more than one thousand small farms. Though Uncle Dave and Ms. Molly disliked selling the family homeplace in their beloved Sugarlands, they didn't hold out like many of his neighbors who "lawed" the government. He was one of those who was overwhelmed by the offer of three or four times his asking price of five hundred dollars. He sold out,

Dave and Mollie Ogle. Circa 1947
(Courtesy of Ogle Grandchildren collection)

and with Molly and his kids made a move closer to civilization

With the advent of land purchases by the park, mountains, "hollers," and valleys emptied leaving only memories and names like Greenbrier Cove, Fighting Creek Gap, Elkmont, Tremont, Cades Coves, and scores of other empty settlements. His small Sugarlands farm lay in a mountain river valley covered in tulip poplars and maples that glowed lemon yellow and burnt orange in October. Old chestnut logs, spotty stone foundations, rotting trunks, rusted plows, and oak shingles that fell into stunted, gnarled apple orchards are the few remnant clues of an olden era so idyllic for many. The area evolved into The Great Smoky Mountain National Park, the most visited in the nation. Now, approximately ten million visitors annually visit and play in what was once Uncle Dave's front yard. Although he farmed his acreage, he was an entrepreneur of sorts. He opened a general store in the Sugarlands and Elkmont, served as postmaster, logged with the Little River Logging company, and guided tourists on fishing jaunts.

As a former resident of the Sugarlands, the old man was brimful of pleasant memories, and we soon visited those mountains often and in every season to camp, hike, and fish. Each ridge and stream was worth at least a half story each trip. They ranged from the time "the grey wolf attacked Clay Ownby's oldest boy ' " to the "biggest speckled trout he ever cotched, snaked him out from the big black hole under Indian Ledge on Little River." I learned something new about the old man and myself with each new outdoor trip . Unconsciously, I was learning a basic value system — a code of ethics to live by, outdoors . Like the day we stopped in a damp, humus filled "holler" to pick ramps, a super strong onion that grows wild in the mountains, to cook with country ham and eggs.

"Don't pull 'em all Boy," he admonished, " most of the fun is not in the eatin but thinkin all winter how good those next year 'ull taste. Always leave some for next year." Somehow he wove conservation and next year's crop into every hunt, every fishing trip, and every venture into the woods.

His demeanor was the epitome of calmness and contentment. Nothing ever seemed to rile him. Most any incident, good or bad, only seemed to trigger a smile and a chuckle. One night later in the summer, his calm was an understatement. It was a moonless, dark night high in the Smokies camping at the Chimneys next to the river. We were camping under a ledge along the west prong of the Little Pigeon River. Around midnight, a black bear walked under my WW II jungle hammock, scraped underneath, and climbed to the rock table-top for fat drippings I had spilled the night before. I was poised for a leap into the underbrush and a stumbling run into the night.

Completely in command of the situation, Uncle Dave spoke softly from his bed on the ground. "Don't be askairt, Boy. Let him finish. They ain't nothing in the woods that'll clean dirty dishes better'n a bear's tongue." I was forced to laugh even if it did come out cracked and falsetto like.

He was a man's man, a fisherman-hunter-outdoorsman's icon, and a mentor. He could pinch the stem from a water soaked sycamore leaf and hide the trap jaws from the wiliest mink; he could sit stump still for a day until he killed his deer, and then carry it four miles out to his smokehouse where it would hang and cure. And he enjoyed every minute of it.

He could tie flies, shoot squirrels through the eye from the tallest trees with a twenty-two short, knew where to find the fattest stickbait for trout, and he knew hundreds of other skills a man should know to survive in and enjoy the outdoors. But the best part for me, he patiently repeated each one until I mastered the skill. I could pretty well hold my own in the woods for a thirteen year-old boy.

Looking back, I would recall that as I've grown older, I marvel at the patience it must have taken. He always followed each lesson with his bywords, as I called them.

"Boy, when you can do it that well – you'll be a man. Then I recon I'll show you Flanders Field." I figured I'd never get there because he'd mentioned that mysterious place for what seemed like years, but he'd never mention more than the name.

The old man knew right where to find the late summer muscadines, how to skin game or fowl without getting hair or feathers on the meat. He always knew where to find the fattest coons as soon as the November full moon caused frosty woods to grow silver fuzz. Fish, game, mink, or ducks, he'd only take what we needed, nothing more, even when the game laws allowed it. Nothing could be more fiery than his grumbling lectures if I got carried away and overkilled on ducks or small game. He always expected me or any of my friends to plan ahead for even more fun next season. Seed, he called it. He probably enjoyed his role as cook as much as any. That long suit of his was the scalding Danish coffee, fist sized biscuits soaked in "red-eye gravy" saddled with center-cut slices of Tennessee, smoked and salt-cured, country ham. Somehow his hot breakfast always seemed to cut the heavy morning fog so the sun could shine through.

The end of our first trapping season brought a bitter lesson. Indirectly, I learned to cope with disappointment, and more. Uncle Dave and I, with much talk on my part, had decided to pool our traps and join forces. With his skill and cunning coupled with my youthful enthusiasm, exuberance, and strong back, I couldn't see how we could make any less than two hundred dollars for the season.

THE BLUE MOUNTAINS SING
of rivers, old men, trails and trout

Ron and Uncle Dave check pelts.
Circa 1949
(Ron Rader family collection)

Muskrat, mink, and raccoon pelt prices were on the rise. Lured by the high prices offered by a Midwest fur buyer's circular, I convinced Uncle Dave that we could get part of their first million from those "St. Louie" buyers. Going against his usual practice of dealing with the local fur buyers he had dealt with for half a century, he consented. When the check came for the furs in March, after six anxious weeks of waiting, it totaled fifty-eight dollars rather than the one hundred sixty I had figured on. The pelts had been graded at least two grades lower than the local bid had been, as is often the case with distant fur buyers. I felt so low I could hardly speak. Now I'd never get a new pair of hip boots and a hunting cap like his.

"Boy," he drawled, "if you could even buy the littlest pleasure we've seen and enjoyed this year, the first bid would start at more than a million dollars. You cain't buy the sight of your first mink of the morning settin' frosty and glowin' goldlike in the first rays of an October mornin' sun. The late afternoon hikes headed home from the trapline with a big hunter's moon fillin' the sky a promisin' another tree crackin' frost. That good smell of crushed walnut hulls all around, and droves of big honkers veein' over us, and callin' mournful like a train way off in the city to the south summers; them thangs caint be bought, and they don't come cheap neither.

"Now I figure a man'll never be able to buy or pay for 'em cause they come from the Almighty for us to enjoy. Way I see it, we're way ahead. We had all them good times and still got money to boot. That fifty eight dollars is just like extry marshmellers on the possum and sweet taters."

The old man never had much education, but he was a Picasso with words. I stood there with my face burning and kinda sweaty, and feeling real guilty at having all that fun, those memories, and still getting the money too. I always had a sneaking suspicion that the old man knew how things would turn out and just wanted to give me an early lesson in the economic reality of an indifferent world.

As I left that day, his parting words rang in my ears: "Eyeball to eyeball, boy, that's the way to deal with any man. That's the reason you can learn so much about a man by playin' poker or huntin' with him. Second best is talking' eyeball to eyeball over a cup of scalding coffee."

He could always sense the mind of a boy. Maybe because he'd always been one himself at heart. He proved it to me during late summer following our disappointing fur selling venture. I had looked longingly for months at the Sears Roebuck catalog admiring the hunting caps. But seven dollars was a lot of money, and fur-selling time wouldn't be here til March. The old man's cap was stained and tattered, yet each time he put it on it looked like a crown —a hunting crown.

After school one autumn afternoon, he was waiting on his porch, its paint peeling from the sag of uneven floor. I, in my usual after school dead run, splashed through the maple leaf reds and yellows in the yard and up the steps. Uncle Dave, with a hooked motion of his right fist filled with dried roots, beckoned me to come sit in the porch swing. I recognized those roots as some of the same ones I'd seen drying in his upstairs attic where he hung our mink and muskrat skins. Oozing fat globules and stretched tightly on pointed yellow pine boards, the pelts always hung wrong-side out near strings of red pepper, old quilts, and these dried roots. Heat from the fireplace and downstairs stove cured and dried most anything stored there.

The old man said matter of factly, "Way this chill has been droppin' on us around sunset, it'll not be long fore the ducks'll fly and coon huntin'll be right. Feller cain't do his best without a good warm huntin' cap—can he boy? "My heart leaped. " Take these ginseng roots and sellum; they'll brang more'n enuff to buy that cap like you'll be needin' in the woods."

I learned that dried ginseng roots were bought in large quantities by pharmaceutical companies for medicinal purposes. Dried, they brought quite a price by the pound. This flowering plant with its cherry red berries grew wild throughout the mountains, but it had all but vanished from the unprotected areas years ago. This was chiefly due to the many ginseng diggers who, like the gold prospector of the old West, spent every waking hour in search of their own brand of growing gold. The plant species had almost followed the fate of the passenger pigeon and the buffalo. Ginseng required many man-hours to discover— one plant at a time, and even longer to dig, wash, and dry its roots. Although it took a lot of dried roots to weigh a pound, the old man always seemed to have a lot.

Uncle Dave's legacy was bound up, with some history thrown in, in a whole lot of conservation, ecology, survival, hunting, fishing, and camping. His early life had not been entirely unglamorous. As a young man he worked as a logger on Little River. He'd ride the company train five to ten miles back in the mountains where he and the lumber crew would live until the end of the month. The Appalachians in the early nineteen hundreds abounded with game. Rainbow trout were caught by the lardcan's full, and turkey and deer were continually hung in the logging camp cooler to cure.

In those early days, the pre-formative ones for the Great Smoky Mountains, young visitors to the mountains often turned out to become distinguished leaders, noted authors, and celebrities. Names like Horace Kepart, Franklin D. Roosevelt, Carlos Campbell, and numerous others frequented the Smokies. Varied in background, they came, but all shared a common interest—a deep love for the outdoors. The dryfly trout rod Uncle Dave treasured came from one such individual. The stranger came to the bunkhouse late one afternoon and talked him into being his guide on a three-day jaunt up near the Appalachian Trail. He wanted to catch the brook or speckled trout in the various headwaters of streams born high near the famous trail. After the fishing trip, Uncle Dave resumed his lumberjacking and promptly forgot the experience.

Several days later at the post office he unwrapped a magnificent handmade bamboo two-piece fly rod—a gift from his fishing companion. Some forty-five years later, there in front of Uncle Dave's fireplace, I got to hold the rod as he oiled the reel. I looked at it closely. The label bore his name and the company's trademark and logo. That casual acquaintance had been a member of a famous outdoor equipment family in New England renowned for their custom made trout rods. Today, they are probably one of the most crafted rod makers in America, the Orvis family. To the old man, the new friend was just another equal, one who shared his same love for this mountain wilderness.

One hazy Indian summer afternoon toward the end of our third summer together, Uncle Dave sent word to my mother that I was to come over after school. Puzzled, I hurried the two miles to his house. We didn't talk much like we usually did. The old man seemed to be preoccupied, on a mission. Instead we hit the woods just behind his barn, and climbed steadily for over two hours out ridges and through deep hollows. The land was strange and unfamiliar, woods I had never explored before. Just before we topped out on the main lead of the mountaintop, we passed through a small natural flat bench covered with small poplars on one end and sheltered by a saucer like lush topography. The other end of the bench was shaped by a small, grassy, spring fed meadow.

A familiar green plant caught my eye. Then another and another, until I was suddenly overwhelmed by the sight of the old man's disclosure—his carpet of ginseng.

This was Flanders's Field, the old man's secret place. His library, his playroom, his den, his safety deposit box—his whole world was suddenly spelled out here. The pinnacle view of the sharp ridges and pastureland far off below was spectacular. I could see why he chose this place to plant his wild ginseng crop. It all became clear. He had carried a hat full of seeds out of his beloved Sugarlands in the Smokies over half a century ago. With each passing season he had reaped the berries, carefully replanted them, until now this wild herb, so carefully cultivated in its natural habitat, covered almost five acres. There must have been several thousand dollars' worth of ginseng in this one spot. There were now two people who always seemed to know the answer to everything that mattered—my dad and now, Uncle Dave.

I was stunned. He was revealing his secret of a lifetime to me. I felt the same way I did once when one of the biggest, reddest, rare fox squirrels I had ever seen ran from tree to tree right in front of me. I couldn't shoot. The woods and this day were near perfect. It was so still, beautiful, and peaceful. To me it seemed like I'd be shooting a gun in church. I sat for more than an hour and watched the red blur of fox squirrel play as two others joined the fun. Finally, as dusk sneaked in, I slipped quietly from the woods.

Now neither of us spoke. I didn't because I didn't know what to say, and he because he didn't have to.

Uncle Dave turned on his heel and set a blistering pace that almost left me behind. Following, I ran through the brush sliding and falling in the slick leaves. Even on the steep slopes of the woods, he was as fast as a graying old fox. We were back home in almost an hour. The only time I'd seen the old man move faster was probably a few summers back. Near his former general store in Elkmont that perched over the stream, we waded side by side upriver in Little River's rocky rapids for trout. The old man was waderless as was I. His work brogans moved uneasily over the rocky bottom in the thigh deep water. He grabbed a low over hanging alder branch to steady himself. Unfortunately, the hornets in the big nest at the limb's end did not want company. Almost walking on water with the agility of a forty year old, he outran me and leaped to the safety of the grass covered bank. His seventies never showed. He got stung only once due to his quickness that got him out of range of the fiery tempered, angry hornets.

I knew something was wrong later the next week when I ran across the wooden bridge that linked his yard with the dust of September pasture. Doc Sam's, also the town's volunteer fire chief, red station wagon was empty and parked in the yard, its siren and red lights muted and resting.

Doc stood in the front yard with one foot on the porch instructing Uncle

THE BLUE MOUNTAINS SING
of rivers, old men, trails and trout

Dave's missus who sat in the off center wooden swing.

As I hit the first wooden step — " Son, he's dying," were his first words. "Never could get him to come in for surgery cause he didn't feel like he'd come out of it. Not much anybody can do. He's seventy-eight and lived a good full life. God knows I'll never live that long. It's just his time."

I couldn't go in. I turned and ran blindly through the brush. When I stopped running, I was in the field of ginseng, his Flanders Field.

It was late in the afternoon of the next day when the ambulance came to pick up his body. From the ginseng patch, as I rolled from my back onto my stomach, I could see it way off down below where the late afternoon sun made the whole pasture and meadows glow in a hazy , burnt orange . Like a big black eraser , the hearse left a trail of smoky tan dust . It hung like talcum in the afternoon rays. It drifted slowly for what seemed like a long time. I kept hoping the ambulance would turn around and start back, that Doc had made a mistake. But it never did.

The smell of crushed ginseng berries hung heavy in the air. I buried my face in my thirteen ounce, tan duck, guaranteed-to-turn-rain hunting cap with the red plaid lining. Suddenly and painfully, I grew older.

A few trout seasons ago, Uncle left a legacy. Those memories of a little southern, Mayberry like village in the foothills of the Smokies, an old clapboard house with walnut trees, an orchard, a creek, and those fine fall days were special. Those years we shared shaped the finest legacy a man can leave. Now that I have an understanding, loving wife, three grown married sons, who love to hunt and fish with me, and three beautiful daughters-in-law who have given us six grandchildren — all of whom adore me—I realize just how strongly that treasure trove of memories has affected my values and life style. The old man's gift was unique and personal — a treasure of virtues.

Somehow such a magnificent legacy never dies. Even now, sixty years later, on any cold, crisp October night with a full moon, when I see a bobbing lantern light blinking high in the Smokies, and hear the bugling of a trailing hound drift down to the valley, I like to think it's the old man up there grinning over another October hunt. And just maybe, he's wondering if I'm still keeping the faith. Who knows, maybe your own story is up there alongside him.

Reflections
Or
"Even fried baloney sandwiches don't taste the same anymore!"

I've shared a lifetime of sketches from my forties and fifties childhood. Those cumulative sixty plus years, understandably, make one ponder the "then" and the "now." The results of our tradeoffs throughout our mountains are worth pondering. Are we better off with our progress? Our economy and quality of life has certainly risen, but at what cost? What have we lost that can never be recovered? If the green disappears from our mountains, what then? Is there an optimum balance in our growth and surroundings? Who should be held accountable to manage, protect, and value it? Are we really good stewards of it all?

Reflections addresses those tradeoffs. In reflecting, I have written fiction, essays, and included other forms of written admonishments and praises to express my personal sentiments about our future. In addition, I have included commentaries, quotes, and admonishments from likeminded and respected ecologists and conservationists. Their words are prophetic and ring true.

The "Commentary on Modern Values" that begins this section will set the tone for Part II.

I hope you too will ponder these prophetic words from the past, and consider what your role, as a steward should be. The future of our mountains and our quality of life depend on it—and on you.

A Commentary on Modern Values

I have discovered many axioms and truths in my attempt to write this book. Many of them seem biblical and prophetic. Several respected naturalists, conservationists, and ecologists seem like prophets as their observations evolve into exhortations and admonishments. Many of their awareness alarms are directed toward our lack of sensitivity toward the nature that surrounds us. From the 1700s to the present day, men with our wilderness concerns at their forefront have cautioned us. I recently discovered Wendell Berry, a present day conservationist, and I view him with great esteem, yet none impacted me like Aldo Leopold.

His common sense views, professional research, and love for nature twanged my heartstrings. Born in 1887, he began a career with the U.S. Forest Service in 1909. The University of Wisconsin created a chair of game management in 1933. In the late 1940s, he wrote *A Sand County Almanac* and died fighting a grass fire on a neighbor's farm in 1949.

His words speak so directly to our own wilderness and area issues today here in the Smoky Mountains that I felt compelled to share some of his comments with you. As a result, I quoted and paraphrased brief portions of the Foreword in his *Sand County Almanac*. I hope that his words give you pause, cause you to reflect, and inspire you to act.

"Some people can live without wilderness and wild things, or at the very least are indifferent to them and can take or leave them. And a minority of others cannot. They value this natural wildness as much as the very air they breathe. Like rivers and wildlife, the wilderness was taken for granted until progress began to slowly eradicate them. Now in our ever increasing race to lift our standard of living even higher, we've created a seemingly insurmountable dilemma. And the question, is our quest for more comfort worth its cost in things wild, natural, and free? For those of the minority, the opportunity to see a wild duck or a stealthy mink is more important than a vacuum cleaner. The chance to find a meadow of rare flowers is a right and is as important as freedom to worship.

"These things of the wild had little human value until the industrial revolution promised us three meals a day. It all comes down to a question of balance between nature and development. The dilemma continues as we, the minority, see little gain in natural balance. Instead, we see the law of diminishing returns as progress rapidly descends. Seemingly, those in opposition, do not."

While conservation has made some strides in recent decades, it "likely will not succeed with any encouraging rate. Why, because it is incompatible with our Abrahamic concept of land. We regard land as a commodity belonging to us." We bought it; therefore, we own it. We feel we can use it for any purpose because it is ours. "When we see land as a part of a community to which we all belong, we may begin to use it with love and respect." We then value it in a holistic way. There is no other way for land to survive mechanized man. We are unable to reap the esthetic harvest it is capable of giving to our culture.

"Ecology's basic concept says that land is a community; to say that it is one to be loved and respected is ethics driven. We have long known the fact that land yields a cultural harvest, an important segment of our heritage. But for a long time now, this fact seems forgotten.

"Certainly, my view of our land and its people is an individual one, a very personal one. It is distorted by personal prejudices, blurred by my life experiences, and touched occasionally by personal bias. But wherever the truth may lie, one thing is crystal clear. Our bigger-better-more-faster society is like a self-consuming being, feeding on itself. It seems so obsessed with its economic health that it has lost its ability to remain healthy. The whole world is so greedy for more bathtubs that it has lost the stability necessary to build them, or even to turn off the tap.

"Nothing could be more exemplary at this juncture in time than a little healthy contempt for this plethora of material blessings. Perhaps a meaningful shift in our values could be achieved by the reappraisal of all things unnatural, tame, and confined in terms of all things wild, natural, and free."

—Aldo Leopold, *A Sand County Almanac, (1949)*

THE BLUE MOUNTAINS SING
of rivers, old men, trails and trout

There are no unsacred places
there are only sacred places
and desecrated places

—Wendell Berry, *The Long Legged House*

In the city , people of different ranks stand scowling and apart;
But when they go to hunt ,to fish, or any other sport
Or occupation in the fields, they are fellows.
Nature thus makes brotherhood;
And if all mankind would study nature,
all mankind would be brothers.

—E.J.Lewis, M.D., *Hints to Sportsmen, 1851*

If a man walks in the woods for love of them half of each day, he is in danger of being regarded as a loafer. But if he spends his days as a speculator, shearing off those woods and making the earth bald before her time, he is deemed industrious and enterprising.—-Henry D Thoreau

CHAPTER FIVE

The Splendor of Solitude

Our Trees: Their Seasons and Their Many Faces

Trees are the very lifeblood of our mountains. Watch the trees carefully and you'll discover the first clues to most any upcoming change in the mountains . Whether it's seasonal, barometric, weather, environmental, or nature based, the signs will usually begin in our trees.

Early Fall

Fall always sneaks in unnoticed sometime in late August. Its rebirth is disguised in hot, sun baked dryness and those first hints of summer's end. Dog days wane and the forest floor crunches. Step into any nearby woodland. You'll feel it rather than see it. Summer's song-bird calls, and chatter, scurrying wildlife, and movement of all things outdoors, slithering, crawling, and flying have almost disappeared. Now, the woods stand still in a strange pregnant silence. They exude an aura that feels overpowering, unnerving, and unfathomable. Unlike summer, the woods now hide secrets, cloak mystery, and offer a mystique not there at midsummer. Only a few weeks earlier these same woods were teeming, alive, and full of nature's dynamic. This forest stillness is the first thing you notice. Any sound, however slight, now seems intrusive and loud.

A faint rustle, magnified in the vacuum, belongs to a squirrel worrying the limbs of an American Beech tree. It hangs upside down chewing beechnuts. Perched tip top like a family's favorite Christmas tree angel , the grey squirrel's mate sprinkles pinecone shards from the peak of a scraggly, lodge pole Virginia pine. Once the cone resembles a well eaten apple core, the squirrel deftly tosses one after another to splash into last year's fluffy leaves below.

Only the glaring, off key, discordant caws of busy-body crows are dominant now. These self-appointed guardian sentinels of all woodlands annoyingly announce you as an off-limits intrusion. Flying from treetop to treetop just overhead, they repeatedly sound their endless, incessant, grating alarm. Vocally, like some sort of black feathered magic markers, they trace your path below. Following overhead, they seem to mark your every step with a grating, raspy caw exchange, a vocal milestone sound inscribed on their noisy flight map.

If you are above three thousand feet in the mountains, there is another bird that can be even noisier. I can only imagine the din if crows were replaced by ravens. However, ravens are seldom seen and tend to avoid humans. To paraphrase Horace Kepart's descriptions of the raven: " Shy of man, intelligent, elusive, hermitlike, called by some a thief, butcher, and pest. It is part mockingbird, sagacious, a mimic with a vocal range some say is unmatched, and it can certainly make the most sounds."

It has been said by old timers and Kephart that it can " cluck, caw, croak, chuckle, squall, plead, bark, heckle, cajole, file a saw, whet a scythe, mimic small birds, pop a cork all with its voice. Yet the raven probably perches on the throne as the master entertainer of the Smokies."

Kepart suggested that Noah learned early on that there would be no peace aboard such a cramped floating craft as the ark, given the number and variety of wild things aboard and given the fact the raven was such a talkative and inquisitive fowl. The two may have clashed and Noah decided to rid himself of this pest and liberated him from the Ark at first opportunity, making the bird the first to ever be banished from the Ark. And some say the Raven, to this day, has remained shy of man ever since the flood.

As September slips in, the woods appear to doze restfully as if in an expectant wait. Even to the automobile driver at roadside, summer's end is evident. The fading transition is signaled first in the trees at roadside. Dusty leaves hang silent, unmoving ,and still. They seem sun faded, lack luster, and maybe tired, not unlike the grimy, sweat dried faces of baseball players in their final inning of their last game at season's end.

The pastures at roadside can't hide the hint of fall. The last cut of hay lies flat and grounded. Its familiar fragrance fills the air. This smell is different from that of summer hay. This last of summer hay fills the air with heavy, sugary sweetness. Sumac, sassafras, along with many wild flowers, and herbs have crept into the field since midsummer, especially at the edges. Mowed, crushed and mingled with the new mown hay, this wild mix adds a peppery, spicy overtone to the hay's fragrant sweetness. This spicy fragrance of fall is distinct, foretelling, and nostalgic.

Leave the pasture and walk deeper in the woods and the silence is really

The Splendor of Solitude

unnerving. The sole song of an afternoon katydid breaks the silence. Singing its raspy song—a flat, sizzling, whirring, buzz—its pitch rising and falling in a continuous rondo. This is a conspicuous and a lone signal that fall is near.

Unless you ventured into these woods in mid-July or early August, you'd never have noticed that this contented woodland silence has gradually deeped. It has fled the cacophony of spring and midsummer.

Now, at center stage, and from here on, the face of the woodland will be orchestrated and directed by the trees not the wildlife. The symphony of the summer woodland is finally at rest. Lounging like a really big family after Sunday mid-day meal at Grandma's house, the woods doze in restful contentment, proud prolific parents savoring their hard work of summer. The results of their summer's production sags from their branches. For these few weeks, their own third quarter, they languish and celebrate their value in nature's cycle. The silence of the woods deepens.

Until Esau explained this somber silence of the woods and made its value come alive, I guess I'd never even thought about it. I did know it was there and that I enjoyed the solitude. On one particular day before he left us, he must have decided that this was the day that Luke and I needed the silence lesson— appreciation, he called it. You'll remember him as our woodsmaster and another in our string of mentors. On this day, he decided to elevate our knowledge. I guess what triggered it was the day before. The three of us had a give and take, a casual conversation and some questions remained. They wafted in the air, unanswered and unanswerable.

"Let's walk and learn something new today," Esau said. He had just walked up and offered us a hike. We had no answers to the why or the where, or even the how far and the how long. We walked for maybe an hour just under the ridgeline of several ridges. We gained altitude with each stride. The ridges became deeper woods on mountainsides. Orienting ourselves at the first rest stop in deep woods, Luke and I realized we had just crossed the peak of one mountain and were starting up another one much higher. We exchanged puzzled glances.

Esau, resting on the ground, said, "Where do you find silence, real silence?"

Luke said, "Uh, in the library, in a closet, or when you stick cotton or your fingers in your ear?"

I said, "The church sanctuary at midweek when nobody is around, maybe your bedroom at midnight, and inside your closet."

Esau said, "Is it perfect silence —perfect solitude? Or can you hear cars outside, planes overhead, or faint conversation somewhere in the distance?"

THE BLUE MOUNTAINS SING
of rivers, old men, trails and trout

"Well, yeah," we both said, "but that..."

He interrupted, "That's not silence, solitude maybe, but not pure silence."

"Well where is pure silence?" Luke asked.

Esau grinned, "I'm going to show you."

"We're deep in the mountains now. It's quiet. Is it noise free? Is there a natural silence? What do you hear?"

I said, "I hear a tractor on somebody's farm, kids laughing in a yard someplace, a dog barking over that way, and just barely that jet up there real high ahead of its trail."

Luke, "Yeah, I hear all that too. How come it sounds so clear the higher we get?"

Esau said, "It's sort of like a lake or large body of water. Sound carries a long distance. People would be shocked if they realized folks quite a distance away could hear most every word they spoke. I can't exactly explain what causes it, but the elevation, wind direction, humidity, and probably other things affect how sound carries. Sound is here; let's go find where it's not."

Two hours and two mountains later, we stood in a deep hollow between two large mountains. The small valley contained a grassy meadow, a few trees, and large grey boulders strung out here and there. A good-sized creek split the meadows middle. It was surprisingly wide and its water surprisingly swift and deep. The water was invisible until a breeze revealed its surface. I had never seen water so clear or, later, feel so cold.

Esau said, "Four hollers converge at the head of this little valley about a mile and a half on up. Each one has a strong spring and a full branch most of the time. That spring over there at the base of that beech tree is the fifth spring, and it'll hurt your teeth. Get you a sip and drink the dew of a pure mountain. Think how cold this would be in January instead of Indian summer."

"What is this place?" Luke asked.

Esau said, " See those tree stumps and those big logs scattered up through there? For some reason they never rotted like most downed wood does. They're mainly beech, hickory, and oaks. That big one there is a chestnut. God only knows why they're down and how long they've been there. The only thing I can figure is water along with freezes and thaws finally emptied their insides. I know one thing-- whatever did it did a good job. They are all perfectly hollow logs with bark still on. You can climb through every one of 'em just like a playground. The same thing happened to those rock overhangs over there. As you walk up through there, ever so often there are big overhangs of rock stickin out of that slope. Several have a little shallow cave underneath. They're not really caves but more like deep bowls stood on their edge, and they only go back about fifty feet in the slope. When you go in one, there's plenty of light, but most of 'em are roomy and deep enough for cover. I figured water has rolled down that slope, split at that upper side and then curled around to wash out the dirt under the overhang."

"It's amazing what water and ice can do over time," Luke said. " I've never seen anything like this."

"Me neither," I said.

"Do you hear any sound that's not a part of nature?" Esau asked. We both shook our heads, afraid to speak and break such a special aura.

"Pick a log and crawl in. They're all slicker'n a minner's belly inside. When you get there, start listening as you go in. Listen hard as you slide deeper in the log. Lie there and listen. Then slide a few feet further and listen for a while. Keep it up til you get to the middle of the log. Give the log time to sing. Then come out.

About forty- five minutes later Esau said, "Come on out."
We stood shoulder to shoulder in front of him.

"Let's lie down in this grass, and you tell me what you heard."

I said, "I know that creek over there has noise, but it's faint sorta evenlike. When I got half way in there, I seemed to hear a low mournful moan like a fiddle rasping real low. I crawled deeper, and it turned into a little higher pitch, maybe like somebody sliding their finger roughlike on a guitar string. It was a kind of wail, maybe something you'd hear from a bird or animal in the woods. I don't know music, so I can't tell ye the chord or note, but it seemed happy. At least it gave me a happy feeling. The deeper I went the more the sound seesawed. They were real slow like in higher notes, like you might hear when the Irish do a jig, but it was slow, and back and forth, like somebody practicing. The whole sound was real faint, and I wondered if I was really hearing some kind of music. Anyway, I don't know what to think."

Luke blurted, "I heard the same thing, but I don't know if my sound was the same."

Esau said, "Now go spend time inside those two overhangs for a while. Be still and act like a deer is in sight and listen."

An hour later, the three of us sat in the grass, cross-legged and in a circle, pondering the strange sounds within the logs and the overhangs.

"It's like the mountain has a soul and is groaning in low musical sounds. The sounds of the cave were sorta the same but not quite like the log. It was a different type of moaning wail, but it still sounded like a violin. It groaned tones sorta like an Indian flute, and the sound ebbed and flowed like a type of music, "Luke's excitement showed.

I said, "Yeah, mine was different like that too. Makes you wonder what each log sounds like and what each little rock outcropping sounds like. I wonder if each one's different."

"You boys are young and your hearing is good. I heard the woods music too when I was younger. It takes real good hearing to hear those sounds. Someday in the future they'll invent somethin' so you can hear those sounds better, and you'll be able to turn up their volume just like on a radio. The main thing is that you know the mountains sing and silence is not quiet but alive with sound.

"The silence of the woods offers us this gift, and we need to enjoy it; learn to stop and listen to what nature is telling you, be grateful for what she is willing to give up on any given day, cause it'll never be the same.

"Now that sound you heard, well, that's just the beginning of a leap of faith. I don't believe that groaning is just sound, it has a purpose, and it's real. My granddad was a spiritual man. Years ago, he told me about those groans. We were in a place just like this. There were logs and outcrops pretty much like these. Nothin' much changes in the woods. Through the years, I've heard those same groans in other spots here in the mountains."

"What'd your granddad say it was?" Luke asked. His eyes widened a bit fearful.

"My granddad said, 'Son, the bible explains it. You read it when you can, but I'm gonna tell you the short version now.'

Esau began, "When we hear groans we usually think it means a person is plumb wore out or hurt. We never think we're listening to something beautiful or sure not somethin' full of hope. The book of Romans tells us that it's hope. We hear three groans in verses eighteen to thirty: The groans of creation, the groans of God's people, and the groans of the Holy Spirit. I think that sound you heard in that log is the sound of God groaning. Maybe he's still making something, or maybe he's moaning because of all the suffering of his people. Or maybe he's groaning because something really good is coming. See, I believe God's still creatin'. God cares about us, knows when we are hurtin', God's excited about tomorrow. We're just gettin' a hint of what it all might mean.

"One thing I know for sure. Right here, we're in a woods full of God's presence. And, this place is special; the sound is real. So maybe the other stuff is true, too. Hope surrounds us all the time, and we're all groanin' in anticipation. Even Creation is crainin' its neck waiting on us, the sons of God, to be completed—to be new creations. The Creation is waitin' for church to be the church and for you and me to be the us that He always planned. I believe that our salvation that everbody talks about is, you know, escapin' this world. That's not the purpose. The purpose is that the world and we might be healed.

"We think we ought to get to live groan-free lives, but we groan because we have the Spirit. The Spirit gives us a taste of the future, the new creation, the first fruits. We long for the full harvest. So we live in the wilderness with only a taste of the Promised Land, but our suffering and our groans are signs of hope.

"All our life, we experience weakness and suffering. Verses twenty-two and twenty-three tell us that both creation and we yearn for something more, yet we don't know what to pray for. At least I don't. Why, we just don't know how to help God advance his purposes. We realize we're not all- powerful like He is. In fact, we probably pray for God to get somethin' out of our lives that God really intends to use maybe as a stepping-stone to reach his purposes.

"So the Spirit helps us in our sorry but hopeful and ignorant state. He 'intercedes for us with groanings too deep for words.' The Spirit searches our hearts. We don't even know what's there down deep. But, the Spirit finds the gold there. The Spirit really knows God's will, and he represents us in a way that we can't. The Spirit melds our pain and our hope with the purposes of God. So because of our ignorance, our prayers may not be on target, but the Spirit can hit the bull's-eye.

"So Creation groans, and we groan. We worry. We wonder if he hears. All the while, God is searchin' our hearts in order to groan with us. The Holy Spirit, all along knowin' our pain, adds his own harmony to the chorus of pain and hope. From inside us, God is groaning to God. So the Spirit expresses God's agony and love for a wounded world.

"To our ears, the groans sound like groans. So we still gotta' remind ourselves that the Maestro isn't finished yet. We gotta wait for the new Creation. God takes the groaning of creation, the groaning of His people, and the groaning of his spirit, and He creates a new world. We may suffer and groan, but because of Romans 8, we do it with patience and eagerness. You know why? Because we know God is working out His purpose for us, and our world, and our place in it.

"So we may bow in worship, but we know we can't stay here. We already have His divine marchin' orders and the human dream he gave us. That thing God calls us to and motivates us to do. He gives us the Holy Spirit to empower us to bring his justice, peace, and love to the world. The kingdom of God is right smack dab here among us. God puts his church right in the middle of his creation as a reminder of what's comin'.

"Now listen to what I say. This is important. In some way, the future is now.

THE BLUE MOUNTAINS SING
of rivers, old men, trails and trout

What we do in this world now changes the new world. Now, maybe some folks would say *affects* or *influences*, I don't care, as long as you understand that, our actions today make a difference in the new world, the new Creation. This means that whatever God is calling you to do, well that's somethin' nobody else can do. We are the wilderness people of God, sufferin' and groanin', prayin' and laborin' on the road to the Promised Land, knowing that all the while God is accomplishing his beautiful purpose. We're a family so we join and work together "So listen real good to the sounds in these woods, our wilderness is right here. Hear the song. Creation groans. We groan. The Spirit groans. We're all groaning to give birth to the new world. We are all singin' together, and the great Maestro is directin'. All those voices harmonize to sing the song of the new world."

"And, remember this: If you listen carefully to Romans 8, you can hear the song. If you can hear it, you can tune your life to it. I pray that you boys hear the song and join the chorus so that the world may know that the new world is coming."

I knew right then this was a place where I needed to pay attention. We both knew. This was a place filled with pristine stillness and natural quietness. I knew this was a special place full of sounds maybe never discovered until now, many already forgotten, and I sensed it was a place that could be instantly changed forever.

Esau said, "Let's sit down. That flat rock oughta make a good table, and we can eat a bite."

"Yeah, but we didn't bring any..." Esau interrupted Luke.

"I've got all we need, and there's spring water right over there."

Esau pulled a cloth bag from his trapper's pack basket. He unfolded what looked like white linen cloth from around a large, perfect wedge of Wisconsin cheddar. He handed each of us a large, lime green apple.

He sliced lunch sized cheese slices for each of us. He said, "These apples are a little tart, but I really like my apples slightly sour. Oh, here, I almost forgot these," as he pulled some sort of crackers from another linen bag. His next move was out of character.

He said, "Guess we better give thanks for all this," and dropped his chin to his chest. We exchanged glances and bowed our heads.

"Lord, you bless us and humble us here today with all this. Fill us with your spirit so that we may leave here and speak in living echoes of your tone."

Esau stopped. He looked into the woods with an absent gaze then said, "The woods always quench that thirst in my soul. Every time I leave here, I am renewed in spirit. Somehow I leave these woods whole, fixed."

The Splendor of Solitude

We sat, slowly chewed our simple dinner and listened and pondered. Finally, Esau started to talk about woods, solitude, sound, and what it all meant.

"The more you listen in this stillness right here, the more you'll not like those back home sounds. I know we make those for a reason, but modern living here in 1949 comes with a price. Nature has always had more sense than any human has ever had or will have. If we listened to actually hear more, our life would be much more livable. Before you leave here today, drink in every drop of the natural sounds that make this silence. They compose a symphony. Notice I said symphony. That's what it is. You have to stop, sit, and become part of it before it'll share its music with you."

He made it sound so good. I looked at the icy water in the spring, and gazed at the pure rush of the creek water headed somewhere down toward a noisy world. Chickadees twittered and flittered from delicate shrub tips. A red squirrel, stuck to a hickory's bark, its rear pointing skyward, looked and sniffed in our direction, chattered, and then went back to his nut search. Rainwater left from an earlier squall still dripped from a few trees at the edge of the meadow. From a basswood tree directly behind us, unusually large water drops made large splats on the neighboring leaf below it. Dragonflies hummed and darted around the meadow near the water, several butterflies swarmed in one spot near a flowering shrub, a wood duck whistled far off in the timber, and the winged whoosh of another duck told me she'd changed her mind about landing. Honeybees worked feverishly on all the tiny wildflower blossoms. Blueberries and wild strawberries looked about ripe on the slope facing us. Blackberries bloomed but seemed a little behind the other wild fruit. Doves cooed, their mating calls sprinkled throughout the woods and announced that they mated longer than most other birds.

A small titmouse bird kept flitting closer as if to strike up a friendship. A humming bird had done the same for over an hour. With lightning speed, it zoomed about three feet from us. In darting hovers, it moved within inches of our faces. Satisfied with each inspection, it sped away to some sort of red flowers near the water that looked like Indian paintbrush flowers. After only a few feeding seconds, the humming bird retired to the delicate branch tip of a river birch, rested, and peered in every direction. Then, after a ninety second rest, it zoomed back to us to repeat its endless inspection flight route.

Esau broke our silence. "There'll be fewer places where you can get away from humans and modern life. Anybody can enjoy this opera of natural sound if they know how to find it and will actually listen. The new Park will help preserve some of it. That will help. Still, if we don't look out for the pitfalls of progress, places like this will disappear. Mechanical sound will drive out natural sound. God added hearing to our senses so we could learn about the world and so we could get information from places where our sight can't reach. Don't get me wrong, I'm not against humans and modern living or progress. I like the luxury and convenience as well as anybody. I'm worried about how many folks are willing to maintain a balance of the modern and the natural worlds.

"If we'd been here at dawn just before the sun came up, you'd have heard one of the sweetest choruses known to man. It's the same music you can hear out your bedroom window, but it's much shorter and may soon disappear. The rush hour, lawnmowers, and the business of the day's routine continually shrink their chorus. The birds everywhere begin their song chorus at dawn; it has a purpose in nature, or so the Indians believed. Anthropologists and ornithologists call this chorus at dawn one of earth's oldest and sweetest songs. Bird experts say that this early morning symphony is composed of mating calls, calls to protect their mates, and to mark their territory. In a noise free time years back, birds and animals were at ease in the forest because they could decipher, prosper, and survive on what they heard. Now, you and I have lost that ability. In fact, animals and birds flee from noise that disrupts their natural cycle and anything that lessens their ability to read their surroundings. Now I've used only birds as an example, but the principle applies to anything wild – flora or fauna.

"Well, I'll stop. I brought you up here so you'd know about such a place such as this. I wanted you to know about natural relationships—ours with the life around us. You are the future. We have outside noise here now. About two hundred families live in the Pigeon Forge area year round, and about half a million people come to our mountains each year in the summer. We've already started to whittle away at our solitude and quietness in our mountains. There's gonna be some hard decisions to make in the years to come. Those choices will be yours. What will you be willing to trade for this right here? The things that you're getting in your barter will look attractive and appealing. You'll think you really need them. They'll be things that are modern, that make money, and that make life more comfortable. They'll be bigger, better, and hold much promise for a better life.

"What you'll have to decide is: Is bigger going to be better, is more of the same what you want, and how can you balance the new with the natural? How much of this are you willing to give for whatever it is you think need or that you'll gain?

"God created this earth and these mountains and told us he expected us to be good stewards of all of it. Later in life, when you ponder your decisions, ask yourself, 'Will the result of my decision make me a faithful custodian of these gifts? Am I extending faithful custodial care toward my spiritual brothers and sisters with the result of my decision?

"A wise man once said, 'If it doesn't feel right, you probably shouldn't do it. ' "
Luke said, "I'm not sure I understand everything you're talking about."
"I think I get parts of it," I said, "but I'm not sure about a lot of it ."
"You will," Esau said. " You will. Let's go."

October

By October, fall is the real Bob Steele. It begins in many ways. The stars align, the solstice, and other astronomical changes occur. The almanac, August ground fogs counted, and the caterpillar's coat assessed, are signs that are subtotaled. All point to upcoming seasonal changes and a caution about winter waiting in the wings. In unison, the gaze of all trees turns skyward, upward, and expectant. Just on time, October's sun begins its fall journey. Its shallowing arc shortens the days, and it partners up with the trees for their final act.

Like the cool down of the runner ending a hard race, the woods, in comfortable transition, relax as they prepare to enjoy less sun and allow nature to color their garments. To insure a magnificent performance, leaves need stress of high summer heat, spring and summer low average rainfall, coupled with dry weather, and followed by some cool autumn nights. Expectantly, they wait patiently in the rehearsal wings, soon to fill center stage. They'll reappear dressed in unmatched finery. In clothing woven and drenched in never- before- revealed exact color shades , they will be stitched to the horizon.

The woods become an unmoving parade. They dazzle, surprise, and overwhelm even the most jaded observer. Their explosive color tapestry gradually oozes like a creeping breeze. The season unrolls this carpet of color like wind across a grain filled prairie. This kaleidoscope of color is the only parade where the entertainment is unmoving and the people parade past.

For a brief few days, a time far too short, these unique entertainers, measured in human terms, visually change the world around them. They evoke a certain welcome spirit of the heart in the observer. The scriptures speak of the much sought after fruit of the spirit. Maybe fall's trees create a welcome spirit of the heart in all of us. People say that fall makes them sentimental. Maybe fall is nature's sermon, its message a reminder to celebrate our own heritage of faithfulness.

While Christmas, for ages, has elevated our spirits and fueled our optimism with "peace on earth and good will to all," just maybe our woods of fall lift our hope and spirit in an even more natural and tangible way. Fall's color season is natural, gradual, free, and makes no demands. It blankets us in a magnificently colored comforter. It is central to a season that reminds us to reflect on who we are.

For years, I've promised myself that one day I'd plant each tree that best depicted our fall colors. I'd then have the ideal fall color mosaic right outside in our yard. Although I've yet to complete my tree bucket list, my favorites and most representative of the Smokies are: Sugar maple's yellow to orange, silver maple's yellow to brown, red maple's red to purple, oak's bright reds, sweet gum's purple, yellow, and red, and the patchwork uniqueness of the gingko, sumac, and persimmon. The River Birch, Hickory, Poplar, and the American Beech are my favorites.

From Art Stupka's notes to the latest Park information, tree description and data are very definitive. In all, some one hundred species of our Appalachian Mountain's native trees are mostly deciduous. Each adds a unique color shade to our Appalachian fall palette.

Our neighbors, the South Carolina low county folks, brag of their comfort food and rightfully so. Certainly, folks in The Great Smoky Mountains own bragging rights too— our comfort views —our days of fall.

Late Fall

Winter's icy winds don't end our fall delights. Some trees, like the evergreens, entertain us even through winter into spring. Once again, the American beech and the oak tree leaves have starring roles. Their leaves don't fall until forced off by spring's buds. These tree species are special. They are winter reminders that the best is yet to come. My favorite, the American beech, never fails to bring joy to my heart as I drive near woods. November's woods are often bleak, dark gray, misty countryside woods. The American beech brightens November and beyond . Its fall golden leaves remain as eggshell white. The bleak woods are dappled encouragingly by the papyrus white pattern of beech trees. This unique egg shell white pops through the darkness grabbing one's gaze even on the dreariest of days.

Less evident than the beech are our several oak species. Less winter spectacular and colorful, they pass to a winter brown and distinguish themselves when their leaves hang on until spring. Their winter sounds are their second contribution. A stiff winter breeze sets off an oak leaf rhapsody in an otherwise silent winter vacuum. Like late summer corn stalks, winter wind plays a raspy, fluttering rhapsody that joins woodland harmonics. This coarse, winter wind oak solo stands alone and apart in the winter woods silence. Absent are most other bird and wildlife sounds. Occasionally, the

The Splendor of Solitude

sound of a deer tip toeing in dry leaves will punctuate this song of the oak.

Late fall woods have a spirit all their own. October color has ripened . This later masterpiece is one devoid of descriptive words. Freezing winds , deep morning frosts, bitingly clear late afternoons, and last rays of sun touch every human sense.

The wilderness in these moments can be surreal and brief. It is a strange occurance you never quite understand. You can only observe it. My friends and I have never resolved this strange and unexplained transition of nature's color and silence. In tandem with those colors and the secretive sounds that some attribute to the little people are the visual miracles the woods can spawn.

I distinctly remember one fall day in November. it was that kind of weather that can be bright , sunny, and crisp one hour and be dark, gloomy, rainy, and windy the next. This day was one of those Jekyll –Hyde days. I had walked to my deer stand in a grove of poplar and hickory trees. The morning was cold, heavily frosted, and the leaves crunched icily. We were promised a bright, sunny, and clear day with a slight warming sun in the forties, maybe the fifties. The predictors were accurate until about early noon. In one hour the wind came up carrying a promise of a weather front change coupled with rain. I was surrounded by swaying trees, above and below my stand, filled with golden yellow leaves. The leaves were tenaciously hanging on until sap dropping winter weather arrived.

My world had gone from bright and sunny to gloom, dismal gray with a midday darkness that only a swamp in late afternoon could bring. I was enveloped in light rain, heavy mist, slight ground fog arising from the forest floor and the kind of dark gloom that crushes your optimism. I couldn't believe the weather change or the transition to dismal that it brought to everything around me. After two hours of this weather downer, I was ready to climb down from my stand and hike back to camp to warm and thaw.

Suddenly, the clouds overhead, for some unexplained reason, had a hole punched in them and the bright sunlight from midmorning barreled into this three hundred fifty acres of wet and misty swamp growth. The entire area as far as I could see was first bright gold. Then huge trees, undergrowth, everything living and dead took on a bright, fluorescent, highlighter, forsythia bush yellow. I was enveloped in color matched only in Alice in Wonderland and the Wizard of Oz minus the characters.

I was totally enveloped in a cheerful yellow. My skin , my camouflage, my metal stand, the fog, mist, leaves, tree trunks, and forest floor were literally bright yellow. The disappearance of dark gloom and the sudden, intense beaming of the sun's brightness was shocking. Nature bathed us all in bright yellow. I barely breathed for some thirty- five minutes, afraid it would disappear. My first thought was grab the camera from my pack and get the picture. I quickly decided not to try to capture this yellow world but to enjoy it while it lasted. So I sat and savored each second. I knew this was one of a kind; this nature's epiphany would be short lived. I carefully studied every leaf, watched every yellow movement around me. I luxuriated in the moment, letting my total being osmose the beauty of something I knew to be fleeting. All too soon, the sun disappeared and the dismal gloom of darkness and mist returned. My world seemed even darker, a more dismal grey day of blackness in the swamp, yet my optimism and uplifted outlook remained. If anything, I was encouraged and elated.

This unique deep woods event was a one of a kind epiphany. One that I would talk about more than the deer that got away. It was a nature reminder. Its lesson is one that airline pilots learn quickly and often speak of. They know better than any of us. No matter how bad and dismal things are on the ground , you need only to rise above the gloom of bad weather through the clouds to find the bright sun and white billowy clouds, their grey dark anger gone and each framed by clear blue sky. Above our dark clouds, we are reminded that all is well, constant, even eternal in nature's world — everything else is temporary, changing, and soon passing. . . *and this too shall pass.*

True Winter

Deep winter calls and the trees take on their new face as guardians against the cold. Stoic in the sleet and wind blasted mountain peaks and constantly battling winter harshness and stress, our giant hemlocks, spruces, and conifers are still evergreen. Below this green line, further down our mountains' side live the hardwood trees. With a few exceptions, the rest of these deciduous trees are now bare. The summer green and fall tapestry are stripped by winter. Their leaves grow the forest floor, a nurture bed for spring growth.

Our woods are filled with skeletal figures like valleys of dry bones, standing instead of lying. Stripped and bare except for limbs and bark, they stand alone in varying shades of leaden grey, brown, and beige. Their lifeblood drops, pausing their energy; they wait for spring. Now all they have is shape. They display it well.

In some ways, trees are more elegant in their winter splendor. Like pen and ink drawings, their trunk, limbs, and twigs are on display as never before. There is something honest and genuine about a tree in winter. Their shape defines who they really are. Harsh winter bares the soul of a tree for all to see.

Their winter shapes display several general silhouettes. And most botanists label their general appearance. Art Stupka and John Morrell were quick to point out these tree details on most any winter hike. The more common ones, they said, were the round, broad, weeping, vase, oval, broad, columnar, pyramidal, and fan. Oaks tend to be broad and spreading , except for the pin oak's pyramidal shape along with the sweet gum. Birches are columnar as is the gingko; red oaks lean toward a fan shape, willows weep, and the American beech, still my favorite, is round. The shagbark hickory has shingle like, grey bark that peels off in sheets and is very rough to the touch. It stands columnar with large trunk and smaller limbs.

I always thought of the American beech as a noble tree. Even in winter, its appearance is one of aristocracy and nobility. Its bark is a satiny smooth grey with leather appearance. Its branch ends in a lacework of tiny twigs, a tapestry against the sky. Again, it remains one of two trees that hold their leaves in the winter. Reversing the stark winter trend of other trees, the woods are brightened by its golden leaves now turned eggshell beige.

The Sycamore is stately and magnificent. It is best known for its winter bark, which drops, peels, and falls creating a stunning mottled tree skin. The Sycamore's trunk is a silver, white, and beige mottled tapestry; its unique artwork lightens winter's day. Under a full moon, the sycamore trunk and limbs take on a bright, star-like glisten that dazzles the eye.

Even if it is deep winter, trees have merely paused. They've stored their energy, dropped their leaves, and diligently prepared for renewal. Soon there will be a transformed life and new buds. They await spring's promise of a new start— as do we all.

For we, along with these wintery sentinels, anxiously await tiny green buds, the crocus, and Easter morning. In fact, the world waits expectantly for the promises of spring, when we , once again renewed, experience and rejoice in the word "risen."

CHAPTER SIX

An Ode to Hunting

Hunting still remains a way of life in the mountains where it first meant survival for the early settlers. It survived even as civilization and modern conveniences came to the mountains and lessened its demanding grip on families. Many folks unaccustomed to the southern Appalachian customs still misunderstand the nature of hunting wild game. Hunting is primordial. It is at home in our DNA and genes. It is a part of our spirit, our soul, an inherited trait.

Let September signal summer's end, and October calls on nature to color the leaves, and you'll see the spirit of hunting began to stir folks. They become restless. Men, especially, have this growing need to get to the woods, to explore, to hunt. This call on their souls is primitive and universal. It is unexplainable.

Formerly a first born of settler survival, you might say hunting has become a ritual, less critical, and free from necessity. It has become an enjoyable foray for a man alone or for a group of men. Among a group of friends, a small game hunt offers camaraderie, an opportunity to socialize, and escape from womenfolk and responsibility. With yesteryear's competitive sports far in their past for most, hunting offers the hunter a different type of competition. Best shot, quickest shot, most rabbits killed, best beagle, worst beagle, and beyond, hunters hotly argued just who owned bragging rights for each throughout any hunt. The joking, grousing, teasing chatter broke the monotony and enlivened the trudge through mud, briars, and misty cold. It was fun filler sandwiched between any rabbit-free actions.

We'd waited expectantly all year for opening day, and it was here. In both the dogs and the hunters, excitement could not have been higher. Quail and rabbits were our primary quarry. We didn't realize it then, but the critters were probably not in very much danger when we entered the pastures.

Hunting season always opened on November 25—Thanksgiving Day. Like Christmas, it never came soon enough, especially if you were fourteen.

THE BLUE MOUNTAINS SING
of rivers, old men, trails and trout

The common custom around Sevier County was to convene at your family's home for holiday lunch, and a gathering of friends would hunt in either the morning or the afternoon after lunch.

One particular November holiday was quite memorable. The kitchen's fragrant smell of sage in turkey dressing and simmering gravy signaled a soon to gather crowd of men and boys in our front yard. Eight or ten friends of both my Dad and me quickly gathered just after dawn. After a brief and swerving ride, our caravan stopped a mile from the river. We piled from Jeeps and pickup trucks and spilled into the brambles, sage, and muddy pasture of the river bottom. Tumbling from their owner's truckbed, a wad of yelping beagles suddenly parted into eight little clones, and their wails grew even louder and longer.

Rabbit beagles, however, always made the difference. Six or seven of the little yelping, yapping critters eagerly chasing in some crazy only god knows pattern, made rabbits run even crazier patterns. The small brown, white, and black canines, their tails wagging excitedly, gurgled and whined as they ran their routes in frenzied anticipation of a catch that always made our spirits rise.

Noses to the ground, this morning's bunch burst into a scurrying search pattern. Their writhing body language assured us there were hundreds of rabbits within sniffing distance. Our group separated as hunters aligned about twenty yards apart; we walked slowly through the roughness of pastureland. Old fencerows matted with briars and honeysuckle, yet unburned brush piles, downed trees, and briar and small sapling thickets were all favorite hiding spots for cottontails.

Our job was to help the beagles by nosily walking through any rough patch likely to hold a rabbit. The now excited yelps of eight beagles rose several octaves and overlapped each other until it became one nearly unbroken wailing and wavering scream. I wondered what it would become when they actually saw a rabbit.

We had one newcomer in the group, Floyd Bydel. He was the new son-in-law of one of the oldest members of the group, Moody Matthews. Moody, a WWII veteran, wounded and survived the Battle of the Bulge, had worked for Bureau of Roads at the Park headquarters since the war ended. He was crusty, loved to joke and was a curmudgeon poster child. Floyd was from Vermont and anything but an outdoorsman. He joined us at the behest of Moody and like most wanted to please his father-in-law. So, he came on the hunt.

Once I became aware of the relationship, I knew what was likely to happen. No sooner had we entered the first thicket when a volley of shots rang out.

An Ode to Hunting

Moody yelled out, "Floyd got him. Good going, Floyd. Just put him in your big back pocket—that is the game pocket. Last time I used that old coat, I fixed the buckle so it will hold some weight now."

The dogs exploded in song and two more rabbits burst into the field and ran straight toward us.

Smoke cleared from an all hunter volley and two hunters said in unison, "We got one, and Floyd got the other one. Nice shot Floyd."

We moved through some heavy brush, slowly pausing to give the beagles their room and search time. Several hunters smiled wryly and exchanged knowing glances. I figured the next shot volley would result in two or three rabbits dead, and, as beginners luck would have it, Floyd would be the lucky hunter with the truest shot. Sure enough, my prediction came true. From the other side of the thicket, four rabbits bounded into the pasture barely ahead of the beagles. Everybody fired this time.

Cal Wiggins, a high school classmate of Moody and owner of the local Chrysler dealership, yelled, "I can't believe it. Floyd killed three with one shot. Man for a beginner you are doin' really good Floyd."

"I'm proud of you Floyd, seeing as how you never hunted before. You are something else with that gun!" Moody said.

Floyd's game pocket was soon bulging. It was an old timey hunting coat. Its game pocket, when unhooked, dropped down and made a seat size ground cloth to give the hunter a dry canvas seat when needed. Rehooked on each corner, it formed a deep hammock like pocket to carry game. At last count, Floyd, expert shooter, had seven rabbits pocketed, and the last shot netted him two more. Nine rabbits at about four or five pounds each meant Floyd was now toting thirty-five to forty-five pounds.

The all- morning, sleety wind in our face forced us all to button up tighter. Floyd alternated hands as the strain of his coat forced him to carry his gun in his right hand and tug his coat collar with his left to ease the choke of forty plus pounds dangling and bouncing on his butt.

Two hours and more than two miles had passed. The last brush pile gave up several rabbits. Two more of which were attributed to Floyd. His side pockets were smaller and could only hold one rabbit each. Ten more pounds did not seem to balance the bulk at his rear. Our pace had slowed. We were all beginning to tire. The cold, the sleet, the mud were beginning to drain all of us —especially Floyd.

We turned toward home, the waiting vehicles, and Thanksgiving dinner. A small honeysuckle patch suddenly yielded three rabbits and a surprise — an unexpected covey of quail.

THE BLUE MOUNTAINS SING
of rivers, old men, trails and trout

Bood Watson said, "Floyd, you got two more. What a shot. I wish we'd had you at the Bulge."

Floyd just stood and stared vacantly. I don't think I've ever seen a hunter more forlorn. It was there on his face. Where could two more rabbits go? Good sport that he was, he gripped a hind leg of one rabbit in his right hand along with his shotgun and gripped two hind legs of the second rabbit in his left.

Floyd said feebly, "I guess if we have to shoot again, I'll have to throw at least one of these down to even raise my gun — maybe both of them! How much further to the truck did you say it was?"

Finally, Moody stopped. The sleet was heavier now. He looked straight at Floyd and said, "Son, you are one hell of a sport. You've been had. This is pretty much a daytime version of a snipe hunt. You ended up ahold of the bag—in this case the rabbits. You went a lot longer than most would. In fact, I don't believe I've ever seen a newcomer in our bunch go as far or as long as you did. You got grit. I'll give you that. Give me all them rabbits; I'll carry 'em back to the truck for you.

"It's time for Thanksgiving. And, right here on this day, we've all got a lot to be thankful for. What a great, great morning this has been."

"Best ever," somebody said.

CHAPTER SEVEN

*Society speaks and all men listen, mountains speak and wise
men listen...I only went out for a walk, and finally concluded to
stay til sundown, for going out, I found , was going in.*

—John Muir

In Quest of More than Trout

My car was parked only minutes behind me at the trailhead. The cool
,mountain breeze smelled moist and familiar; the sounds from the river's
rush rode on it. I had stepped back in time. Trudging through morning
woods not quite awake yet, except for a mocking bird and two twittering
chickadees, I felt like I was coming home. Home, today, was one of the
many deep cleavages in our Appalachian mountain chain. This particular
cleavage formed an almost perfect vee. And for about two thousand feet to
the ridge tops that defined it, its hardwood covered slopes were comfortable
for walking. Its gorge cradled one of my favorite rivers. Soon, the shafts of
sunlight would disappear. This was low country compared to the rapidly
ascending terrain at both sides and that loomed above and ahead of me.

As the gorge deepened and the sides grew steeper, I would soon enter
what the Cherokees called " the land of the noonday sun." The terrain was
so deep in fact that the sun's rays shone only for a brief period at midday.
For the remainder of the day, this area was shadowed into darkness with no
direct sun. I didn't plan to travel that deeply into the gorge mainly because
hiking would become difficult. Most productive fisherman, as they fish up
stream, try to anticipate and plan their route ahead for the next rapids or
pool. Trout are very wary, suspicious, and acutely aware of movement and
changing shadows.

Success begins with positioning yourself low, shielded by trees, boulders,
anything natural with minimal wading disturbance. Blending with the
surroundings and positioning so that you optimize your casts are a must.

THE BLUE MOUNTAINS SING
of rivers, old men, trails and trout

Your fly should be placed well above the trout, float naturally with the current, and drift into the river pocket most likely to hold a feeding trout. Since you are surrounded by overhanging tree limbs, bankside vegetation, and other obstacles, using a seven and a half to eight foot fly rod with room to cast a fly line twenty to thirty feet to a prime trout haven makes your casting position and location all important. Stealth is imperative. Slippery rocks, strong current, position of the sun, and your attempts to hide while wading offer quite the challenge. Stalking the trout is very much like stalking the deer.

Trout fishing in the mountains has always helped center me. It grounds me. There is something pure and unvarnished here that keeps me returning. Solitude and pristineness are difficult to find. Ten million people visit our Park. If I want to fish the way I did growing up in the 1950s, I have to plan to go where others can't or won't go. An old sales quote for success sums it up: " Success results from your willingness to make those efforts that no one else is willing to make." Today, midway into a fishing wade, you're suddenly confronted with rafters, tubers, swimmers sunning on rocks, and picnickers. I still search for that 1950s solitude. Now, it's much more difficult to discover.

Today's hike for trout began first in dense woods , mixed with occasional open areas that suggested the life of an early settler. Grassy spots, underbrush, and blackberry briars, gave hints of an age old pasture now unused and overgrown. These ghostly homeplace pastures and yards once held sounds akin to farm life and family. Most spaces were fringed by a few unkempt apple and pear trees in need of pruning. Here and there shards of man's attempt to survive peeked out from the tangle of brushy undergrowth that held leaves piled from the wind. A rusted railroad rail, a leaning metal cog of some sort, and occasional stacks of stone spoke of unfinished fences and cabin foundations with their chestnut logs long gone.

Rounding a bend in the trail, the coldness, in a heavy moist breeze, told me my morning trout fishing adventure was near. The trail dipped close to the river now. A familiar beach, sandy with pea gravel, greeted me. The sun had peeped through the trees in a few places. The vodka clear water shimmered here in the shallows. I always waded in the stream at this sandy spot. Its gradual slope began with sand, then gravel, and gradually the bottom became studded with the roundness of brown river rocks. They formed the rounded slickness of a riverbed floor and deeper water. At ankle depth, the hundreds of multicolored stones that formed the bottom were mostly flat and varied in size. Their rustic colors ranged from browns and beiges through blues and grays to clays and oranges. More colorful in the sun, as

In Quest of More Than Trout

a group they looked deceptively like a level terrace, the work of a master artist or stone mason. In knee deep water, the larger stones were somewhat uniform, underwater protrusions in all directions, their roundness neatly mounted in sand pockets surrounding them. The rock shadows deceptively belied a smooth flat walking surface. Their underwater lie had tricked me often in the past. I don't remember many trout ventures when I didn't slip and fall at least twice. Chest waders are clumsy and can be dangerous for wading the streams of the mountains. Most locals wade in felt bottom wading shoes and endure the icy mountain water. Before the advent of felt bottom shoes, the old timers fished in leather soled farm brogans. As water neared my crotch, I knew the same icy coldness that numbed my toes would now grow. The current and the cold would now tug at my knees and lower thighs, and cause my pant legs to flutter as the stream clawed at my legs.

I stood midstream trying to osmose the serenity these woods and waters always offer. Up ahead was a string of deeper, long, still pools, their surface punctuated with grey granite boulders of all sizes. At either end, the deep pools are sandwiched between rushing shallow rapids. This pattern would be repeated for miles upstream and down. The water in mountain rivers is always fascinating. Rushing mountain water like the campfire's flames, form once-only patterns. They are seldom repeated and are continually changing. The images froth and dance in bubbling rushes by and around boulders in mid-stream displaying a uniqueness owned only by waters of the mountain. Dancing, gurgling, hissing, spewing and shimmering, the river sung and danced, in its rush, its unrelenting wildness, its race down. Like the snowflake that has no equal, the mountain river painted aliveness eternal in its watery dance of gurgling images. The river's work is endless, ageless, and unique. Its very nature draws us to it. We are in awe of its sounds, movements, fragrance, and majesty.

In its solitary setting absent of civilization, the language of the river can be felt and heard. Numbers of times in the mountains the waters have offered a surreal experience. It's more commonly experienced by fishermen who escape modern society, withdraw to the mountains, and use a fishing experience to find the offerings of the mountains. Often, the pilgrim encounters silence, mystique, and a surreal face of nature.

I distinctly remember one such experience. It happened in the headwaters of a trout stream high in the Smokies. In our teens, it was customary for me and my fishing buddy to rise well before dawn, drive to, and enter the park at one of its many graveled roads. At road's end and blocked by the park gate, we'd park at river's edge and hike the gravel road for two or three miles further ahead into fresh fishing water. Once we reached our fishing entry point, we'd leave the road walk through brush, woods , and brambles maybe one half to three quarter's mile to reach the water. Once we entered the water and waded, we leapfrogged each other for the rest of the day. One fisherman would begin fishing, and the other would walk along the bank seventy-five to one hundred yards ahead, depending on the terrain, walking difficulty, and thickness of foliage. The second fisherman would enter the water, begin to fish, and his partner would fish until he saw wet rocks or footprints in the sand, signs that signaled him to exit, hike upstream, and leapfrog his partner. This would allow him his one hundred yards of undisturbed fishing water. As a result, unless you took an agreed break or joined up for lunch, you were alone in remote wilderness, never hearing any human sound for the entire day.

My day, alone, was filled with the gurgling, murmuring, often up and down roar of the water's rush. The breeze, often the wind, together with foliage, the trees, the sway of leaves, and the constant motion of tree tops formed rushing, unending sounds of silence. It soon became a continuous symphony that the woods always play in their summer aliveness. When you are alone, this solitude and tranquility create an ambience Kepart and Muir so often refer to ——the voice of the wilderness. Its silence, when free of human sound, can be rather deafening, yet the silence is not silent but alive.

Wading in a remote trout stream, relatively alone, you sense this aura that belongs only to the wilderness. It can take on a surreal, even unnerving feel. It seems to surround you. At times the silence and its rush envelop you like mist or fog. This daily flow of nature in its surround sound, gradually begins to resemble many tiny, low voices, murmuring among themselves. Their words or meaning are undistinguishable, yet they make one think of a swarm of gentle bees murmuring to each other as they busily go about their work , talking over, around, and through each other in a constant tapestry of busy sound.

Each conversation seems equal in level, maybe with a bit of clarity and emotion but none shouting over the other. If I could put fitting descriptive words to this occurrence, I'd describe it as a high pitched mix of joyful, happy, bubbling, excited, playful, and eager activity—a seize the moment sharing by nature's "little people." It's what I might expect to hear from five or six otters playfully swimming, chasing, and chattering excitedly as they enjoy each other and the moment.

The Cherokees described the hush of the woods, the rustle of the leaves, and the bevvy of faint voices so common in their woods. They equated them to the Irish leprechaun. They called them "the little people" too. Kepart speaks of this same surreal experience in some of his writings. Until recently, I was unaware others had similar experiences until I read the Kepart and Cherokees' accounts. I have experienced it a number of times through the years in the Smokies.

I, along with others, have experienced this same type occurrence in other locales outside the mountains. While aboard a U.S. Navy destroyer participating in military exercises in the Mediterranean, we had a few days shore leave and travelled to Rome. We visited the coliseum and the catacombs in Rome. There was a total silence there. In fact, when we were there, it was treated as a religious site , and silence was required and enforced. Even with street traffic and other visitors and tourists nearby, the public silence inside was eerie. It was silent with no outside human sounds. My fellow officers, surprised, said that they heard what sounded like faint chaos, a low roar that rose and fell, and many faint screams. Visitor guides explained these sounds in the silence as screams of slaughtered Christians and battling gladiators. Similarly, I have heard many civil war buffs who frequent the Civil War battlefields say that on days when they are alone in the field of such silent stillness, they, too, have heard the voices and screams of war.

Wherever the answer lies, I often wonder if those woodsy and watery voices of "the little people" that reside on some of my favorite trout streams might actually be the happy words of joy, the playful excitement of the Cherokee Indians, and the settlers who were here before me. Could these sounds mirror a people whose lives were lived in contentment and harmony? Are they people filled with a special joy in the day's replay of people enjoying a life fully lived while they accepted the bountiful gifts offered by the mountains? And on this day, maybe they were a people grateful and respectful of that promise of what each day, especially this day, brings.

A scolding blue jay reminded me why I stood there knee deep in one of my favorite fishing spots. I'd already tied on a Hare's Ear. This mental reminiscing of the past hour prompted me to change. One of the first trout flies that I'd ever used was a Royal Coachman. A dependable fly in the 1950s and one we all used heavily. It always seemed to produce back then, why not now. I changed. I flipped a long first cast roll across the current into the darkened swirl split by an automobile sized boulder. My only guide that would signal action was the loop where my fly line joined its nine foot, three- X ,tapered leader. The loop floated at an angle and the tiniest twitch would signal a strike by a hungry trout. I repeated the casts and waded through three pools. Near the head of the fourth, spongy green moss covered a granite rock. The rock, a fine slide for a child, was covered in a thin layer of wet, spinach like, slick moss. I cast about thirty feet into the strong current rush at its upper tip protruding deep into the hole. A flash of reddish silver slammed the nymph. The old bamboo rod bent and snapped into a deep arc. I tightened the line and let the trout move at will. If a greater rush of adrenalin exists in the outdoors, I don't know where to find it. As the twelve inch rainbow tired, I gently eased him to my side, slipped my fingers under the belly, and cradled him at the water's surface. I knelt and studied the trout closely. In bright sunlight, a native rainbow trout's color mosaic is spectacular. Carefully keeping the glistening rainbow half submerged, I let him slither free. I have tried, and I've never found words that precisely define such beauty. This watery peacock is an image defined only by itself and God. I guess that's why I believe so strongly in God. Times like this one reminded me why the wilderness had always been so precious to me. This continuing cycle of nature was returning to its own original state. In fact, that very day the way it came to me.

Everything in the mountains is pristine, pure, and filled with the promise—what you see is what you get. It's a refuge away from that life where things, places and people try to be what they are not. Each hike I make and each fish I touch promise me unchanging truth and undying absolutes. In these waters and in these mountains, I find truth tightly wrapped in hope.

CHAPTER EIGHT

The woods were made for the hunters of dreams
The brooks for the fishers of songs
... To the hunters who hunt for the gunless game
The woods and streams belong

—Sam Walter Foss: *The Bloodless Sportsman 1898*

From The Front Porch:
Respect for the Mountains

The old man seemed pensive. This afternoon he was not in his usual joking mood ,even his crustiness was absent. His mood was puzzling, for the day itself could not have been better. The breeze drifted in from the rows of sweet corn in the pasture to the west and said something. It spoke of Indian summer. October was near. The old man seemed deep in thought. He and his two grandsons sat on the front porch. He slumped, moving ever so slightly in his hickory rocking chair. The two boys, his grandsons, thirteen and eight, sat side by side in the porch swing. The oak swing was two generations old now. Its worn chains were rusted, creaky, and needed replacing, but never had been. No words had been spoken for almost an hour. The serenity that surrounded them made it easy to doze after Sunday dinner. The front porch faced the creek, the bottomland pasture, and the woodlands to the northeast edge of the farm. The only sounds were those that belonged here, generic sounds so farm familiar on any lazy summer day. Contentment seemed to envelop the entire homeplace. From the apple trees behind the farmhouse to the bee hives in the walnut tree grove, the sounds of security stretched lazily out across honeysuckle tangled fencerows at the east pasture's edge; everything living seemed to just be going about their business, singing.

The only sounds were comfort sounds, the creak of the front-porch swing, faint gurgles and murmurs from the creek, three or four hens scratched selectively at the edge of the yard, clucking in shared gossipy chatter. The slam of the kitchen screen door at the back of the old farmhouse broke the mood, an exclamation point in their lazy vacuum of sound. Drawn from their dreamy Sunday reverie, the lounging trio reluctantly returned to the now, pulled there by sounds of their grandmother busily finishing her Sunday kitchen cleanup.

"This day is escaping," the oldest grandson proclaimed silently to himself. First, it would be the mockingbird, on his usual perch on the chimney cap, always first up and last to bed. With his cacophonic repertoire of two dozen or more birdcalls, he would loudly announce dusk was not far away in the same way he had announced morning's arrival at first light earlier.

Up at the barn, the proudest rooster would flap to the tallest post at the edge of the hog lot. He would once again crowingly proclaim the day's end, which was a repeat of this morning when he announced the arrival of dawn and later at sunrise. The only discordant sounds at day's close were ones that seemed to clash with all else. They came from those of the farm's exotic birds running wild and free. While it was still light, Grannies' peafowls, all nine of them, would begin their shrieking jungle like screaming calls. They would fly to roost into the nine hedge apple trees that lined the yard. As was the custom of the day, at least on this farm, the apple tree trunks were white washed twice each year. They gave the appearance of a perfectly even eight foot tall, living white fence encircling the yard . They separated the yard from the dusty driveway, were cloned in height, and they formed a near perfect rectangular outline that lined the edge of the lush yard.

Soon, the whippoorwills would begin at the creek and dusk would drape the fade of the sunset. Finally, a family of hoot owls would call to the other. Each would drop from its secure roost amidst poles empty of tobacco this early in the year. For a time, these owls, the last farm criers of coming darkness, would glide along the divide between dusk and pitch darkness looking for rodents and calling to each other.

Finally, the old man spoke. The boys exchanged quick glances; they had already anticipated it. They knew the familiar signal. It was the creak of the loose porch plank under his rocker. It always made the same sound when he shifted his weight before he was about to speak.

"I've lived here in the county all of my eighty years. This farm and this house have been home for the last sixty years. At one time, I knew every person in this town and nearly all in the county except for the young kids. I was raised in the mountains, hunted and fished 'em, and only come out when the new Park bought us out. I've been right here ever since. Then, I worked off and on for the Park doin' a lot of different thangs. I worked

From the Front Porch: Respect for the Mountains

for 'em because I believed in what they was tryin' to do. I wanted to help someways. I learned a whole lot.

"We live in the best place in the entire world. Our mountains are the best in the world. Now, everbody probably thinks where they live is best. That's OK. That's good, and they should think well of where they live. Everbody should think a lot of their homeplace. Now with that said upfront, our homeplace mountains are the best they is. And I thank you boys is old enough to realize it, know it, and respect it.

"Now that respect part is important. It's just like havin' a treasure hoard of gold or diamonds. If you had sich a treasure trove you'd make sure it was secure, protected, safe, and you'd even defend it, just like our country. Now, we've got to always treat our homeplace and our mountains just like treasure cause they are.

"And the mountains, well they're just like them tomater plants out there in the garden. They need protectin', fertilizin', and cari'n so they'll grow and produce. It's the same with our mountains and ever thang in 'em. We've got to do it cause their ain't nobody else but us humans that care.

"I want you boys to promise you'll always do that. I need to know that you'll always help keep our mountains, rivers, wildlife, and ever thang in it, safe and growin'. It's important that you respect the mountains, show it in the way you treat 'em, and teach other people to have that same respect for all our nature. You've gotta have the same respect for them as you do people.

"Now, I know from them looks on your faces that you are thinkin', 'What's he talkin about?' And you are a wonderin' treasure? Where's the gold? These woods ain't no treasure'! And I'm uh tellin' you right now— they are! And you can take that to the bank. Now, you need to know just why our mountains are like treasures and why I'm tellin you they have such great value. So I'm going to tell you. Go ask your Nana to please fill us up another big pitcher of ice tea with plenty of fresh lemon. And don't spill any, cause she'll be madder n' Hobbs. You boys bring it back out here on the porch and let's talk a while longer.

Taking a big sip of iced tea, the old man began. "These mountains are different. They're made up of a bunch of working parts, parts that nobody or no place on earth has. Even if they've got some of these parts, they're not all together in one place like in our mountains.Now the government , the Department of Interior, has collected a bunch of information. So as not to bore you, I'll squeeze it down and just tell you what the Park Service generally says about itself. And I'm gonna shorten that on down and just tell you what I think you should know.

THE BLUE MOUNTAINS SING
of rivers, old men, trails and trout

"Fair enough?" The boys nodded.

"Our Great Smoky National Mountain Park was established on June of 1934. It took eleven million dollars to buy the land and eight years to do it. Old man Rockefeller helped us out during the Depression when he kicked in about five million."

"You mean he just gave it and never got nothin back?" said the older boy.

The old man nodded, " And President Franklin D. Roosevelt drove up through here and dedicated in September of 1940.

"If you were an eagle and flew over it, the national park would look like a big horse blanket that straddles the Appalachian's spine. It probably has more than five hundred twenty thousand acres of wilderness and streams. The horse blanket's edges would lap over deep into two states, Tennessee and North Carolina."

"Can you drive or walk it all?" asked the younger.

The old man smiled and said , " I don't know if anybody's ever done it, but here is what the park service says is the opportunity if you do try it. There are somewhere around four hundred miles of roads, nearly eight hundred miles of hiking trails. The trail lengths are from half-mile to seventy miles. "

"How much are mountains and how much are water?" asked both boys almost at once.

"Well, the Park says it protects eight hundred square miles of these mountains. They say we got the world's best examples of deciduous forest, and more different plants and animals than anybody else can match.

"And here it is," he said, turning the page and paraphrasing. "The Park is ninety-five percent woods, and, sadly, only twenty-five percent that was never logged. That ranger bunch had nearly everbody helpin 'em do a good job though. Now, they protect more than one hundred different types of native trees; fifteen of them are national champion trees. In the 1920s Horace Kepart 's tree count was close. Don't ask me the why difference.

"You all asked me yesterday about why we have all those different flowers and shrubs that other people don't have in their parks back home. Well, the Park explains it pretty good right here.

"According to their public documents, our mountains are some of the oldest on earth. Some big Ice Age glaciers pushed south , some say from 20,000 to 500,000 years ago and stopped just short of the Smokies. They formed a junction of southern and northern plant life. The just pushed and squeezed till the spine of the Appalachians squished up. That made our mountains become part south and part north. The pressure caused our mountains to squirt up and that's what gives us our different mountain elevation and altitude. Over time, it gave us sixteen hundred species of flowering plants and four thousand non-flowering plants. Rhododendron, mountain laurel, and azalea first sprung from those weathered rock crevices. If you were a southern plant you thrived lower down ,and if you were a northern plant, home for you was in the higher elevation. In fact, we have some plants that no one else has and at least three of 'em are protected and endangered. And to help everything along, the park gets about eighty inches of rain each year."

"Wow," both boys breathed in unison. Their attention was growing more focused.

"You know when we hiked last year to Spence Field and Russell Field?" said the old man.

"And somebody threw up from eatin' too many blueberries," laughed the older making the younger scowl.

The old man continued, "For some reason in some of our mountain crags, the shrubs take over and the tree-free zones are called balds or laurel slicks. Some old timers called them 'plain hells.'

"I remember my granddad taking me hunting and warning that some men had gone in some spots and were unable to come out for days. Many laurel thickets in our mountains are dense tangles even a small animal can't make it through."

"What about the animals and the bears and stuff. How many are there. Do they know?" the older asked.

The younger jumped to his feet, "Whatcha think they do, jis go around the woods countin' stuff? Everybody in the fifth grade knows you caint do that."

"Actually , son, that's exactly what they do," said the old man.

"They have hundreds of folks studying that very question each year. Right now, according to park records, there are fifty-five hundred known species of plants, sixty-six or more mammals, more than two hundred forty species of birds, sixty native fish species, and more than eighty types of reptiles and amphibians, including twenty-three species of snakes. Remember, only two are poisonous, the rattlesnake and the copperhead. They call us the 'salamander capitol of the world' with thirty salamander species and thirteen kinds of toads and frogs, at last count.

The old man eyed them and said, "And the answer to the question that started this whole discussion and one you 've been waiting for: Our American black bear total is approximately fifteen hundred bears or two bears per square mile, and the Park says we've got the largest protected bear habitat in the East."

"I'm gonna write this down and tell'em at school. I can't believe there's that much stuff in the park," said the younger.

THE BLUE MOUNTAINS SING
of rivers, old men, trails and trout

"You remember when we trout fished and had to scramble hard and slide and wade around those big boulders in the river at the Chimney Campgrounds? Do you know generally how they got there?" the old man waited for it to sink in. Their silence said they didn't.

"Well, I'll tell you briefly.

"That Ice Age freeze and thaw was rough. So hard it actually shaped the Smokies. Those big boulders we climbed across and those others scattered around actually froze so hard and thawed so quick they broke up, tore loose, and rolled into the stream beds. You can see the proof of it in all those rock seams and layers that we passed by on the trails. They were part of the pressure and push that finally shoved our mountain peaks into being. They say those rock seams are made mostly of sediment and part of a core that was about fifty thousand feet thick, and they were laid more than six hundred million years ago."

"I can't even imagine how old that is," said the older.

"Six hundred million years," said the younger. "He just said it."

"As far as plants and trees go, the Park says that when you climb from one of its rivers to one of its craggy peaks, you hike through the same floral zones you would see if you walked from mid-Georgia to southern Canada. Boys, think about it this way. If we started at the river in Sugarlands and hiked to some of our highest peaks, we'd begin our hike surrounded by sycamores, willows, persimmons, chinquapins, elms, and gums. As we gain elevation, we pretty soon enter a zone of beech, birch, two of my favorites. The basswood, cucumber, butternut, holly, sourwood, ash, maple buckeye, poplar, and hemlock are all there. Once we reach three thousand feet, the white oak is replaced with the equally valuable mountain oak. Beech, birch, and buckeye, live at five thousand feet, as once did the chestnut. Above that, we get to a level called the sub artic zone where black spruce, balsam, striped maple, red cherry, and service berry ("sarvis") hang out.

"Listen, the Park and the geologists call our Great Smoky Mountains the master chain of the Appalachian system. They form the greatest mountain mass of highland east of the Rocky Mountains. In their two thousand mile Alabama to Newfoundland stretch, no mountains rise like the Smokies. You'd have to go fur piece to match their elevation.

Looking at the older, the old man said, " You were asking about how big they were. The Park says that they have thirty forested peaks topping five thousand feet and sixteen of them beyond six thousand feet."

"There must be a negative somewhere," said the older refusing to accept its face value.

The old man nodded and sighed, " If there is a negative, I'd have to say

From the Front Porch: Respect for the Mountains

I'm disappointed in our mountain views. They're disappearing. When I was a boy, we could see forever from these mountain tops. They say ozone does it. Its killed thirty plant species, and they say you can see twenty-two miles on a good day. Before ozone, when we only had mountain haze , they say we could see ninety- three miles. I've lived here all my life, and I say we can't see shit now! What the coal burning smoke don't hide the developers do.

He stood and stretched, "Anyway, I guess all this has been on mind to tell you boys. I won't always be around here to remind you of the *'what was.'* You both are just like me. You like to fish, hike, camp, and swim in our outdoors. But, it can't last if we take away all the green and mess up the water. No farmer would treat his farm the way we've treated most of our mountains and streams. Today, ours is the most visited park and every year we get more than ten million visitors. We provide 'em tourism services to get our income.

"It's a tough balancing act for everybody. It's one you all will have to wrestle with if you live here after college. Just remember, people come here for the mountains and the water—for the green. They could shop, eat, and spend the night anywhere. They come to the mountains to find peace and freedom from civilization. .All that other stuff that grows our economy and makes us money is not the reason they come.

"Just remember, if we don't protect and manage our woods 'n waters, visitors will find another spot. Why we locals want the same thing. Most everbody hungers for solitude and a wilderness spot they can find his or her quiet place. They want to tell their children of those good ole days in the Smokies where they once found peace and joy. Some will speak of how they wish the mountains were that way, again.

"Now, my final point. Is this not a greater treasure, greater than even gold and silver? You can see why we got to be so protective of these mountains? We had better become a best friend and steward. There's no more of it left; it's all we got. And that's why we've got to git others to do the same."

The boys looked at each other; then their gaze met his. Their throats tightened at the tears that had welled up in the old man's eyes.

CHAPTER NINE

The Oak Tree Chronicles

The old man's soliloquy yesterday afternoon about respecting the mountains was still fresh in the boys' minds as they poked at their breakfast. They were still trying to wrap their understanding around everything he'd said. They hoped he'd be his seemingly old carefree self today. And hopefully, he'd gotten what was bothering him off his chest. But his body language said that was not to be. In fact, it looked like today's tension would be even higher and maybe even turn dramatic.

"Get in the truck, boys. We're going to a funeral."

As soon as the old man uttered the words, the chorus of moans and rolling of eyes began. His two young grandsons grimaced like a new school year was about to begin.

The younger one spoke first, "Not another funeral, Poppi. This is the seventh one we've been to this year. All with you."

His brother added, "Yeah, funerals are for old people. Most of the time we don't even know who it is laying there anyhow, cause most of the time they're old, your friend, and we never knew them to start with. Why go and look at 'em if you don't even know 'em?"

The old man was solemn. He continued loading his old cross cut saw into the truck, "This is not a regular funeral. This one is special. It's one of my dearest friends, and you all are going to help with the funeral."

The boys quickly looked at each other and the older boy swallowed hard before asking, "Help? Surely, you're not asking us to, to…"

"Why no, just shut up and get in the truck."

The trip was only a few miles, but time enough for their thoughts to go to all sorts of imagined places, scenes that only naïve youngsters could conjure. Winding across several ridges, through lush woodlands, they reached a ridge top. The truck stopped. Through the windshield, the view below them was the view an eagle might have. Woodlands and countryside were wrapped around in an arc with their small town at the center. The Pigeon

THE BLUE MOUNTAINS SING
of rivers, old men, trails and trout

River formed a shimmering line that divided the land below almost equally. The old man got out and walked over to a monstrous yet grizzled tree. After studying the many ascending limbs, some forty feet in length or more, he slowly gazed skyward.

"It's nearly ninety feet to the tip top of this white oak. It was majestic, once. Most of its life, in fact. All these other trees all around us are just simply background scenery, but this one is special. Its special in a lot of ways. This tree has stood sentinel on guard for maybe three or four hundred years."

Certainly, it had stood solid, towering, and more like a monument as long as he could remember.

"Boys, if this oak had a soul it could have been my favorite aunt or grandmother. She raised us when we were outside. Her August shade was wide and cool. Even in the hottest dog day stifle she cooled our burning bare feet. Her sparse skirts of cool green fescue and clover delighted us all. We were the kids of Pigeon Forge summers, and she made sure we appreciated her. Her cool shade even soothed our sunburn better than the coldest bed sheets in the night."

It was not until years later that he would realize how important this aging old oak had been to his youthful wellbeing. For kids all up and down the valley, she stood for everything that was good in their outdoors. We never realized how much we depended on her, he thought, chasing, scrambling, racing, and climbing over, up, and through her huge branches.

He looked at the boys, and pointed at the oak, "She served as storm shelter, tree-house holder, everybody's rope swing support, hideout, picnic shelter, and back rest for dreamers. We even used her shadow to keep the ice cream freezer cold. Her treetop canopy always blocked August's sun. Most important, this oak tree was a sentinel and an observer of all things Pigeon Forge and of all things Smoky Mountain for, at best guess, close to three hundred eighty years."

He remembered the trees beauty was ever-changing. The lime green leaves turned to reddish flame when October sun dropped low in the West. At summer's end, she nurtured and fed any and all local acorn loving varmints, just as she had nurtured him and his friends all spring and summer. Squirrels, raccoons, birds, rabbits, and even an occasional black bear or deer sneaked in for a snack. Some roosted, some ate, and some just dropped in merely to be social.

The boys looked at each other. The old man seemed even more lost in thought, and his pauses between the thoughts he shared grew longer. It made them nervous. They'd never seen him like this.

"This was a special tree, one you hid behind in sadness or one that took

194

your anger and frustration and kept them hidden. Neighborhood kids knew they could safely share their deepest concerns here. She listened to those secrets and hid 'em. Funny thing is, those unanswered questions were ones that every generation thinks belong only to them. She knew their pleas would always be the same, ones she would hear again with each generation. Among them, were secrets of pain, loneliness, loves lost, and loves gained. Some shared targets of their anger, others who wronged, betrayed, or bullied them; the old tree heard them all."

The tree really listened, he remembered, whether you leaned against the rough bark with your forehead or talked intently to it high in its canopy astride one of its many forty foot limbs. The height of the climber's perch was dictated by the weight of the emotional burden and level of despair. The questions were eclectic but common: Do you think the prettiest girl in the fifth grade likes me? Will I make the fifth grade basketball team? Will Santa bring me what I asked for? Do you think my dog will ever come home? Who keeps stealing my lunch at school? Why do our two ponies always get out and come to the school yard? Do you really think if I hit that sixth grader right in the nose he'll stop bullying me? Do you think I'm saved? What is sex, exactly? Will my Dad be OK over in Germany fighting the Nazis and Japs. He won't get hurt will he? Are we poor or rich? Does my mother love my little baby brother more than me? He and the tree had a special secret, a buried treasure secret. It must have been the late 1940s. He was sure the details would come back to him as the boys sawed.

Like the Blue Mountains in the distance, he and his friends had assumed this friend, haven, and playground—this mighty white oak —would always be there. She had stoically withstood midwinter blizzards, had not even bowed under layer after layer of ice that could have toppled a ship. Her limbs and leaves had whipped and bent in the most vicious of summers' thunder and windstorms. At times, she had bent and swayed frightfully as lightning bolts and cracks of thunder rode tornado-like forces on summer's angry wind. Even though she stood tallest on the ridge top, she evaded a lifetime of danger and remained unscathed.

It seemed everything his gaze fell on now was an integral part of his boyhood. When he left for college, this classic poster picture of a white oak looked the same as when he was five, yet this tree would not reveal its age to him. At ninety feet tall with a girth diameter of six feet, her growth rings were testament to that historic patchwork that nurtured her and to the times that had evolved around her. With lower limbs that reached a horizontal forty feet or more, there must be a clue to her age.

"Boys, no one really knows how old a tree like this is. About the only way is to count the growth rings while you cut or once it's cut down. A forester's opinion is usually based on research and data, but even professional opinions can vary. Generally, each year's growth is affected by weather pattern, wind, water, humidity, sun, temperature, technology, civilization, farms, development, and man. Many questions go unanswered. When were the tree's stunting years of drought and icy blizzards? What year was it starved for lack of enough nutrients or minerals? Which year stunted its growth because of too much rain, too little rain, or too much ice? As the animals struggled to survive, did deer, rabbits, or some small animal girdle the oaks bark setting it back early in its life?

"Time has really taken a toll on this huge oak. Sometime ago, I'm not really sure when, a lightning bolt destroyed a major limb and split the trunk. Now, all that's left is a screwed up canopy and this skeletal silhouette of a crippled giant."

Sap oozed several places from its base. The old man knew the tree must come down. It was time, but it was hard for a lot of reasons. Shouldering his long crosscut saw, he told the boys to get out of the truck and follow him. His tone was serious and intentional. Somehow the boys sensed they needed to pay attention.

He talked as he walked back toward the tree. "Any tree is both an observer and mapper of our history. It tells us who we were and shows who we've become. Most folks don't think about it, but trees are actually active participants in our society, and I mean more than their most basic role of processing carbon dioxide to oxygen that give us breath."

Taking one look at the saw, their grandfather, and then the tree, the older boy quickly realized the magnitude of the task at hand. Indifferent to the gravity of the moment, he made a suggestion, "How come we aren't using your chain saw? We could cut this thing down a whole lot quicker and not be out here..."

The old man interrupted, "Because this is very special tree. And it deserves a proper end to its life. Really, we should'a gathered up a bunch of local folks who remember. They needed to come, to congregate, to reminisce, and to mourn.

The two boys stared at each other in blank wonderment.

"These branches are as intertwined in the lives of many others as much as they are in mine. In fact, your lives too. This tree stood watch over us all."

The younger boy's imagination leaped to the Saturday morning movies he loved, "You mean like the pioneer scout guarding the wagon train against Indians or, or, the sergeant on watch protecting his men against the Japs and Nazis... or ,or, or."

His grandfather nodded and gave a faint grin, "Yeah, something like that."

Running his thumb over a saw tooth, he continued, "Boys, in the early days of logging and on into farm life here in the mountains, these cross cut saws were all they had. Anything that was felled in the forest, fell by the use of an axe and a crosscut saw like this one. The people who pulled on each end of the saw were called sawyers. So kneel down here, both of you."

Puzzled, the boys dropped to their knees as the old man touched each of their shoulders with the saw's wooden handle.

He said solemnly, "So in honor of the great and full life of my friend here and for all it meant to me and my friends, on this day, on this high ridge, in the heart of these Great Smoky Mountains —I dub you sawyer 'the Younger.' He knighted the younger boy. He repeated the same exact words for the oldest boy, ...I dub you sawyer ' The Older. ' " He touched each of their shoulders with the saw's hickory handle. It looked cracked and worn smooth, darkened to a dull patina that could have been grease and sweat.

"This tree is regal. It's pure royalty. Now, you've been properly knighted. Only royalty should destroy royalty."

"All right," said the Younger with a quick pump up and down with his bent forearm, as if he'd just scored a goal. The Older glanced at his little brother, his lips winced in a slightly melancholy smile. He was reminded of his own carefree fun at that age, but his eyes drifted back quickly, riveted on his grandfather's eyes. He studied them intently. While he had looked into them countless times, today he examined his grandfather's blue eyes and sun creased face as if he was really seeing the old man for the first time. The boy sensed the importance of this moment to his grandfather. He didn't really understand, but he sensed it.

Turning to his brother he said, "Let's help Poppi celebrate."

The old man took a deep breath. Slowly, his gaze rose upward, from the oak's gnarled, exposed roots, slowly along its gray bark, past the many scarred, aging, stunted limbs. Finally, his gaze rested on the very tiptop of the old oak. It was if he was trying to breathe in, and by osmosis, retain every molecule of the oak's aura before it was too late. Somehow, he was hoping he could keep something substantial and tangible from this moment, something that would transform itself into more than just a memory. He longed for something that had shape that would touch all his senses, something he could physically touch, recall, and savor time and time again. But he knew he was dreaming a senseless dream, maybe in another life but not here, not now.

Although he couldn't fathom the emotion this moment was wrapped in, the older boy began to realize that this was a heavy time for his grandfather.

THE BLUE MOUNTAINS SING
of rivers, old men, trails and trout

Not quite old enough to understand, he, nonetheless, wanted to respect it for what it was and for what it meant to the old man. He sensed somehow that the next few hours were going to be very difficult for his grandfather.

Choking at the lump banding his throat, the old man's double bit axe finally severed a large bark wedge that would guide this mighty oak, his dying friend, in its fall to its best and final resting spot.

With the enthusiasm of someone who had never ached from pain of manual labor, the younger boy enthusiastically grabbed the saw, "I want to pull it first."

"OK," said the older, "but you better pull your share or we'll be here 'til you move up to the fifth grade." The rhythmic bite of the saw teeth piled sawdust from the wound of the old veteran tree. Given the size, age, and experience of the two young sawyers, the pile grew at a surprisingly fast rate.

The sawdust smelled fresh, sweet, and familiar. The old man couldn't help but consider the paradox; the killing, death, and burial of a woodland giant was accompanied by maybe the most pleasing outdoor fragrance. It seemed this dismal scene should certainly not be coupled with anything pleasant, fragrant, or sweet.

Still unable to read the emotion on his grandfather's face, the young sawyer tried to please him with some recently gained school knowledge. "Poppi, at school they said you could count how old a tree was by the number of rings it has inside."

"Yes, that first ring you just cut was 2011. The Park labeled it the year the first tornado ever recorded touched down in the western end of the Great Smoky Mountains National Park with winds of nearly two hundred miles per hour and destroying 4500 acres of wilderness.

The saw quickly bit through four growth rings back to 2007.

The old man laid his hand on the older sawyer and paused their efforts. "Every ten or twelve rings normally would approximate ten years or a decade. The weather may have altered the count a little, but our count will be close. Now our Park coupled with the National Park Service has lots of information, timelines, and statistics that tell us what happened each year. So I'm gonna tell you parts I've read, some parts I know, and some I remember from John Morrell, Art Stupka, and all those rangers and staff."

"OK," said both boys. Their sighs foretold their ebbing enthusiasm for this upcoming and apparent civic lesson. They knew their granddad. This was not a new drill.

The old man began. "This decade had a lot of firsts. The U.S. Fish and Wildlife Service removed the Bald Eagle from the endangered list. The largest living eastern Hemlock tree ever documented was and is located in the Greenbrier area of the Park. The Park's black bear population totaled fifteen hundred, up from five hundred in 1976 or two bears per square mile of park land."

"I'm already gettin tired, "said the younger sawyer.

"Pull," said the older sawyer.

Five more years of tree history spilled to the forest floor, back to 2001, which saw brook trout restored to eleven park streams and seventeen elk restored after a 150 year absence.

A decade of growth rings had disappeared in no time. As the younger sawyer gritted his teeth, to keep up with the older sawyer's pulls, the saw bit into the 1990s. Back to 1998, the Park recorded every living species in the Park. Then to 1994 when the Park reported 137 otter and closed its restoration program.

"Those 1990s rings right there are important. Park environmental and weather timelines reported what they called "The Storm of the Century." It sliced across the United States and buried the Smoky Mountains in its deepest snow and cold in 'The Blizzard of '93.' They say it was the worst since the second greatest storm in 1888. In 1992, Elkmont's summer home leases expired—seventy-four cottages, including the Appalachian club, outbuildings, and the Wonderland Hotel."

"I can go faster than this," said a determined younger sawyer, hoping his pulls would prove his mettle.

"You've already reached the 1980s. In 1987 fall forest fires burned throughout Tennessee. The Park labeled it a strong decade for conservation and wildlife. Four peregrine falcons were released and Abrahams Creek got the release of ten otters mid-decade. An eagle alarm sounded with the sad report that only one active bald eagle nest existed in Tennessee and only a total of sixteen hundred active nests in all forty-eight states, according to various National Wildlife Association timelines.

"This old guardian oak has stood sentinel duty and looked out over much of our Appalachian history. It served in silent service to animals large and small, to town youngsters and oldsters, and it provided a slew of varied human services. It was a town crier who observed and listened rather than shouted. She stood silent, observed, and then recorded our local history. You're cutting into her archive rings, and I'm serving as her color commentator."

Three decades of observed history have just spewed from her trunk. The seventies were a bit of a paradox. That decade saw both outcries of alarm and some red flags that jump started conservation efforts.

"Your saw just sliced into 1976 and in two pulls you've reached 1970.

THE BLUE MOUNTAINS SING
of rivers, old men, trails and trout

In the this decade the Park reported the total black bear population at five hundred, the Clean Water Act is signed, and DDT is banned. According to the U. S. Census, Tennessee had 3,926,018 people in 1970."

Like runners at mid marathon, both sawyers were focused and struggling to maintain a rhythm. Their breathing was labored and left little energy for wisecracks.

The old man added, "In less than fifteen minutes, your saw teeth have reached into the sixties decade. Tourism and hospitality growth in Pigeon Forge exploded. Restaurants, motels, craft, and retail shops occupied. Roadside lots were auctioned earlier in the mid-1950s, according to Veta King, historian at the Pigeon Forge Library. Most auctioned lots came from the Conner and Lafollette farms, farms that had formed the rural heart of Pigeon Forge . Now the new highway was built.

"Right there, your saw just struck a monumental event in 1961. Not more than a quarter mile away from this spot, a significant historical event occurred and few people gave it much attention. Pigeon Forge became a city governed by three commissioners. The census reported Pigeon Forge population total as 974 permanent residents. Few could predict that by 2009, the city would grow to 6,429 permanent residents. Approximately one thousand people per decade would choose to permanently reside here.

"O.K. you boys are into the 1950s. If this tree could talk it'd tell you lots of stuff you don't know, since it can't talk, I'm gonna tell you." The old man said, " The Pigeon Forge Pottery housed in the renovated Butler family barn burned. I never knew that its replacement would become so famous and prized. The new construction became an icon. Thirty six street side lots along US Hwy 441 were auctioned as final part of the new US Hwy 441 construction in the mid-fifties. Pigeon Forge's commercial face and focus changed from riverside to highway side—people's back door became their front door because of the highway. The unincorporated greater area of Pigeon Forge's population was 650. Two southbound lanes of U.S. Highway 441 were paved. Fort Weare Game Park opened. I remember those years very well."

Finally, sawdust of the 1940s decade drifted out.

"Near the end of the 1940s decade, the Pigeon Forge Pottery began operation in the old renovated Butler family barn across Mill Street opposite the Old mill. Doug and Ruth Ferguson and daughters Sarah and Ester moved into a newly renovated second floor apartment that replaced the barn's loft. The entire remodeled first floor of the barn served as the production and retail area for pottery makin'."

When the boys' pulls reached their rhythmic balance, the melody from the crosscut's rhythm made his mind wander. This sameness pushed him deeper into what once was and would never be again.

He remembered, Right here in this spot , somewhere around 1948 an eleven year-old boy buried a tin box. Having just finished reading Robinson Crusoe, he decided a time capsule could serve two purposes. One, future pilgrims would know what Pigeon Forge was like in the last century. And the second, as a cache that might hold treasures sure to serve him well in his future life or some emergency. He selected a metal lunchbox, his favorite that had never allowed a crushed banana.

It was richly adorned with Red Ryder riding hard across the dusty plains. Following closely behind was a dust covered Little Beaver, always faithful and also covered in the same dust since he never got to ride in front. He was leaning forward astride his pony trying to catch up to big Red. The treasure box contents were highly prized and would be sought after by many: Two large dough roller marbles, scarred and chipped having survived four grade levels of pig eye marble games at two a day recesses; an empty Prince Albert tobacco can containing four perfect arrowheads earned by following the neighbor's plow every afternoon for two weeks; the first yo-yo, maybe some little alien kid from Mars would use it; a Case pocket knife with one blade broken off when he tried to open a walnut; a picture of Penelope Laudermilk, the prettiest girl in school; a second Prince Albert can filled with rabbit tobacco from the sage field next door; three long range twenty two shells for any survival tough spot; three pictures of his best buddies in the fifth grade; a pack of twenty-four firecrackers direct from China; a small box of wax coated matches with the corn cob pipe just like Tom Sawyer and Huck Finn's that he'd carved, hollowed and trimmed from corn cob and a cane pole; a bottle of Hawbaker's muskrat lure—guaranteed to catch even the wiliest muskrat with its secret ingredient, anise; two fish hooks and two trout flies carefully attached to felt and placed gingerly in a small match box.

He followed that up with a eight by ten, black and white, glossy picture of Lash Larue. Always faithful to his Boy Scout motto, the *Be Prepared* part, that he took seriously, he had secured one of a boy's most prized dreams for the future. He carefully placed the hermetically sealed, guaranteed against all defects, one size fits all, regular style condom in a sheet of Alcoa aluminum foil, and carefully wrapped it as insurance against all future needs, elements, and catastrophes. How it came to be in his possession came at a great deal of anxiety, stress, and debate. He had paid a high emotional price to possess it. There were six M-80 firecrackers and four pair of wax lips he'd saved from last summer's school trip to Lookout Mountain in Chattanooga. Finally, he put in a paper back copy of Jack London's *Call of the Wild*. Using black enamel paint and the twisted end of a frayed cotton rope for a brush, he carefully painted his name and inscribed the following: "Buried under my friend and my favorite —the biggest of white oak trees in this the year of our Lord on June 3, 1949." Having carefully wrapped the tin box in an Irish potato burlap sack, he dug deep at the tree base and carefully buried his Red Ryder lunch boxed treasure deep under the largest and knobbiest of all the gnarly roots in a spot closest to the trunk.

The sound of the saw reaching 1946 drew the old man from his reverie.

"Boys, there was a mountain crisis here. In 1946, a B-29 Bomber crashed and burned just fifty feet below the road at Newfound Gap and Clingman's Dome killing thirteen Army personnel. Investigators believed an altitude increase of only fifty feet would have saved the plane. In the mid- 1940s Tennessee government purchased the land for the new highway. Around that same period, the National Park Service and the U.S. Forestry Service proudly announced the birth of Smoky the Bear. This bear logo dramatically reduced forest fires in the next decade.

"This was about the time World War II ended. Between 1945 and 1947, the way of life in our Smoky Mountains was forever changed as fathers, brothers, husbands, and women family members returned from the World War II. The economy boomed, the GI bill meant college for many, women moved from their sole provider wartime independence to partnership marriages, and America's promise of the good life now seemed real and within everybody's grasp.

"That's the 1942 ring. According to the Park's CCC booklet *History of the Civilian Conservation Corps*, WWII costs caused a frugal congress to refuse to refund the program. Its young men had provided nine years of CCC services constructing the Park. In their formal statement at the closing, the National Service eloquently confirmed the contributions of those educated, outstanding, and energetic young men:'. . . That magnificent army of youth and peace that put into action the awakening of the people to the facts of conservation and recreation.'

"That same year, the atomic energy plant at Oak Ridge began the development of the atomic bomb. Nineteen forty one was special for us. Its events changed our little mountain communities forever, when President Theodore Roosevelt in May dedicated The Great Smoky Mountain National Park. It also signaled tragedy as Japan attacked Pearl Harbor and U.S. entered World War II. In the first year of this decade, eagles gained protection, and the last remaining Peregrine was sighted in the Park.

"The decade of the 1930s was eventful, especially in the Park. The decade included my June of 1938 birthday. According to Park records, the CCC boys battled twenty fires that consumed 929 acres and recorded 19,422 man-hours fighting the blaze. CCC enrollment was 4,350 men and they completed eight fire towers in the mid-1930s. Arthur Stupka became The Great Smoky Mountain National Park's first naturalist. He will later become a national icon in study and survey of flora and fauna.

"A mid-decade flu epidemic swept through the mountains taking children four years and younger within three days. The TVA (Tennessee Valley Authority) was established.

"That same year, the new Park struggled for identity and mission. Park documents showed that Superintendent Ross Eakins's monthly report was optimistic about the current state of its wildlife '... On July 11, a fisherman was fined three hundred dollars in federal court. He was carrying 137 rainbow trout that he said he had caught in less than four hours . . . so fishing must be pretty good over in Deep Creek.' He was named the Park's first superintendent around 1931. They say that he was so busy taming poaching, squatting, and moonshining, he had little time to practice park management.

"It was in the Thirties that the Tennessee Public Service Company began to provide Pigeon Forge with electricity at the beginning of the decade. Prior to this time, the Old Mill generated electricity to only a few homes. The Chestnut blight arrived from Asia in the Great Smoky Mountains. It soon infected ninety- nine percent of the Park's dominant tree species. Chestnut trees occupied up to forty percent of Parkland.

"The Stock market crashed in 1929. At Elkmont, "Rooster" Cogburn, in his private plane, crashed where the Elkmont Campground is now. The State of Tennessee built the Little River road from Townsend to Elkmont on the old railroad grade in the latter part of the 1920s decade.

"Boys, 1927 was really significant locally. Dr. Robert F. Thomas, a Methodist missionary and physician, came to Pittman Center. His story is rich and goes deep here in the mountains. Most of us or our families were doctored or ministered to by this fine man. He was a friend to us all, and I don't know of a man any more beloved. In 1960, I remember introducing him as our lay speaker at our church one Sunday. Part of the introduction aptly summed him up. '. . . I am pleased to introduce a man who is at peace with himself and with God more so than any man I've ever seen.' He visited my father–in–law's car dealership monthly for an oil change, and meticulously recorded the maintenance details in his Blue Horse note pad.

"Boys, your sawdust pile and the tree ring say it's about 1920 or earlier.

"Now, let's see. I believe some Pigeon Forge prosperity happened in the 1920s. Veta King's documentation talked about those details. Jehu Conner sold his farm to the Park, moved from North Carolina, and paid fifteen thousand dollars for a one hundred thirty acre Pigeon Forge river bottom farm. That same farm tract was later split by a four-lane highway in the 1940s. Another local milestone happened around 1926; Barber Tebo Watson and his wife Becky opened a general store, restaurant, and barbershop in Pigeon Forge's town center. Tebo would become a local icon and colorful barber.

"A lake I would swim in years later was formed in the mid-twenties at Elkmont. A lake and power plant were built using water from Little River. The lake site was located directly across from the Wonderland Club Hotel and near the boy's camp."

His mind wandered. His gaze dropped as he watched a spider weave its web on a very familiar root at the tree's base, it was the one with his carved initials. His mind wandered as the boy's crosscut reached a rhythmic drone. The sound pushed him deeper into what had been and would never be again.

He had left out that condom part of his old man reminesces. They didn't need to know. Some things are better left unsaid.

It seemed like last year; it was so vivid. He remembered four eleven year olds and a condom dilemma had required much deliberation and study. Their Huck Finn-Tom Sawyer quartet argued and agonized for hours over the best way to get a condom. Their town was small and all four boys were eleven years old. In the end, the bottom line was there were only two places in town where condoms were available. Doc Allison's Drugstore was downtown, convenient, and easy. Doc Allison peering condescendingly out over his horn rim spectacles would not be easy. Floyd's Filling Station and Garage had a condom machine in the men's bathroom according to the eighth graders at school. At the vote, Floyd's Garage won hands down. Nobody wanted to face Doc Allison and be on the receiving end of his famous doubting gaze.

Especially when he would likely ask, loudly, "And so what does an eleven year old boy need with a condom?" Boy, that was sure to draw an audience. Besides, Doc greeted and handed out those church paper programs at the front door of the First Baptist church every Sunday, ushered visitors, and passed the offering plate every Sunday morning.

"Yeah and remember, his daughter Mary Beth is in our class," Henry blurted out excitedly. With the *where* out of the way, the boys had to decide the *who* would go to Floyds, and then the *how*. They drew straws. Just before they declared a loser or winner, depending on your viewpoint, they unanimously appointed Henry as the *who,* since he was the tallest of the four. No doubt, the short straw drawer breathed a great sigh of relief.

Henry, tightly gripping five quarters in a sweaty palm, marched rigidly up to Floyd's front door, turned crisply with a military left face , and marched around the corner of the garage where both the men's and women's restrooms were side by side and opened to the outside. The men's restroom door had grease smudges over chalky, white scales. The blue E was missing from its weathered label — M N. Luke grabbed his collar, and yanked him back just before he entered the women's restroom.

"Damn, Henry, tune up your glasses," Luke pulled him toward the adjacent door. Apologetic and afraid Henry might back out, Luke said sympathetically, "But I can see how you'd miss the door, since its misspelled," as he smoothed the back of Henry's collar down with his palm. Sheepishly, Luke turned to the others with a "I'm sorry, do-you-think-he'll- back-out "look. Henry popped into the small bathroom as soon as his three guards pledged their loyalty, protection, and lookout diligence.

Just as quickly, he poked his head back out around the half opened door. Henry looked like someone preparing to make his first parachute jump from an airplane one that also served as his first time in the air. Peering through thick lens of his horn rims at his three young sentinels standing guard outside, he said, "You all three are dead if any stranger so much as even looks at this door."

He turned quickly, dropped the toilet lid in order to reach the condom machine and climbed aboard. He first read the label with a telephone number for a T Gravely in case the machine didn't work or for refills. Right above it were four slots. Each slot had the style listed across the top. The four musketeers had done their homework, just like all the smart, professional criminals did in the Humphrey Bogart movies. The group had loud, heated arguments debating which style condom to get. They had explored the merits of each style like seasoned, Valentino professionals. Each knowing full well that no one present had ever even seen an unused condom nor much less had used one.

However, arguing the merits of a condom and speculating on its various features and benefits gave real meaning to the adage: "In any endeavor, the greatest reward is not in reaching the destination but in the journey."

Henry looked carefully at each slot and slowly read the styles: *Glo-in-the-Dark, Rough Rider, Ultra-Thin,* and *Regular.* They had agreed on this choice almost a week ago. They chose regular. It sounded average, middle-of-the-road, traditional, like safer ground, and most of all—a comfortable fit.

Twitching nervously outside the men's room door, the three young musketeer guards eyed an older gentlemen. He had just pulled up to the gas pump in his 1949 Buick and began to fill his car.

"Oh gawd, it's Mr. Franklin. He'll try to get in here for sure," Luke squealed thru clenched teeth.

"Why'd you say that?"

"Cause, he teaches my brother's seventh grade math class and has to go pee about twenty times a day. Every time he leaves the room my brother kisses Freda Langley right on the mouth."

"How come?"

"Cause he likes to kiss her on the mouth, I guess."

"No, I mean how come he pees so much?"

"Oh, I don't know. I think its cause he has bladder problems or a swelled potentate."

"What's a potentate?"

"I think it's some kind of muscle that wraps around your bladder and makes your pee pressure really hard."

"You know like your solid stomach muscle," chimed the third musketeer.

"Oh. Thank gawd, he's leaving," said Luke in a breath of relief, his first oxygen since the man started the gas pump. Mr. Franklin revved up the Buick and left.

Almost in tandem with the teacher's exit, Henry burst through the door clutching five foil packages in his hand yelling, "Got em, I got em, by gawd, I got em!" Leaping in antelope bounds ahead of his three protectors, he yelled over his shoulder, "Run hard and then split up. Take separate roads. Don't meet back at the tree house until things cool off! Be sure nobody is after us."

It took about fifteen minutes to reach the hideout. They figured that was enough cool off time since the deed. Like eager bank robbers dividing their booty, each grabbed a condom, their own personal condom, from the pile, and left the fifth one lying there. This fifth condom was to be their training aid. Eight hands excitedly tore at the seal and completely unrolled the training condom.

Henry pushed his glasses back in place on his nose, flipped his brown forelock, and pinched the condom between his forefinger and thumb. Dangling it at arm's length like a dangerous snake, he treated it as if it had germs, fleas, or cooties were readily poised to leap on any one of the quartet. No one spoke. Each one studied this thin opaque pouch intently. An observer might believe they were on the threshold of a medical discovery, a scientific breakthrough for all humanity. Finally, their pondering assessment became words.

"I believe the Japs put the wrong size label on that thing. Look how long it is."

"Yeah, and look how big around it is."

"Dumbass, it said one size fits all," said Luke.

"Well, I've not ever seen any man with one big enough to fit that."

"How many men you seen naked?"

"Well, my pa, I guess, and my grandpa. And that sure as hell wouldn't fit grandpa. He'd need the little finger from a doctor's glove."

They all cackled, nervously.

"Yeah and look how big around it is. How do they expect us eleven-year old kids to use that thing?" said a disappointed Luke.

Henry, always the analytical, said," I'm worried. You think we may be that much littler than everybody else?"

"Nah," said Luke with a deep sigh," but I'd hoped to use that thing at least by the time I was twenty-five. Looks like I'll play hell doin' that now. Even if I ate Wheaties and spinach three meals a day, I still don't ever see this damn boot sock fittin' me."

The shorter of the four boys, still very concerned, asked Henry, "Did you look real good at those quarter slots? Are you real sure they didn't have a small or boy's size in that machine?"

"Hell no, I'm sure they didn't."

Now, after all this, they ended with more questions than when they started. Solemnly, they made a sacred, spit–in-your palm-first- handshake, and sealed pact. Each boy would hide his condom in his most secret hiding place, one known only to him.

The smaller of the four left them one parting warning, "Better keep em out of your pockets, boys. The last thing any of us want is for one of these damn things to shoot up in the wash water in our mom's washing machine, and just float there." A chorus of laughing cackles exploded at the mental picture. Leap frogging and shoving each other, the four musketeers relieved their excitement in yells and high pitched laughter. Just ahead an unfortunate chicken stepped into the gravel road, it set off an explosion of screams as the four gave chase. From the old white oak, their volume trailed off, as they grew smaller in the distance. Soon outdistanced by a terrified chicken, they playfully moved away in search of yet another adventure in preteen misdeeds.

"What are you smiling at Poppi?" said sawyer the Younger. Returning from boyhood memories, the old man felt as if he was almost there, he felt reluctant to return to the now.

"OK, you're getting into the early 1900s," said the old man. Saw teeth bite deeper into the oak, sawdust piles higher, the two young sawyers grimace, and sweat.

THE BLUE MOUNTAINS SING
of rivers, old men, trails and trout

"I'm tired. I'm sweaty, and I'm hot. This sawdust itches. How much longer? And why do we need to know all this stuff you're saying?" asked the Younger.

The old man said, "Because every boy needs to know where he came from and understand what and who got him there. It's the only way he'll ever know who he really is when he becomes a man."

"Oh," responded the Younger.

"Now boys, you're cutting into the first decade of the 1900s. President Woodrow Wilson created the National Park Service, and designed it to 'conserve the scenery and the natural and historic objects [and] leave them unimpaired for the enjoyment of future generations.' That was good news for you boys and all of us. Right now, today, the Environmental News Network says we have 77.5 million acres preserved in the Park system. How about that?

"The Sevier County mail delivery started. A thirteen-mile mail route named the STAR route was established around mid-decade and ran daily from Gatlinburg through Pigeon Forge to Sevierville. The Park's Elkmont study mentions at Elkmont, the Boy Scout Camp Helpful, Camp Townsend, was established. During this decade, the Wonderland Hotel at Elkmont with new owners was renamed the Wonderland Club. Slightly earlier, The Appalachian Club at Elkmont, got land for a playground and permission to dam the river for a pool.

"That same year, my grandfather began his medical practice. The Montgomery *Vindicator* news read: 'Dr. John W. Ogle and wife Blanche began his medical practice in Pigeon Forge at their home in String Town, a row of nice residences bankside, overlooking the Little Pigeon River on US Highway 441.' The Bureau of Forestry became the U.S. Forest Service."

Refreshed from their break along with a quart of ice tea, the young sawyers are reflective, more focused on their Poppi and his perspective. For the last two hours, their fatigue has gradually been replaced by growing interest and at times, awe.

"All that Elkmont logging had quite a history. You didn't realize that when we fished Jake's Creek last year did you?" he asked. "You're into the early 1900 decade ring. The Park's study, the History of Elkmont timelined the growth. Little River Logging Company (LRLC) and the Little River Railroad (LRRR) opened logging at Elkmont and Jakes Creek, and, according to Park documents, this was the peak year for timber production in the Appalachians. Daily train excursion service to and from Elkmont began, and the Elkmont Company store and post office began. Elkmont Hotel was constructed along with Elkmont school. The Little River

Logging Company began logging along the west fork of Little River and Little River Railroad was chartered.

"Since I'm telling you about conservation and local mountain history, a few significant things happened nationally that you need to know cause they had an impact on us and our area.

"For instance, your tree ring indicates we've cut to around 1901. Well, President Teddy Roosevelt's first message to Congress pushed hard for forest and water conservation and reclamation. John Muir wrote *Our National Parks*. Some folks said it was so popular it was reprinted a dozen times.

"Now we don't have buffalo here but what happened in the West made us think about our own conservation needs in Tennessee. A U.S. Conservation timeline stated that a 1900 report, estimated to be thirty million in 1800, had dropped to fewer than forty animals. They said most of 'em were killed just after the Civil War, when the US Army removed the buffalo in order to discourage and move more Indians onto reservations.

"In this last decade of the 1800s, the rings you just splintered, the Great Blizzard of 1888 slammed the nation and Tennesseans. Around mid-decade winter, smallpox threatened Tennessee and reached epidemic levels. Veta King's chronicles pointed out that in 1881, citizens rejoiced as Pigeon Forge Methodist church was built, and the flooding Little Pigeon River destroyed the Old Mill wooden bridge in downtown Pigeon Forge in the 1870s.

"Your old oak's sawdust says we're into the 1870s and 1860s. Yellowstone became the nation's first national park; 1866 brings healing news as Tennessee is the first state readmitted to the union; 1865 appears in the sawdust – the Civil War ends – and former vice president and now president, Andrew Johnson faced a daunting task. He must reunite the North he served with the South he called home. All this is important.

"And that tree ring of 1863 brings up a fact you boys probably did not know. Pigeon Forge's new industry was short lived when Union army uniforms were made in the Old Mill, according to Veta King's *History of Pigeon Forge*.

"Those next two rings represent countrywide dissention. Emotions exploded in 1861 and the Civil War began. Although a slaveholder, Andrew Johnson refused to side with his state when it seceded. He was the only Southerner to gain his seat in the U.S. Senate. Lincoln appointed him military governor of Tennessee.

"Tennessee Conservation timelines recorded that here in Tennessee, our last elk was killed around 1850. Elk, like many other Tennessee wildlife species, disappeared due to overhunting and habitat loss. Life was hard. Our grandfathers were not as well clothed, fed, and housed as we are today. Small and large game made the difference in their day to day existence. Their priority was short term family survival not conservation."

Listening to the excited reenactment of the old man's historical facts , the young sawyers realized their saw's spill truly was *historic* sawdust — valuable recorded knowledge.

Their saw reached 1841.

"If this oak could speak, right now is when it would probably shout the news," said the old man. "Pigeon Forge Library documents tell us that William Love became Pigeon Forge's first Postmaster. The Sevier County Turnpike Company took advantage of large land grants issued in 1800s in order to construct a road from the top of the Smoky Mountains through Pigeon Forge to Sevierville's southern border. Our county was about to really change."

For several morning hours, with very few breaks only made tolerable by more of Nana's unsweetened ice tea, Poppi, much like a ship's captain, had been urging them on, calling for smoother pulls, and dispensing all manner of facts and directions. Tired now, the young sawyers noted the conspicuous absence of any physical exertion on behalf of the old man— like pulling the crosscut. The exchanges of steely-eyed glances between the sweaty, dust-encrusted brother sawyers spoke volumes. They were used to it. The Older thought, the old man always ignored this oversight. It seemed a common occurrence especially where and when old men and boys come together. Freedom from hard labor always appeared to be an entitlement, one that was seemingly reserved only for old codgers.

Poppi continued, "You just hit 1838 when Tennessee became the first state to pass the temperance law." At the mention of this single fact, Poppi's mood seemed to darken, the Older noticed.

What happened next, toward the tail of 1838, seemed to deepen his already black mood. He spoke of the Trail of Tears as the Cherokee Indians were removed from the Great Smoky Mountains and ordered on a death march to Oklahoma. Over time the U.S. had broken seventy-eight treaties with the Cherokee and other tribes. The Older thought, "Why did I never hear about that before?"

The sap dulled saw pulled coarsely into 1830. "William Love, son of Isaac Love, built Pigeon Forge's mill. A decade earlier, father Isaac built three forges and a furnace near this same site. His product, bar iron, contributed to the town's name. Five more states are admitted to the U.S. —Tennessee, Ohio, Louisiana, Indiana, and Mississippi," the old man shouted proudly.

When the saw hit 1812 the old man proclaimed tragedy, "Tennessee's catastrophe, the worst earthquake in U.S. history, happened in northwestern Tennessee. A woods and farmland area dropped several feet. Tidal waves were created on the Mississippi River, and it flowed backward into the depression. It filled the thirteen thousand acre bowl and became Reelfoot Lake. Remember, we fished for crappie down there and duck hunted there two winters ago. The country cookin' at Bluebank café—that's where we got those plates of big ole fried crappie."

For three hours now, the old man, like some filibustering, white haired senator, had recited relevant East Tennessee facts, colorful historic anecdotes, significant things that had impacted local generations of their neighbors and kin. He had made most every growth ring come alive. And this grandmother or father tree, old by four times great, had survived it all.

The old man continued, "You've sliced into 1796. Tennessee adopted its constitution tryin for statehood; Andrew Jackson helped to draw it up. Tennessee became the sixteenth state and John Sevier its first governor. Records state Tennessee's population was 77,000. Our county—Sevier— was formed in 1794. We did that two years before Tennessee even became a state.

"We're getting there now boys, its nearly the end —or the beginning. Your Tennessee history books will tell you all this, if they haven't already. There's the 1789 ring when North Carolina gave the Tennessee region to the U.S.; it became a new territory, the territory of the United States South of the River Ohio, and William Blount its first and only governor.

"Here's where it started, you've sawed into 1784. Let's see. Three of our counties in East Tennessee form the State of Franklin, which seceded from North Carolina for four years, came about then. Greeneville was the capital, and John Sevier was their governor.

"Now, stop your yawn cause we are gettin to some Pigeon Forge stuff. You've backed up one year to 1783. Colonel Samuel Wear, Sevier County's most prominent early settler, built a fort in the Pigeon Forge area. He provided refuge to settlers during the last Native American raids of the 1790s, so the Pigeon Forge Library documents say.

"The preceding year, 1782, is the USA's founding year. The Bald Eagle was so unique to North America that our Founding Fathers made it our national emblem. Ironically, the day our national emblem was adopted, our country may have had as many as 100,000 nesting eagles, according to a U.S. Conservation timeline.

The saw moves swiftly through the first decade of the 1700s. The young sawyers are glad the end seems near. The old man spoke of the this first era that began the Cherokee plight.

THE BLUE MOUNTAINS SING
of rivers, old men, trails and trout

"A U.S. Health and Welfare timeline described this early era as a pre-white settler span, and an era significant to Cherokee history. European epidemics were introduced into the southeastern U.S. in 1540 by the Desoto expedition. It was estimated to have killed at least seventy-five percent of the original native population. How much the Cherokee suffered from this disaster in unknown, but their population in 1674 was about fifty thousand. Then, a series of smallpox epidemics cut their numbers in half, and the Cherokee tribes remained fairly stable at about twenty five thousand until their removal to Oklahoma during the 1830s.

The saw blade binds and stops at ring year 1673, and the old man said, " James Needham and Gabriel Arthur of England explore the Tennessee River Valley."

Leaping through the 1600s, the saw finds the 1540 ring.

"Finally, we are there," said the old man, "Spanish explorer Hernando De Soto was the first white man known to come to our area. The dominant tribes were the Cherokee, Shawnee, and the Chickasaw. Forty-eight years earlier, 1492, before European settlers first sailed to America's shores, our Bald Eagles may have numbered 500,000, and the.."

A sharp crackling sound interrupted the old man before he began his closing. The rendition of the colorful past —his and the tree's was lost in the tree's movement. The sound of wood grain shifting drowned out all sound around them.

At first, the tree only sighed and leaned, then it groaned almost mournfully, and with a creaking wail it leaned for a long time and then slowly fell. There was no celebration. The old man cast his eyes downward in an attempt to hide the swell of emotion he thought he was prepared for but could not contain. The exhausted young sawyers tried to avoid letting their eyes meet, unable to face the gravity of what they have just done. Hushed, the boys stood stoic in a dark but a new awareness. Sweat rivulets pushed sawdust bits down their sunburned cheeks. Tears of youth blended with rivulets of sweat. The three stood silent, overwhelmed by this single moment. Three generations stood slightly stooped. The fourth was laid at rest. On this day, and in this place, at this moment, each of them was changed. None present could truly know the gravity of this act nor could they know the lasting impact it would have on each of their lives. This day will transform each of them forever.

CHAPTER TEN

Here is calm so deep, grasses cease waiting...wonderful how completely everything in wild nature fits into us, as if part and parent of us. The sun shines not on us, but in us. The rivers flow not passed, but through us, thrilling, tingling, vibrating every fiber and cell, and substance of our bodies, making the soul to glide and sing. . . When I discovered a new plant , I sat down beside it for a minute or a day, to make its acquaintance and hear what it had to tell...I asked the boulders I met, whence they came and whither they are going.—John Muir

Once When The Trout Spoke

The grassy, wild flowered riverbank was maybe three feet above the stream's, glass clear water. Small clumps of wild grass and weeds, so common to the Smokies, dotted the bank's edge. Its shelf held random green clumps so consistent that they appeared planted by something other than nature. This riverside flat made for good walking, and a hiker could depend on it to cushion the uneven terrain just off the river. It was rich carpet that always afforded flora surprises to anyone perceptive enough to look. This morning was different. Standing on the bank and peering into the long, dark pool dappled with light spots of emerald green was a man. The old man's gait and movement suggested a somewhat unsteadiness of balance. From below the water's surface near the sandy bottom, his silhouette was black against the morning light. The water's current and the surface ripples distorted his outline and made the man grow tall, short, thin, wide, then tall again. The old man's gaze slowly scanned the entire length of this secluded mountain pool. He was in the steep "land of the noonday sun" here, and his sacrifice to climb here must have been arduous. Obviously, he began his hike in the early dawn, maybe even before daylight. He watched a single mayfly drop to the pool's surface and begin to flutter. Then the old man turned and left, hobbling back in the same direction from which he had come.

The mayfly had stopped its fluttering and instead it drifted lazily. Rather than trying to escape, it seemed to be content in its ride on the current, which had slowed considerably now that it had reached the deeper pool.

The midday sun would soon chase the last of the river's morning mist skyward. It would be at midday, when nature's second act would come alive both above and below the surface of the Little Pigeon River's icy clearness. Bright sunshine would fashion a mottled tapestry on the river, one of contrast, one of brightness alternated with darkness, one that existed only at the pleasure of the woods, as the sun's rays tried to once again penetrate the forest canopy. The entire river surface would soon be overlaid with an alternating, random, uneven pattern of sunshine and shade artistry.

The drift of this single mayfly suddenly gained speed. The water swirled it around a gray granite boulder. It danced atop the white frothy fingers created by shallow rapids that sent it swiftly toward a circling eddy vortex near the slick, mossy stones at bank's edge. A young trout had observed the insect's movement for some time.

Perfectly positioned in line with the mayflies drift, Spec, a native, twelve inch brook trout, waited patiently. No sense in rushing this one, he thought. In his book, there was something to be said for civility. It was a given that trout protocol demanded you play by the rules and wait for your food choice to arrive in your lane and in your inline drift. You never poach another trout's food lane. The river's current was usually a fair provider. He'd never suffered for lack of insects, larvae, creepers, pupae, crawlers, or other river bounty that sped downstream in his lane. Just as Spec flexed caudal and pectoral fins in a surge toward the awaiting winged delicacy, a sudden scattering of bottom feeder minnows, knotty heads, silversides, and pesky surface feeding minnows exploded to his right. A large, four pound, female, brown trout rushed from the bank's overhang, sped right at and then past Spec. Her cavernous mouth captured a few of the unfortunate fleeing minnows as she engulfed the mayfly with a crushing leap and entry splash. Only an eagle plunging into the water could have made a bigger splash.

It was a small insect, a wispy mayfly, thought Spec, not a duck or a Kingfisher. Boy, talk about hogging overkill not to mention rudeness. That was his intended lunch, well within his lane and certainly in-line with his position. Any fish who is anybody knows trout protocol and proper etiquette. You coexist with your sisters and brothers, heads pointed upstream, moving gracefully, prudently and ever so slightly ahead or slipping sideways with the current. Like a squadron of bees or a flock of geese in formation, you

Once When The Trout Spoke

respect the drift zone of others. But, that huge female brown had exploded from the hidden darkness of probably a muskrat hole in the bank shelf . Spec felt lucky she missed him. With the spread of that cavernous sized mouth, she was four pounds if she weighed and ounce.

"Fat, overweight, pushy opportunist," grumbled Spec aloud. "I've had it with this entire river stretch. First, hundreds of tiny minnows always swarm to grab at my morsels, then this self-centered heavyweight poacher. None of them care who they offend or bully. I'm going to find someplace secluded, where there are no so-called neighbors." Feeling a bit guilty, he tempered his last thought. "Well, I do love all flora and most of the fauna, its fish that I can't stand. Everything is always fine in the abstract," he thought, chiding himself again. *His decision was final ;* Spec had had enough. He angrily churned every fin forward and surged upstream toward new and unexplored waters.

"No sir, the last thing I want is to always be looking over my dorsal fin afraid of another cavernous mouth coming at me."

First one then another—riffles, long still pools, rapids, riffles, long still pools, more rapids. He navigated through this river pattern rondo swimming upstream for more than half a day.

Finally, with a tired thrust of his tail, Spec cleared the last of a long stretch of frothing rapids. The pool he entered was a deep and moss green. It was as near perfect mountain pool as ever he'd seen. Trees lined both banks, shady in the right areas but sunny toward the pools head. Boulders, large and small, created lots of rushing current. The right bank was shadowed and shady. At midday, those deep under cuts and the pool's deepest water would hide him. To any predator, the view would be one of a green, deep darkness. The left side was mostly sandy, accented with a large grey boulder here and there. A gentle slope held promise of all day sunshine, and there were a few rocks along the edge that the sun would bake throughout the day. Layer upon layer of granite slabs sandwiched with crevices filled the upper right bank at the pool's head. A sharp left bend in the river just above the pool's upper end formed a one half mile long rapid created by the shallow rocky bottom. Here, the river was at its swiftest, and it rushed in a constant roar as it loaded itself with oxygen, larvae, and all things edible for trout.

A large chestnut tree, a casualty of the 1930s blight, rested partially in and partially out of the water in the upper reach of the pool. The large slick trunk rested on the bank while its tree top limbs, now useless, protruded sadly. The few that remained were broken, splintered, irregular ladder stubs and soggily preserved in the icy water.

A few moss-covered rocks, their flat surface slick and wet, dotted the pool here and there like unfinished walkways. Each rock was kept moist by the churning mist. As the water's current struck the rough, craggy, uneven notches and splits of their granite sides, the boulders responded as they sent out small ripples and surging waves that raced out then back in a reliable and constant rhythm. Their gurgle and flow earned them their place in the ranks of those unique performers in nature's endless symphony and woodland showcase.

Shivering excitedly, Spec said to himself, "This is gonna be perfect! I'm so excited! I never in my wildest fantasy ever thought I'd discover a spot like this!"

Then, wonder of wonders, hatching mayflies were drifting, fluttering by the dozens, no, by the scores, and they were undisturbed. Spec gawked; he'd never seen such an undisturbed sight. He was more accustomed to an average food drift with pesky minnows and bottom feeders constantly slurping and swishing, as they bumped into, over, and under each other. They became wild and frenzied at the sight of each and every insect.

Spec was in awe, "This is perfect, and I'm ..."

Just as he started to say he was alone, a ghostlike shadow moved up alongside his drift lane. A much larger and much older fish eased up on his right.

"Good morning, young man, welcome to today's mayfly fest."

Spec, startled, dropped his head and his pectoral fins submissively, "Sorry, sir, I thought I was alone in this more than perfect pool; I am so sorry to intrude."

The old rainbow, his bright colorful stripe cheerfully radiant, "Young man, quite the contrary, you are most welcome to enjoy it all. Just eat away."

Spec's gills opened and closed nervously as he eyed the older trout with short sideways studied glances so characteristic of an unsure youngster.

Suddenly, Spec excitedly exclaimed in a burst of tiny bubbles, "You're rainbow trout! How did you get way up here? You're not from here are you? Where are you from?"

The old rainbow chuckled, "Slow down, slow down—one question at a time. I know I am a puzzle to a youngster native brook trout like yourself. Especially, one whose piscatorial history and genealogy smacks of descriptors like native and mountain bred. Besides, mine is a long story.

"But first, " said the old rainbow, " what brings you up into this new territory?"

Spec, struggled to hold his spot next to the wily old rainbow, his pectoral fins fighting the current. He drifted right and then left, then back again . Trying to get accustomed to this new water current, he overcompensated. His over steered caudal fin, his rudder, repeatedly pushed him into the old

Once When The Trout Spoke

rainbow. Embarrassed, he was afraid that to the old gent he might appear, bumbling, out of control, unskilled, or worse, a mere naïve youngster.

But his imagined inadequacies vanished when his words tumbled out excitedly as he shared the story of his plight earlier in the day. As he relived the morning, the stress reignited and caused his words to stumble, bump, and fall over each other. A steady stream of irregular shaped and mixed sized bubbles began exiting his mouth. It was obvious they were the result of his pent up anger coupled with his frustration and excitement.

"I just got tired of the silversides, knotty heads snatching every gnat, insect, larva, and every other edible critter. Then that big thug of brown trout grabbed my mayfly like a big hoggy elephant. That whole bunch— why they are nothing but one big flail, swarm, snatch, blast, of surge, poach, and gulp. Right there in my home pool where I'd spent my entire life. Not one fish, outside of my few trout friends, has any social skills, follows any kind of trout protocol or uses any etiquette. "

Having drifted too far to the left, Spec suddenly caught himself. His thoughts returned to the present, somewhat, and he quickly eased back alongside the old rainbow.

"By the way, I'm Spec."

The old rainbow, smiled, gills extended widely, "You can call me Rainey. Yes, what you encountered this morning is a pity but common. Women, most of the time, tend to be calm and nurturing. It's their nature at least in the Pisces world. But threaten their babies or get in the way of their mission, and its every trout for herself. Go ahead and take this next mayfly, while I talk."

Spec moved self-consciously toward the surface hoping to look skillful. Surprising himself, he barely dimpled the water as he rose and took the resting mayfly.

He turned and sped back behind and below the old rainbow. As he moved slowly up current and alongside, he eyed the old fish on his right from tail to head.

"Your colors are very pure, deep, and bright. Are you a native rainbow?"

Rainey replied, "Actually, I was fishery raised many years ago in a village called Merlintown. At that time, before I arrived here, this was originally an expanse of deep wilderness. And it was being logged. Every hill, ridge, and hollow was almost bare except for slag and stubble. Rail tracks were laid in places, forest undergrowth destroyed as logs were slid or rolled to logging roads or the streams. Horses, people, even houses were moved to and fro. Sleds and skids scraped the earth. Sometimes when the rivers flooded, loggers moved the logs downstream on swollen river current. Some loggers lived in tent camps instead of riding the last logging train of the day out to their home village. At days end, those who remained often hunted and fished. The woods and waters suffered a lot of wear and tear."

Spec, wild-eyed and listening in awe blurted, "Really, all that happened right here?"

"Son, go ahead and take that grub, but please leave the shiny green larvae for me. They're my favorites. You asked how I got here. Well, there was one young logger who was a true visionary and an excellent fly fisherman, a purist. He never used bait, tied his own flies, and took only meat that he would eat. More often than not, he released the trout he would catch, gingerly returning them to the water for next time. Sometimes he'd just sit by a stream and observe everything. He'd study the wind, the clouds, the weather, the insects, the water's bottom, and rock shapes. He'd watch each bird, learn its call as well as its songs, he'd see where it nested, and what it ate. Best I could tell, I believed he learned all their sounds by heart and could sound them as well as the bird could. He'd sit for hours watching and studying every animal from the smallest to the largest. Sometimes he'd sketch with pen and ink. I believe he learned to be in harmony with woods and waters and everything in it.

The old rainbow paused looking away, "Hold on, that's caddis larvae that just washed loose upstream; must have been a deer or bear wading or something." He moved stealthily, with seemingly little effort, and captured both morsels in one move and then returned alongside Spec in one single motion. His gills opened and closed rhythmically signaling his contentment.

Waiting until his mouth was empty, he continued. "The young logger knew the logging would one day cease. Somehow, he realized someone must champion his concern for the wilderness and the wildlife it sheltered and nurtured. He was born and raised in a farm family. They only had a few farm acres in the nearby Sugarland's, but they managed to scratch out a living. The young logger grew to manhood and tried many ventures. He owned a mountain grocery store, served as postmaster, guided wealthy city merchants to hunt, fish, and camp. All the while, the local logging effort provided him additional income as a logger. He figured the logging would only last a couple more years. He knew as soon as the suitable trees that were most valued by loggers disappeared so would the loggers and their support operations."

"Did it really all disappear," asked Spec still bewildered.

"Hold it, there's a big stonefly nymph, I love them."

Moving slightly he dined for the third time in an hour.

"Anyway, this young logger was determined to make a difference in his world that now was almost scraped bare. He loaded me and about two hundred of my brothers and sisters in a fifty gallon metal milk can at the fishery. He carried us on horseback here to the mountains where he strapped the can into his tall, trapper's pack basket. With us sloshing all around in the can lashed to his back and him, sometimes on all fours, he clawed and dragged us way up here to these headwaters. He freed us a ways downstream in a pool that I now believe was special to him."

"Did you see him ever again?" queried Spec.

"I saw him quite often along the stream until the logging stopped. Then, they all left, but he often returned to the stream. He hiked in to camp and fish occasionally. It was like magic—the change that followed. The wilderness, the trees, and the wildlife returned quicker than anyone ever dreamed. Soon it was difficult to discern where logging had been except for the diameter of the trees. And the young logger was meticulous and determined as if he was on a mission. Ah yes, what a purist he was. Slender bamboo trout rod and his perfectly tied flies.

Rainey paused, "Let's move to the old chestnut tree there and stay close to the trunk in the shadows. That kingfisher is always an aggravation. He usually takes mostly bottom feeders dumb enough to rise to the surface at the wrong time. He seems nervous and agitated. All his noisy shrieking, he's way too loud even with his normal loudmouth attitude. See that mink there on that flat rock. That's why mister kingfisher is upset. He's so possessive. That mink is stalking a fish that he believes is his. Some of his jitters are very real cause he's well aware of what his own fate could be if he were to fly to low or relax his vigilance. Although mink prefer fish, they especially prize anything that has wings. It must run in the family because his cousin, the weasel, has the same proclivity.

Rainey stopped and looked at his young friend and back to the sandy bottom. "See that tiny crayfish speeding with the current? Let me see your capture speed."

In mere seconds, Spec returned to his former spot alongside Rainey.

"Well done my young Brookie. That's about as good a swim and scoop trout dash as I've ever seen. Ah, to be a fledgling trout once more — energy, speed, agility. Where did they go?" sighed Rainey. Rainey continued, "Now where was I? Oh yes, you asked earlier how had I lived so long and survived so successfully. Well, I matched wits with many, many fishermen through the years, even my logger friend. He was stealthy, quiet, and careful. Not like those muddling fools who wade downstream, throw stupid looking flies, sloshing about like a bear wrestling up a trapped trout, or even worse, using a baited hook.

THE BLUE MOUNTAINS SING
of rivers, old men, trails and trout

"My early life in a hatchery enabled me to study men. They have certain routines, certain interests, work habits, and leisure habits. I studied them intensely maybe because there was nothing else to do. There were no predators, and we were provided plenty of food. When I got here, my fight to survive was whetted by competing against the woods full of natural enemies of the trout. I had to learn to find my own food, and out maneuver, and out think the fishermen. I honed my skills well. My will to survive all these threats, within and without, developed my survival skills to near perfection. For several years now, I've enjoyed this survival game. It keeps me alert. At my age, there's little that I haven't already seen several times before."

"You actually enjoy defying disaster?" Spec asked in a hushed tone.

Rainey continued his soliloquy, "The basic makeup of trout like us helped me get there. You see, we trout are made of two basic things —appetite and suspicion. Watch it, don't take that mayfly Spec! I know it's an easy drift, but it's not natural if you look closely. Why is it moving faster than the current and on a slight angle? It's because a fisherman above us has let his line drag at the end of the drift — its unnatural. I saw his shadow pass over us a few minutes back as he stepped between the sun and us. If you swam about twenty yards upstream, you'd see his waders.

"But back to my young logger. He would never tolerate anyone who violated his sense of fairness and conservation. His core values were solid. I always appreciated that about him. He was a strong believer in the natural law of nature. He believed there was a right way and a wrong way to be a part of our mountains and rivers. You violate those natural laws, and you'd soon see there was a side of him that was not all about harmony, and then he could be quick to anger. Right then and there he could get down to the brass tacks with any man or animal taking the side of wrong.

"I remember one time in particular several years ago, he was younger, and he came upon two knuckleheads stomping around on the riverbank, yelling and laughing loudly. I'd seen and heard them long before he came. Cautious, I sought shelter in the darkness of a flood washed muskrat den to listen and observe. Below me, further downstream, the two were creating loud thunk noises under the water. I could feel the concussion and vibrations whump me broadside. Even though I was way upstream, it was still very uncomfortable. My side started to throb and hurt, but I stayed and watched.

"The two were filling glass jugs with lime, soda, and vinegar and capping them quickly and tossing them into deep pools. The gas build-up created a small bomb. The underwater explosion created concussion that

Once When The Trout Spoke

stunned any fish in the deep pool.

"Wading, yelling, and scooping, the two rogues were filling a burlap sack with our piscatorial brothers and sisters. Some years before, others of their kind had used half sticks of dynamite when the logging operation was around. Dynamite was always plentiful on construction jobs.

"I never saw the young logger so violent, angry, or loud before or since that day. He was on the two like a mountain lion. The first man had just screwed a cap on his jug. Two lightning fast blows to his face caused him to clasp the jug to his chest tightly in surprise, as both he and his jug were launched midstream. The second man turned toward the commotion just before a swift jab reeled him backward with a broken nose.

"The underwater thunk of the first man's jug still held football fashion his chest was quickly followed by two solid blows to the second man's distended stomach. The two- hour lunch of moonshine and pig's ears the duo had finished earlier, under the current circumstances, was not much help. While the second man hurled his stomach contents projectile fashion into the water, his body, its limbs flailing, sailed even further midstream. His landing barely missed a big, slick moss covered boulder. However, his splash bested his partner's landing by more than ten feet.

"After a while, calm returned to the river. The men grew sober, remorseful. I guess the icy water helped on two counts. Shaking their bowed heads they admitted to the young logger that they realized what they had done was wrong and probably illegal.

"The young logger spoke, 'Boys, all the logging is over. It has been for several months. The government bought all these woods as far as the eye can see from the top. In fact, the government bought all these mountains all the way into North Carolina. All this is going to be a national park. Think about it. Every mountain, tree, and river and every living thing in them are all goin' to be protected. Not only that, the protection is gonna help em' grow and get even better. Why before long, we'll have trees bigger than any of us has ever seen. There'll be pure cold clear streams, and woods just full of all kinds of critters. Probably, we're gonna have ever live thing the good Lord meant to be here. And the rivers and creeks will be full of trout mainly because they got helped, along the way, to grow and multiply. Think about it — your kids, my kids, their children's children will have a fine mountain place to enjoy. Everybody will want to come to these mountains because they are untamed, natural. They'll be pure, free, and unspoiled. And the great thing about all this, everything we like about the mountains will get even better every year. That is, if we respect 'em and take care of 'em. The good Lord knew what he was doing when he gave us this. Now, from here on, we have to help Him out. We got to be good stewards of His gift.

"'Now, if you want to get fish, and I mean learn to fish with a rod, I'll help teach you. But you've got to promise me you'll only keep enough for one day's meal and throw any little ones back.'"

Rainey, continued, "My side hurt from the thumps, and my nerves were shot from seeing so much violence, so I moved back upstream to my favorite pool. When I took that last look back over my dorsal fin, the scene back downstream was quite comical. The young logger stood in midstream patiently showing the two reformed, repentant knuckleheads, one standing on either side.

"He was saying 'load, load, load, and cast' as the two attempted to place a trout fly lightly near a midsized boulder. Each of them alternated as they awkwardly tried to use his rod. One caster wore part of a shirt with no front, his bare bleeding chest uncovered. His upper torso was encircled only by the back of a ragged shirt back, ragged sleeves, and a partial shirt collar. The entire front was missing. .

"With the back of his left hand, the second prodigal son wiped blood that continually oozed from his now crooked nose. His right hand held the slender bamboo rod, as he awkwardly tried to keep in rhythm with the young logger's chorus –'load, load, and cast'. Yes sir, those two soggy, shivering beginners would have a ways to go before they'd ever catch any fish."

Rainey's belly moved vigorously his chuckle clear evidence that he was enjoying reliving that incident and the logger's retribution as much now as he did then.

Spec inquired, "have you ever visited downstream or other pools"?

Rainey gazed wistfully, "Yes, I tried it way on downstream at times, but didn't like it. Lots of metal here and there, remnants of civilization, settlers, and logging operations. I've moved with the times, but I always liked it up here, best."

Rainey rose to engulf a particularly fat mayfly with hardly a dimple. His excellent feeding skills hid the fact that he was even feeding. "Helps avoid problems," Rainey said, acknowledging Specs quizzical look.

"Our lineage is quite interesting, my young Spec. There are four genera of our type fishes in the North America. You belong to one and I belong to another. While we are very much related, still we are quite different. You are really from the Char family and have close cousins in the lake trout and the Dolly Varden, a very beautiful fish like you. You are known as a Brook trout and the locals here in the mountains call you speckled. Your formal name or species is Salve Linus fontinalis and with your permission I plan to still call you, Spec.

"My ancestry is quite interesting as well. My scientific name is Oncorhynchus mykiss. My close cousins are the steelhead, red salmon, Coho and silver salmon. And, I'm still Rainey. You are really from the Char family and have close cousins in the lake trout and the Dolly Varden, a very beautiful fish like you. You are also known as a Brook trout, and the locals here in the mountains call you speckled. Your formal name or species is *Salve Linus fontinalis* and with your permission I plan to still call you, Spec."

"Sure," said Spec submissively.

Spec confessed, "Till now, I really thought you were one of us. And that tiny bright thing on your fin is strange, but I gotta admit it is handsome. You seem worldly beyond any trout I've ever known."

Rainey responded. " I must truly answer in the affirmative. I am more worldly than most of our Pisces neighbors. Since I was fishery raised, men fed me daily. My five years there provided much insight into their species. I saw their manners and their deviousness. I saw them in action and at rest. I learned their motives and their consistent patterns.

"You've noticed my right pectoral fin and its adornment. That is a tiny metal stud with the letter S on it. The young logger decorated each of us with one just before he released us years ago. Man banded ducks; he adorned us. He went to such a great physical effort to get us here. I guess his emotional attachment to us is partly the reason for the tag. The S was important to him."

"So don't you fear fisherman and people just the same?" queried Spec in an anxious tone.

The bubbles from Rainey's mouth grew much larger than Spec had seen before as he retorted, "Are you so young that you have not yet enjoyed the thrill of the match ,the tension of gamesmanship, and the elation of escape? There is an unmatched aliveness that comes from using your hard earned skill and cunning to survive the encounter and live to compete another day.

"Peril and coping is at the core of our species. Yes sir, my young Spec, basically, we are made up of two traits, a voracious stomach, which often makes us out as idiots, and our paranoia, which can teach us wisdom. We remain forever resilient because we are curious, and we can adapt.

"As trout, the superior line of the piscatorial family, genus, and specie, we survive by three qualities that make up our innate nature. These are our best qualities: hunger, suspicion, and intellectual superiority. These mountains offer us few challenges beyond a few of our natural predators like the mink, otter, the kingfisher, and a few other unskilled fowl.

THE BLUE MOUNTAINS SING
of rivers, old men, trails and trout

"But back to your experience with rude piscatorial behavior. I can't tolerate rude behavior in a man or woman. Cannibals are disgusting. They destroy the social amenities of the woods and waters. Being from within the ranks of the most elite piscatorians in these waters, we, you and I, have very limited friendships and social circles, and even fewer opportunities to enlarge them. Therefore, it behooves us to cultivate and nurture friendship, fraternity, and fellowship. As for me, I'm happy to line up in any water occupied with any well-conducted trout that has the decency and civility to respect my line of drift. 'Noblese oblige' the French call it."

Spec's puzzled wonderment became words. "You must be really old, considering when the young logger released you here?"

Rainey pondered the question, his gaze fixed way upstream, "Actually my age and experience have helped me survive for a long time, one building on the other. Quite candidly, everyone and everything around me seem very young. All my friends and siblings have disappeared. I don't know who, if any, are left. It is very lonely to be in my situation. I grow lonelier by the day. The only thing that keeps me optimistic is the next wits match with fishermen or maybe with anyone who would attempt to catch me, even those natural predators who aim to eat me. All have some merit in my view. At times though, I wonder if maybe God forgot all about me. He just kept taking each of those who meant something to me, one by one. I've been alone for a long time now."

Upstream, a mayfly landed delicately and an emerging nymph trailed underwater just a few feet behind.

"What a gift, a gourmet treat from on..."Speck was interrupted by the surging backwash of Rainey's caudal fin as it propelled this huge trout on a mission.

He engulfed both the nymph and the fly, and as he started to return to his original station in the school, he stopped a few yards short. Suddenly, Rainey was in the fight for his life. A 3X tapered three-pound monofilament tippet had once again connected him to his latest adversary, a fisherman. Time and time again he ran for the safety of chestnut tree's stumpy limbs as he'd always done. It had saved him hundreds of times. A quick turn, a deft wrap, and a quick break had always worked, always freed him.

Today, however, was different. The fisherman at the other end continually tightened the range of the line causing Rainey's fighting, leaping circles to decrease ,and he kept falling a few feet short of the saving grace of the old chestnut log. His fighting, struggling, swim escape route now became circular and smaller. Finally, he was too tired to fight both current and captor. Exhausted, he gave up the fight.

Once When The Trout Spoke

The fisherman eased the old rainbow to a sandy beach in the notch of a sun dimpled, grassy flat spot at the bank.

"Well, I knew you'd run for your chestnut like you've always done for others in the past. Guess I finally outsmarted you." Lifting the huge rainbow gently into the grass, the old gentleman used both hands as if to safely hold an infant. "My, you're quite a rainbow. Deepest colors I've seen in a long time. Wait a minute. Do I know you?"

The old man's index finger, its joints swollen and arthritic, gently traced the deep red lateral line of the old rainbow until his fingertip stopped at the tiny metal medallion attached to Rainey's pectoral fin.

"S for Sugarlands," he said in loud surprise. A bright, shiny glint from noonday sun reflected from the metal's scarred, scratched face. The reminder was twofold. One was the sudden appearance of an old friend, his long ago rainbow fish; the second reminder was the shocking contrast between the then with the now. Suddenly, he was filled with a deep sadness. His thoughts moved to his old homeplace at riverside in the Sugarlands. Today, that scene seemed far away, long ago and at times, a never was.

"Why you're ...you really are....My God ...hello old friend. I didn't know if any of you all were still round. I'd seen you up here in this pool through the years, but I didn't even dream you were one of my two hundred. Lord, Lord, you are old. Well, me too. Getting so I can't hop rocks, I can barely wade, and can't hardly even see good enough to tie on a fly but what a great journey we've had – you and me. Words can't express how I feel on knowing you survived and are still here. How in blazes did you ever survive all these years? I wish you could talk. I'd love to hear every inch of your story.

"Here, let me get you back in the water so we both can enjoy our visit. This could be our last one, you never know. What a magnificent place you've found to live in. If I was a fish, I don't think I could find one any better. Of all my time in these mountains, I don't believe I've ever seen one so perfect and serene. Why this place is almost mystical. The trees, the rocks, the current, the view of the sky from here. My Lord , it really is an enchanted little slice of heaven. In fact, you maybe don't need to go to heaven when you die. Maybe God will just leave you here."

Seeing Rainey's gills pulsing normally, the old fisherman gently turned loose of Rainey's tail. Returning to midstream, Rainey turned to face his speckled friend. The stooped figure of his old friend who freed him stood studiously on the bank. He continued speaking to Rainey, but Rainey, now beneath the surface, could only see his lips moving. The only sound now was rushing current.

THE BLUE MOUNTAINS SING
of rivers, old men, trails and trout

Elated at the find of the aging trouted friend, the old man continued to speak to his rediscovery, Rainey, and he stooped to water's edge. His fingers searched, poked, and explored a sunken nest of twigs, leaves and woods residue in a small eddy. Finally, he found what he was looking for. He collected a fistful of tiny, flat, brownish, rectangular, and leathery looking things that at first appeared like bits of bark. Each looked like a tiny stretcher with wooden handles on either side. These were stickbait. A small twig on each side of a leathery like pouch helped house the larva of Caddis Fly.

When they were peeled open, a small yellowish white grub much like a tiny hellgrammite was exposed. These larvae were prized food of any trout lucky enough to find even one. That would be very seldom or never because they had to be removed from their cocoon, and that was an almost impossible task for a trout. Unless some animal like a raccoon, bear, or other critter removed them and accidentally dropped one, a stickbait grub was rarely, if ever, available to a trout. The best a fish might hope for would be angry floodwaters or some other act of nature that might somehow release them free of their cocoon. Spec had never ever seen that happen.

Rainey drifted back alongside Speck. Exhaling his anxiety, Spec spoke excitedly and very relieved, "Boy, I thought you were a goner."

Rainey was silent for a long pause, as if taking in everything that had happened. "Well, I kinda thought that was my logger friend. Though he's changed alot physically, his movements, the flies, rod and delivery were very familiar.

"You mean you did that on purpose?" Speck shouted in disbelief. "I can't believe you'd take such a death defying risk. Caution and discernment have been your first and middle name. You've even taught me that!"

Rainey turned and faced him head on, the current pushing him forward and forcing them nose to nose as Rainey's fins continually pushed backwards against current at his back, talking as he attempted to hold his position in the strong current.

"Speck, old friends grow dearer as each year passes. That old man, who once was my young logger friend, is probably the only reason I'm still alive. He brought me here. No telling where I'd have been placed out of that fishery when the time came, but it sure would not have been piscatorial heaven on earth like this place is."

Speck still trying to sort out the last half hour said, "Then you tried to get caught? Took a chance on that being your old friend? Took a chance he'd recognize you and not eat you? And you knew you two might be reunited and actually enjoy a visit on dry land! Jumping Jehoshaphat! But how could you have known ?"

Once When The Trout Spoke

Rainey smiled, "Skill and cunning, my boy—skill and cunning." Before he could respond, Speck's gaze turned from Rainey, now in his face, and upstream to where a small tiny grub floated mysteriously near them as if tossed.

"Quick, don't let it get away; I've only had one of those in my entire life. Wait a minute, Rainey. That's your old friend there, he's tossing those peeled stickbait in to us — or better said, to you. Look at 'em. They are everywhere. Water sakes, this has to be fish heaven." Speck stopped short and said, "Go ahead Rainey, those are really for you."

Rainey moved ceremoniously underneath first one then another, as he barely dimpled the water. The old fisherman, still standing just off the bank ankle deep in the icy water, smiled a knowing smile, and nodded approvingly. His gaze fixed on Rainey as he tossed several tiny larva almost on top of the old rainbow. In a ceremonial salute, Rainey exploded in a leap high above the water, his twisting return slapped the surface loudly as he grabbed the floating yellow grub.

Spec had never ever seen Rainey leap from the water, nor had he ever seen any trout that large clear the surface or leap so high, not even one much younger.

Finally, shuffling uneasily across the slippery shallow rocks, the old man climbed the streamside bank until he reached the grassy level spot where he stood earlier. His gait was a bit wobbly, and he seemed stiff and even a bit unsteady just standing there. He picked up his fly rod, and appearing unsure, he walked only a few paces through the lush green grass to the wood's edge where he paused, turned , and looked back over his shoulder at the river.

For a time, he simply looked back at Rainey's watery haven. He seemed reluctant to leave, as if trying to make a decision. Finally, he turned his body so that he fully faced the river. He peered down the wet path he had just trod, its Queen Anne 's Lace stems still bent exactly the way his shoes left them. He took the rod from his right hand with his left, lifted his right arm with his open palm high in the air, his fingertips pointing to skyward, and stood stone still for what seemed like several minutes.

Rainey dropped his nose prayerfully. Sensing the solemnness of the moment and its gravity for his new mentor and friend, Spec gulped back a sudden rush of his own sadness. Deep sadness was new to Spec, it was unexpected and heavy, a choking blanket of darkness. When they looked up the old man was gone.

CHAPTER ELEVEN

Our Remembrances of Christmases Past

The duck blind had been quiet for a time, boringly quiet.

Rafe, my hunting-everything buddy ever since our teens, broke the silence, "It's almost Christmas and I dread it." That tired exclamation drew in perfect unison of agreeing "UhHuhs "from the all four of us.

The lack of midday ducks had us all running through the proverbial daytimer in our heads. That's the reason men come to the woods to camp, hike, fish and hunt. You're supposed to be able to leave all that stuff at home and refresh your mind, yet here we were with the beginning of boredom that resulted from a morning with no ducks, time on our hands, nothing to do except deal involuntarily and wrestle with all those upcoming challenges we thought were left back at home. Evidently, five hundred miles was not far enough away from our professions to erase the upcoming demands there, even if we were only to be away four days.

Susy and Cain, our two labs, whined, twitched, and squirmed their rumps, feeling a retriever's own brand of discomfort and boredom. They had sat poised and ready to leap, swim and retrieve since five a.m. Now, they sat scrunched on their hindquarters unsteadily trying to sit on their small wooden deck. Typically, the dog ledge of a duck blind is a balcony like short extension of the floor, uncovered, has a sloping forty-five degree wooden ramp designed for footing when they return from their swimming retrieve. Barely wide enough for two dog butts, it didn't allow them any room to stretch out and they grew increasingly bored and stiff.

So even they probably knew what topic would fill the next two hours left before sunset.

"Yeah, Christmas is only five weeks away. They had Christmas deco in the retail stores the day after Halloween and carols on the radio," Tad chimed in. The cobalt dazzle of this perfect bluebird sky overhead was birdless, certainly duckless, except for a few crows and the long glide of an occasional eagle searching for an unwary fish that might venture too near the surface.

THE BLUE MOUNTAINS SING
of rivers, old men, trails and trout

Even nature's perfection on this day could not hold our attention.

Trying to escape our boredom, our conversation drifted into a stream of "Christmas remember whens." Childhood remembrances of Christmases past tumbled out as we shared our favorites. Those most memorable and poignant were the ones we all said we missed most. The holiday highlights seemed deeply attached to anticipation, excitement, smells, sights and sounds. Taste, unexpectedly, came in lower on the scale. Almost to a man, their eyes took on a faraway gaze, slight smiles framed their recall as treasured long ago Christmas thoughts spilled out.

Suddenly, chords and words of Christmas leapt out from somewhere deep in my psyche. The faint melody seemed a part of the breeze. The oak leaves scratched and the brushed cover of our blind swayed. Even the wispy bamboo cane seemed to flutter in some sort of strange rhythm.

"…Oh come all ye faithful, come and behold…"

Was that really music?

Our one and two liner -liner memories spewed from our Christmas Past. They tumbled out methodically as if our plan had been to take turns, though we had not:

"…string thin tinfoil icicles thoughtfully and evenly draped on a fresh cut evergreen tree, 498 total strips,cause the dog ate two."

"…lights with aluminum star backs, first the back and then the bulb, always red and green; one sick bulb darkened them all."

"…Angels singing sweetly and the mountains whispering in reply: Christ the Lord the Newborn King has come…"

I shook my head to clear my mind. Where was this music coming from?

"…the family favorite ornament rested at tree top, and everybody's story differed on the ornament's ancestry."

"…spun glass angel hair pulled and stretched into veil thin spider webs that enveloped the tree, and hands, arms, back, and neck of the pullers itched and burned incessantly."

"…house front windows were filled with glass globed window wreaths with real lighted candles accompanied my much praying and handwringing."

"…all lights and wreaths were turned off by unplugging each individual cord from the wall outlet."

"…sleepily crawling through evergreen underbrush and behind couches and chests plugging and unplugging before bedtime was not a favorite pastime for most kids."

They laughed.

"…This, this is Christ our King. It is He — the one whom shepherds guard and angels sing…"

Our Rememberance of Christmases Past

I knew the words to nearly every Christmas hymn. After seventy-four years, you don't need the book. These lyrics were not familiar and not just words from any Christmas hymn I'd heard.

One by one they continued, "Granny's shortening bread made in tins and her creamy egg custard."

I tried to listen, to share. Because of this strange music, I couldn't concentrate.

"...cranberry salad tart with lime slices and crunchy with chopped celery and stack cake with each of twelve layers sandwiched by spicy apple butter laced with ground peppermint Christmas candy."

Stack cake was always at its moistest and best two days after it was baked, I thought.

"... boiling, pouring, cooling, pulling, eating homemade creamy vanilla taffy. We boxed a dozen or so tins for gifts."

"...ole timey chess pie born two hours ago. It was best when you ate it still hot, and you cooled your tongue with ice cold milk morning fresh from Mrs. Lawson's cow or Ruby Allen's cow."

"...country ham n' red eye gravy simmering and waiting for the cat head biscuits to brown."

"...fudge with walnuts and pecans cracked in October. Sliced apples, dried in Granny's attic, were best simmered in brown sugar, butter, and cinnamon."

"...grandmother's house with the family gathering of twenty-six strong for picnic ham, roasted chicken, dressing, and six different kinds of cake... kids ate in the kitchen...grownups at the large dining room table."

"...cooking aromas danced with the spicy smell of a real Christmas tree and fourteen real evergreen wreaths."

I had not heard the music for a while. Had it left?

"...*Christ the Savior is born; Christ* our *Savior is born...*"

It wouldn't stop. This was not just a hymn. These lyrics were not verses strung throughout any hymn I knew.

"...the ritual of the arriving proverbial relative always unsteady, rosy faced, and especially happy, and the same departing relative more unsteady, rosier faced, yawningly happily."

"...celebrating Christmas Eve and Day with one gross of fire crackers twenty-four to a pack, Chinese made, forty-nine cents, plus tax."

"...the annual gift-concocting ritual that began immediately after Thanksgiving. The family bake off of thirty-two fruit cakes as gifts for friends placed in a decorative tin container. Many recipients, I believe, secretly felt a fruit cake should be for enemies, not friends, and most recipients would never admit that they secretly hated fruit cake."

THE BLUE MOUNTAINS SING
of rivers, old men, trails and trout

They cackled with laughter unaware of my total disconnect with the game of the moment.

Maybe if I joined in and spoke more often maybe this surreal music would leave. I started to share one of my own memories, but the music interfered.

"...O Holy child descend on us we pray..."

Bored, there we were, each one reliving physical, tangible, highlights of the season . What started as fun now suddenly seemed shallow to me. This music made me feel guilty. Had no one else heard it? I began to get nervous. I'm not believing this.

My buddies droned on in their reverie.

"...the favorite mother–daughter annual holiday trip: Catch Trailways Bus at Bruce Street's Sandwich Shop to Knoxville's Gay street for the Christmas parade. Proceed to Millers department store along with mother-daughter friends, choose a doll for Christmas, have lunch at Gay Street's S&W Cafeteria, catch a return ride on the street car to the bus depot for return home on a Trailways Bus."

Where was this music coming from? It continued.

"... Hail the heaven-born Prince, born to raise us from the earth, born to give us a second birth..."

As quickly as it began, our fun and laughter waned. Rob paused and his mood changed, " You know most families dread those days. Family tensions reawaken at Christmas. Seems like they simmer all year and then flame up and darken what should be a joyous family occasion but I'll have to give it to Christmas, the true holiday spirit is resilient. Somehow, in the end, we always manage to gather, share love, and renew our friendship despite any complex family dynamics. For once, I'd like to learn how to be proactive instead of reactive.

"The holiday spirit is the heart of the season. I guess it's up to us to make sure it transcends everything else. You gotta admit the Christmas celebration in today's world is one that, for the most part, seems to ignore the real reason for the season.

Once again, the breeze continued its gentle whisper and, for me, it carried music.

"You know," he continued, "the more I think about it we can make each Christmas special. We could recreate and renew the way our family celebrates it. See, we personalize it. First , we set aside a time when we revisit, and talk about our favorite remembrances, things we cherished most, share our favorite highlights of Christmas Past and of our own family's Christmas past, just like we did here today.

Our Rememberance of Christmases Past

"I guess it could be sort of a Christmas accounting of our holiday family heritage. Then, we could add one new thing like a new family tradition. It would have to be something the entire family agreed was worthy. A single thing that enriched our holiday. I guess then it could join our Christmas Future."

He paused and breathed. His gaze begged for acceptance,

"...*O come to us, abide with us our Lord Emmanuel...*"

Still puzzled, I looked all around. Evidently, I was the only one who heard it.

Our hunting group, usually joking and animated, was studiously silent, lost in thought, I suspected. Dusk dropped sooner than we anticipated. We packed gear, climbed backwards down the wooden ladder down in to the boat, carefully balancing its load, cleaning the blind as we exited . The silence continued, broken only by the few words meant to calm the dogs. They were so relieved to stretch and leave that their bouncing excitement rocked the already unsteady boat. I guess we were all rethinking our own Christmas tradition. This spontaneous sharing between old friends ended as sort of an "aha," a bulb that suddenly lit, an epiphany of sorts.

The musical strains returned, rising and falling, with a faintness as if from organ pipes, the melody quickened in the rhythmic beat of small waves, keeping synchronous time against the metal side of the john boat.

The lyrics were louder now, this time riding organ strains.

"...*Peace on earth and good will to men...*"

Now that one I had heard before.

Surprising myself as well as them, my own words welled up from deep somewhere inside. I began to sing in low tones in time with the wavelets lapping against the metals. Distracted, I sung to myself. I was somewhere else, but I guess they heard.

"...*In this bleakness of this winter eve , icy winds moan. I cry out to the mountains and the waters. I have little to give. What can I give Him? Give Him my heart...*"

The organ music lifted louder, and words I'd never heard at Christmas or in any song, wafted forth.

"...*Filled with shepherd excitement I loudly proclaim: This is our Lord and Savior, my Lord and Savior — this is Jesus Christ the King...*"

"...*The Alpha and Omega — He truly is the Emmanuel— the sole reason for the season...*"

Unconsciously, I mumbled under my breath, "Happy Birthday, Jesus."

We left with no ducks; I believe we left with much more. In the eyes of the others , I thought I saw something different, something not there this morning. Was it some sort of renewal, some sort of inspiring commitment, some sort of resolve , maybe it was renewed hope. I don't know exactly, but it had nothing to do with ducks or hunting. Whatever it was, a newness shone in their eyes and voices. I pray it did the same in mine.

History is important. So is the nurture of our family heritage, especially at Christmas.

CHAPTER TWELVE

To those who would allow a human flood across the land at the expense of all other creatures, the prophet Isaiah warns: "Woe to you who add house to house and join field to field till no space is left and you live alone in the land"—Isaiah:5-8

A Smoky Mountain Fable
- Or, Is It?-

"I don't really have a name, I guess. But, if it'll make you feel better, just call me Gabe. I'm just sitting here resting trying to gather my thoughts, mainly, on what I'd seen today. HE asked me to do some stuff for Him, you know usual stuff like HE always does. He does it all the time. You know little odd jobs here and there. Like maintenance, clean up, people stuff, and relationship stuff, mostly.

"Well, I'd just got back from that little ole planet next to Jupiter. Don't really know its name. In fact, I don't even know if it has one. Anyway, He asked me to help with some stuff— just for Him. And believe you me, it was a tiring trip. Even if it is just one light-year from here, I'm still tuckered out. I know they're well-meant words, but I don't believe I ever really realized exactly what they meant, or at least I didn't til now. We must be His hands and feet, for who else is there?

"OK, OK, maybe the meaning has crossed my mind a few times. Maybe like the time He turned on the rainwater for forty days and nights. He was really on a mission that time. He flooded the whole thing. The earth was completely underwater. Not even a mountain tip was showing. Except for Noah, his family, and all their animal pets, nothing was left alive. He started His earth all over. Finally, when He pulled the plug, it took about fifteen months for the earth to drain. Don't ask me where all that water went, cause

THE BLUE MOUNTAINS SING
of rivers, old men, trails and trout

I never asked Him and sure wasn't going to. He wanted me there the day Noah left the ark. So the minute the ramp touched ground, and the first animals started walking down, I made sure I was there. Whoo-wee, I don't believe I've ever seen so many animals. Have you ever seen the earth after fifteen months underwater? Can you imagine earth with not a living thing anywhere? Talk about a mess, yes sir, I can tell you, there was plenty to do. I really had to rest up after that.

"But back to the here and now, I'd just got back from my latest errand — adventuring for Him. I knew He'd ask. He always does when I come back.

Always from behind a wall, from another room , or out of sight, He'd say, "Well, how 'd it go?" and "What'd you think ?"

This time He asked, "Did you go by that wilderness of mine, My Appalachian mountains on your way back?"

"I did."

"So, what did you think? "

"Well, your wilderness is still stunning and majestic, but it seems to be fading and disappearing. The part that's left seems diminished, tired, and worn. Your woods and waters aren't pristine any longer. Both of 'em are disappearing right along with the wildlife. It seems to me your flora and fauna are disappearing first and most. Your people, and it's not just those mountain folks either, but people all over the world seem to be falling away from You and Your plans for them. I'm sure this isn't what You planned or wanted for Your people.

"But You know all this already, I'm sure. With all due respect, I've often wondered why You even ask my opinion each time You send me out. You created all this. You are all-knowing and all-powerful—the Alpha and Omega—the Creator of all of this."

"Yes, I do already know, but your opinion really does matter to me. It's part of that 'free will and love one another' thing I gave to everyone."

Then, the inflection in His voice changed. As He began, His words seemed tinged, and wrapped in a weary, disappointed sigh.

"You know Eden, My garden, was perfect, and I meant for it to be perfect. I created it. I created the perfect human couple—a man and a woman. I wanted them to live there, enjoy it, and prosper. I intended for them to have freedom of choice and not to be controlled by Me like puppets on a string.

"All too soon, they had to leave the Garden. They were on their own. Now, their world would gradually become a fallen world. One filled with evil. Their progeny soon inhabited the earth. Through the generations, time and time again, my people have drawn near to Me, and then drifted away to their own devices believing their life choices were best. Over and over,

A Smoky Mountain Fable–Or Is It?

their history repeats itself. One generation draws near to Me, follows My commandments, puts Me first, depends on Me, and follows My directions and My wishes for them. The next generation , well, they believe they know best and become self-centered, follow their own inclination, and harden their heart against My guidance. They forget who I am.

"From the very beginning, I assured my people I knew each one by name, knew them in the womb, and knew every hair on their head. I created each one for a special purpose. I have a life plan for each one. I know what I am about. In my blueprint for each of them, their life plan, I assured them that I would promise them a life in abundance, a prosperous journey, one that would fulfill them, and fill them with joy."

"...For I know the plans I have for you," declares the Lord," plans to prosper you and not to harm you, plans to give you hope and a future. Then you will call upon me and come and pray to me and I will listen to you. You will seek me and find me when you seek me with all your heart. I will be found by you," declares the Lord.—Jeremiah 29: 11-14

"Through the later centuries, I inspired my people to record these promises in My scriptures so that future generations might know My personalized plan for each one of them. I wanted to make certain that they might hold fast to Me, and that they might listen and hear sacred words, My words that I created just for them. I knew the difficulty they'd face. I wanted to make sure they understood the importance of My admonition 'to be in the world but not of it.'

"Time after time, I've called them to be My people, to honor My requests, to follow Me, and to glorify My Father. My life plan for them was perfect in every way. The freedom of choice that I gave them even today continues to get in the way when they choose anything but Me. And most still continue to live their life in self-centeredness rather than God centeredness.

"And, time after time, generation after generation, in this back and forth spiritual tug of war, they gravitate toward worldly things, and follow their own will. They grasp independence in pursuit of what they believe to be best for them, despite My mentoring, warnings, and at times my interventions. They harden their hearts toward Me and fall away.

"The fruit of the Spirit virtues were especially ingrained in them. These were tools to be exercised and used as they deal with each other and with Me. Instead, as My people become *'of the world'* and secular, their entire life plan begins to go awry. Those virtues then become distorted by sin and are transformed:

"*Love* becomes hate; *joy* becomes sorrow; *peace* becomes war and turmoil; *patience* becomes coldness; *kindness* becomes uncaring ; *faithfulness* becomes disloyalty ; *gentleness* becomes hurtful; *self-control* becomes self-centeredness filled with ' me' demands.

"Their wrong choices gradually distort the fruit of the Spirit; they stain the way people deal with each other and with themselves. Their traits and actions transform into greed , self-centeredness, *and a* lessening concern for others. They become aloof, arrogant , and rude. Their God-given gifts and talents, that I placed in them, they use to spawn false pride, disrespect, and disloyalty. These are actions they continue to direct toward Me and toward others. They live lives that nurture false character , pride, and opportunism. And, sadly all these can deepen. In their most extreme distortions they are recognized as: Murder, lying, cheating, stealing, and violence, coupled with a yearning to escape the reality of their world. The peril of ignoring My Word is addressed in My commandments and throughout My scripture. Yet, My Word continues to go unheeded.

"If they do not draw near to Me, each generation gradually becomes comfortable living in their world or 'of the world.' They remove Me, My name, or any mention of Me from most of the tapestry of their world."

"What you saw in that Great Smoky Mountain wilderness is a partial result, a reflection, of that of which I have spoken. It is the result of yet another generation of My people, who have become distant to Me, and hardened their hearts toward Me. They become a people who show a growing disrespect of Me and for My gift to them—a natural wilderness. I told them in the book of Isaiah. The worst form of avarice is at work.

"The wilderness you've seen throughout the world and specifically My Appalachian wilderness, I created as a backup to the Garden of Eden. I fashioned magnificent flora, fauna, wildlife, woods and rivers. Forced to substitute, I designed it as a habitat for My people who would now dwell in a fallen world. Compared to Eden, it is a less than a perfect homeland, and one far short of the home I had planned for My people—My Eden.

"Yet, in this substitute world, I created nature's harmony, rhythms, and heavenly spectacles. Of all my people thus far, the earliest Indians may have been the few who best grasped nature's rhythm, its circle of life, its interdependence. Rightfully so, they viewed themselves as only an equal link in this cycle. They saw every part of nature as having great value, as sacred, and deserving of their highest respect. They respected all outdoors as a vital part of their being. That entire rhapsody of nature, I put there to remind My people that I am their God, love them unconditionally, and will be with them always. My directions were that they should value this earth, and every living thing that I placed upon it as worthy of respect. Each living thing had a place, and its existence was meaningful in My plan. This was

A Smoky Mountain Fable–Or Is It?

an ongoing gift—a living gift—and I expected them to practice an earthly stewardship, to grow and preserve my gift.

"Once again, I wait patiently for My people, for their response and their return. As always, their free will struggles with the choice between rejection or acceptance of My free gift, the assurance of their eternal life, and their acceptance of My unconditional love.

My Word was clear, is still clear.

"Seek ye the Lord while he may be found; call on Him while he is near. Let the wicked forsake His way and the evil man his thoughts. Let him turn to the Lord and He will have mercy on him and to our God for He will freely pardon.

For my thoughts are not your thoughts, neither are your ways my ways declares the Lord.

As the heavens are higher than the earth, so are my ways higher than your ways, and my thoughts than your thoughts.

As the rain and the snow come down from heaven, and do not return to it without watering the earth and making it bud and flourish, so that it yields seed for the sower and bread for the eater, so is my word that goes out from my mouth: It will not return to me empty, but will accomplish what I desire and achieve the purpose for which I sent it."—Isaiah 55: 6-11

"What you observed in those magnificent mountains and waters was gradual destruction and pollution caused by My people. It actually is a reflection of their disrespect for Me and many of My commands. Everything negative in their lives is an extension of their disregard for Me and My love for them. When My people harden their hearts and turn from me, you can see the indirect results in their lives. This is but one facet of their lives, this lack of stewardship toward my land, their home. But if you look closely into the many other facets of their personal lives , you'll find their disregard for Me yielding the same result of self-destruction and pollution.

"It is manifested in a multitude of ways like: Divorce, violence, war, separating me from schools and state, drugs, gangs, the poor, the widows and the orphans ignored, dysfunctional families, child and spouse abuse, pornography, abortion, hypocrisy in the church, sexual deviation and licentiousness, greed in the marketplace and government, broken homes and families, and I could go on. My people always seem intent on destroying the very quality of life I created for them.

"Generation after generation, each has managed to destroy those most basic and sacred foundation stones that undergird their own prosperity and happiness. Although some follow my call, most of My people seem uncaring and disrespectful of Me. They disrespect My offer, My gifts, and the life plan I intended for them. They continue to follow their own choices and their own path. You can see where it has led them. History repeats itself. Nowhere is it more evident, than when I first brought My people out of bondage.

In following my direction to populate the earth, each generation did so, but they ignored My exhortation to do so in My Father's name. Now, worldwide, my people live lives based on the wrong core values. They've embraced new values authored by this fallen world, not by My Word. They've substituted their own new choices for the ones I set for them at the beginning of time. My guidelines are timeless, unchanging, eternal —for they are My Word. The result of My people's choice of misdirected paths creates a world population whose misery and suffering grow. Time after time I've seen the result of what one generation turns a blind eye towards and ignores; the next generation embraces. As a result, the suffering of My people grows harsher, harder, and more intense. Their human despair increases at an ever quickening tempo, and their aimless grief hurts Me deeply.

"I spoke in my scriptures of My promises and My truths for all My people. I created a living roadmap that leads them out of their present day wilderness. Too many times to count, I have restored MY people, numerous generations of their forefathers, to a richer and fulfilling life. Each time, I fulfilled My promises to them. I can and will do so once again.

I wait for them
to place Me above all things of their world
And to glorify Me as their Creator and their Father
I wait for them to walk and talk with me, continually, just as they
would their best friend
.. I love them.
I am with them always and I will never forsake them
They are My people
I wait

Hear my Word! My people!

... if my people who are called by my name will humble themselves and pray and seek my face and turn from their wicked ways, then I will hear from heaven and will forgive their sin and will heal their land.—Chronicles7:14

Society speaks and all men listen; mountains speak and wise men listen.

—John Muir

Thank You, Lord

The sky told me my day was near the end. I sat on a rock and looked west. It was the first time that day I'd had a panoramic view. I'd walked and fished all day surrounded by tree canopy with only an occasional blue sky sliver overhead. The rock made a fine rest seat, and the view reminded me there was a God. I was not far from the trail end and the sunset promised some artistic gifts only nature offers.

The clouds were washboard ripples and waves of color. They stretched across the entire horizon, and chameleon like they moved through one color into another. Fiery orange and coral colored the woods in an afternoon blood red. Molten lava colors of varying shades rolled and churned one layer over another. The top cloud layer of somber gray lay above and sheltered the lower layers. Its lower edges drifted slowly to lavender. Then a low refrain floated in from somewhere: *Lavender blue, dilly dilly, lavender blue.* The coral red layer nearest the sun turned salmon and moved through orange then became lemon yellow. The lavender turned pink. Then the entire color spectrum moved from hot color layers to faint water color pastels until only a faint pink melded with the darker gray. The sun, in its afternoon finality, blended its last gasp of color into navy blue, and the Blue Mountains ended their song for the day.

All sorts of praise thoughts raced through my brain. Bits and pieces of praise hymns welled up. I felt like I needed to thank somebody, but there was no hostess nor host. I grabbed a pen. Some scribbled thoughts would have to do. I looked up and gave thanks for the moment, that brief epiphany. The words that follow were my feeble attempt to capture what I saw, an effort to describe the indescribable. Nature's scenes always transcend words. I could only express feelings.

Your Mountains, Lord

Surely the presence of your Spirit is in these Your Mountains, Lord

Lord, My God

When through your woods and icy rivers pure, I wander

Lord, the spirit of your mighty works fills my heart

And I can only stand silent and still

in my awesome wonder

So very small, insignificant, temporary and alone

Overwhelmed

at these your mighty works

I delight in your moon and stars and trees

I hear the mighty thunder

Marvel at your lightning and storm chased clouds

Feel your breeze whisper secrets to the trees

Truly, my cup runneth over

When I in awesome wonder consider all these works you have made

Beyond belief, and by You, I am immeasurably blessed by

All this

Your power throughout the universe displayed

Your blessings overwhelm me

I stand overcome

By your unconditional love

To thee and thee alone

I praise you—Holy, Holy, and Holy

Then, sings my soul of grateful thanks

To You, My Savior God, to you

How great Thou art, How great Thou art

When in your mountains and forest countryside, I walk

See the sky with circling hawk, your trees with birds aloft

When I view your magnificence from mountain top grandeur

And hear the creek and feel the morn mist

See the cobalt sky and all beneath it

Each step is yet another renewing, a nature's gift that fills my soul

How great thou art, Lord, How great thou art

In this your gift of beauty so purely wild

you offer epiphanies of joy that further fill my heart

Truly, sings my soul, my Saviour God to thee

How great Thou art,

How wonderfully great Thou art

Maranantha, Jesus

And when Christ shall come with shout of acclamation

And take me home

What more joy than this shall fill my heart

Then, I shall bow in humble adoration

And there again proclaim, my God, how truly great Thou art.

Works Cited

It takes many people and many texts and documents to create a word journey such as mine. Much of the documentation contributed further to my understanding of The Great Smoky Mountains Appalachian range, the Great Smoky Mountains National Park, and Sevier County.

Much of the statistical, historical, and cultural information came from the various documents at the Great Smoky Mountains National Park headquarters and the Great Smoky Mountain Association. Quotations from biblical scriptures were drawn from The Holy Bible New International Version 2011. The Appendix B, Cultural and Historic Landscape Assessment for the Elkmont Historic District document, was especially helpful.

Special thanks goes to Aldo Leopold's work, *Sand County Almanac*, and to Roland Pertwee's article. Their works helped spawn ideas and concepts that made *two* of my conservation chapters possible. I was able to "show rather than tell" because of their inspiration.

For the purpose of this book, I have quoted briefly from the following material.

Manuscripts
Berry, Wendell. *The Long Legged House*. Harcourt, Brace & World, 1965.
Brill, David. "The Nation's Best-loved Park, at 75," *Smokies Life Magazine* 2, no. 2 (2009): 13-23.
Bush, Florence Cope. *Dorie, Woman of the Mountains*. The University of Tennessee Press, 1992.
Camp LeConte for Boys, Summer 1935.Smoky Mountain Historical Society Journal and Newsletter, Spring   2007, vol. XXXIII.
Cotham, Steve. *The Great Smoky Mountains National Park*. Acadia Publishing, 2006.
Foss, Sam Walter. *The Bloodless Sportsman*.1898.
Jolley, Harley E. *The CCCs in the Smokies*. Great Smoky Mountains Association, 2001, 1-9.
Kephart, Horace. *Our Southern Highlands*. MacMillan Company, University of Tennessee Press, 2006.
King, Veta. *A History of Pigeon Forge*. The Mountain Press, 2006, 1-3.
———. Pigeon Forge, Images of America. Charleston, S. C., Acadia Publishing, 2010, 7-8.
Leopold, Aldo. *A Sand County Almanac*. Oxford University Press, 1949.
Lewis, E.J., MD. *Hints to a Sportsman*, 1851.
Morrell, Virginia. "The Sound of Silence," *Conde Nast Traveler*, January 2012.
Pertwee, Roland. "Fish Are Such Liars," *Saturday Evening Post*. 1927.
The Holy Bible, New International Version, NIV. Biblica, 2011.
Thompson, John M. *Wildlands of the Upper South*, National Geographic Society Press, 2004.
Wuerther, George. *Great Smoky Mountains, A Visitor's Companion*. Pennsylvania: Stackpole, 2003, 1-5.

Special Notations
As requested
THE HOLY BIBLE, NEW INTERNATIONAL VERSION®, NIV® Copyright © 1973, 1978, 1984, 2011 by Biblica, Inc.™ Used by permission. All rights reserved worldwide. http://bible.cc/isaiah/5-8.htm

Electronic Resources:
America's Best History, US Timeline 1940s. http://americasbesthistory.com/abhtimeline1940.html/
E-Reference Desk, Tennessee History Timeline. http://www.e-referencedesk.com/resources/state-history-timeline/tennessee.html/
Historic Timeline of Tennessee. http://www.history-timelines.org.uk/american-timelines/42-tennessee-history-timeline.htm/
Maples, Mike. "Historical Events of Tennessee: Parts One and Two." http://gosmokies.knoxnews.com/profiles/blogs/historical-events-of-tennessee-part-two?xg_source=activity/
Muir, John. http://www.best-quotes-poems.com/quotations/
National Park Service History Timelines. http://www.nps.gov/history/history/
New World Encyclopedia. http://www.newworldencyclopedia.org/entry/Info:main_page/ tennessee - new world encyclopedia.mht
Radford University, Environmental History Guideline. "1890 to 1920—The Progressive Era." http://www.radford.edu/~wkovarik/envhist/5progressive.html/

————. "1920 to 1940 – The Roaring Twenties." http://www.radford.edu/~wkovarik/envhist/6twenties.html/

————. "Industrial Revolution: 1810 1890." http://www.radford.edu/~wkovarik/envhist/4industrial.html/

Tennessee Wilderness Society, Timeline of Wilderness History and Conservation, The Wilderness Society.mht. http://wilderness.org/

Timeline of Conservation. https://docs.google.com/document/d/17yGGth8-Nj90Q-1aiZoCQTslV_uiBdgmxB04uhqT8VM/preview?pli=1

Timeline of Wilderness History and Conservation. https://docs.google.com/document/d/17yGGth8-Nj90Q-1aiZoCQTslV_uiBdgmxB04uhqT8VM/preview?pli=1#heading=h.26w4j5320vyw

USGS Science for the Changing World. *http://www.usgs.gov/pubprod/*

National Park Service, Department of the Interior. *http://parkplanning.nps.gov/document.cfm?parkID=382&projectID=15794&documentID=26126*

Or (in mauscripts)

Appendix B Cultural and Historic Landscape Assessment for the Elkmont Historic District, Great Smoky Mountains National Park, Sevier County, Tennessee. Authored b: M. Todd Cleveland, TRC Garrow Associates, Inc. Atlanta, Ga. TRC Project No> 02387 April 2004

Wood, Harold. Favorite Quotations from John Muir. http://www.sierraclub.org/john_muir_exhibit/writings/favorite_quotations.aspx/

Wildlife Federation , http://www.nwf.org/Who-We-Are.aspx

Photographs and Permissions

Pages:

23 Pigeon Forge valley and view of LeConte. 1954 (Tennessee Library and Archives collection)
24 Stringtown homes in early twenties. (Pigeon forge library and Jim Whaley)
30 Pigeon Forge elementary school class. (Ron Rader family collection)
32 Unpaved US Hwy 441. (Pigeon Forge library)
    Aerial of 1950s Pigeon Forge town center with paved road. (Pigeon Forge Library)
33 Center of Pigeon Forge. 1954 (Pigeon Forge library)
37 Windswept —our second home. 1960. (Ron Rader family collection)
46 Aerial view of midfifties Pigeon Forge. (Pigeon Forge library)
47 A Windswept birthday. (Ron Rader family collection)
49 Our eighth grade team. (Ron Rader family collection)
54 The many faces of the Little Pigeon.
56 Dad in CCC's. (Ron Rader family collection)
    Sgt. Al Rader with some of his squad members. (Ron Rader family collection)
57 Military family trio at Five Oaks. (Ron Rader family collection)
59 Early Windswept Days Gallery. . (Ron Rader family collection)
60 Local childhood. . (Ron Rader family collection) (Howard Davenport family collection)
67 Retired GSMNP friends tour Spence Field—photographer, Charlie Grossman. (Ron Rader family collection)
69 Pop greets Granny at back door of Five Oaks. (Ron Rader family collection)
    Later generation at Five Oaks —1945. (Ron Rader family collection)
70 Five Oaks living. (Ron Rader family collection)
73 Moonglow, her colt, and me at Five Oaks driveway. (Ron Rader family collection)
76 Pop and his mother and his note to her. (Ron Rader family collection)
80 My early years at Five Oaks. (Ron Rader family collection)
81 Five Oaks reunion in the yard under the oak tree canopy in 1937. (Ron Rader family collection)
82 Summer and cousins in yard at Five Oaks. (Ron Rader family collection)
    Ogle uncles with their Tennessee Walking horses. (Ron Rader family collection)
84 Pop with new yearling. (Ron Rader family collection)
87 Granny Ogle on her one hundredth birthday. (Ron Rader family collection)
88 Five Oaks Picture Gallery. (Ron Rader family collection)
93 A young Uncle Harry with favorite hounds. (Harry Ogle family collection)
94 Mill Creek farm in 1928. (Harry Ogle family collection)

Thanks to my friends who contributed and labored with me

I owe a special debt of gratitude to the following people:

Annette Hardigan, archivist, the Great Smoky Mountain National Park

Retired educators who graciously read and edited my manuscript: *Glen Cardwell, Shirley Delozier*, and *Norma Blair.*

Veta Wilson King, Pigeon Forge Library historian and author, for her overwhelming resource, picture, and verbal information. Her books and her advice certainly enriched my manuscript. She also read my manuscript and provided feedback.

Greg Johnson for his "been there, done that" coaching and his service as a resource provider.

Lori Hill who found time away from her photography business, teaching honors English at Sevier County High School, and even summer vacation at the beach to edit. She relentlessly edited my copy three times.

Carroll McMahan, Special Projects Director at Sevierville Chamber of Commerce, was helpful in endless ways. The recently published author of *Sevierville,* Carroll not only read my manuscript, but also provided me resources, ideas, pictures, and many helpful suggestions at just the right time.

Cathy Kodra, author, poet, and friend, her counsel and encouragement was priceless.

Several close friends who read and gave me verbal feedback. *Mary Bob Rowe, Andrea Cooper Roe*, and *Kay Henry Gill.*

Jim Richardson, a close friend since childhood and Forge brother, read and edited my manuscript, and talked me through many publishing choices. As a thorough hiker of the entire length of the Appalachian Trail in 2005, Jim wrote his trail memoirs entitled *One Man's Journey* and published it the same year. His prior experience in working with publishers was very helpful.

Aaron Barnhart, graphics professional and a writer's godsend, was the perfect fit. He is very competent, considers the mountains his second home, and immediately took my manuscript to heart as a labor of love. Hiking is his second love so my work quickly became his friend.

Melissa and Don Fields who do their magic on old pictures. They transform the old until they become the new.

Steve Hemp, Director of Interpretive Products & Services, author , and superb writer about all things Great Smoky Mountains, made time to help me over numerous hurdles that manuscript writing creates. His knowledge of both writing and publishing and his willingness to share it with me is appreciated beyond words.

Robert Tino for his magnificent artistry. Using his gift of art, he made my work even more special.

Appendix

May 1937 Mother's Day Picture at Five Oaks Farm
Home of Dr. John W. Ogle, M.D. and wife Blanche Wayland Ogle

Left to right:

- Alvin Clarke Rader: ("Al" husband of Louise Ogle Rader; father of "Ron"ald Holt Rader and John Richard "Rick" Rader, Pigeon Forge.)

- Louise Ogle Rader: (only daughter of Dr. and Blanche Ogle and Al's wife)

- Helen Adcock : (niece of Dot Adcock ; Aunt Josie's husband)

- Stuart Adcock: (aunt Josie's son and owner of WROL radio station on Gay street in Knoxville)

- Mrs. Blanche Wayland Ogle: (wife of Dr John and mother of Harry, John D., Louise, and Dr. Homer Ogle)

- Bill Stone: (husband of Ruth Stone, aunt Josie's son-in-law, and owner of Stone Produce on Market St.

- Josie Adcock: (sister of Anah Ogle Seaton and Dr. John W. Ogle)

- Frankie Fleming: (aunt Frank was wife of Decatur Fleming and third sister of Dr. John W. Ogle)

- Ruth Stone: (aunt Josie's daughter and wife of Bill Stone)

- Charlesy Adcock - in front of Ruth-: (Stuart Adcock's daughter and aunt Josie's daughter)

- Martha Jane Waters - the honoree-:(Grandma Ogle was Dr. John W. Ogle's mother)

- Ruth White Adcock: (Stuart's wife)

- Jane Seaton -in front of Ruth Adcock-: (later married Clyde Blalock)

- Dr. John W. Ogle, M.D.: (wife was Blanche Wayland Ogle and father of Harry, Louise, John D., and Homer)

- Hugh Fleming-in front of Dr. John-:(son of Decatur and Aunt Frank Fleming)

- James Wilson Wayland: (Blanche Wayland Ogle's father, his wife Sara Wilson Butler, Blanche's mother, was not present in picture)

- Wesley Seaton: (husband of Anah Ogle Seaton, Dr. John's sister, and was a Pigeon Forge merchant)

- Anah Ogle Seaton: (wife of Wesley and Dr. john's sister)

- John D. Ogle – on the horse at rear-: (third child born to Dr. John and Blanche Wayland Ogle; would later marry Antoinette Ogle, daughter of Charlie and Hattie Ogle of Gatlinburg, and father Gloria, Jim, David and Sarah Ogle, The children would form Five Oaks Corporation and the related outlet mall)

Note: Dr. John W. Ogle was a physician, surgeon, and family doctor. His practice was located next door in a small one-story brick office just left of the house. Currently, Old MacDonald Mini Golf sits on the edge at the edge of the site.

The author and his wife Jane live on a lake in the Great Smoky Mountains of East Tennessee. Retired from the University of Tennessee, he continues as a commercial real estate advisor with Sperry Van Ness–RM Moore Commercial Real Estate LLC in Sevierville, Tennessee. In reality, he is a vagabond trout fisherman wandering aimlessly in the mountains.

He may be reached at: ronrader@live.com

21772819R00135

Made in the USA
Charleston, SC
05 September 2013